Dear Reader:

The book you are abouthe
St. Martin's True Cri *ork
Times* calls "the leader fer
you a fascinating account of the latest, most sensational crime
that has captured the national attention. St. Martin's is the pub-
lisher of bestselling true crime author and crime journalist
Kieran Crowley, who explores the dark, deadly links between a
prominent Manhattan surgeon and the disappearance of his
wife fifteen years earlier in THE SURGEON'S WIFE. Suzy
Spencer's BREAKING POINT guides readers through the tor-
tuous twists and turns in the case of Andrea Yates, the Houston
mother who drowned her five young children in the family's
bathtub. In Edgar Award-nominated DARK DREAMS, legendary FBI profiler Roy Hazelwood and bestselling crime author Stephen G. Michaud shine light on the inner workings of
America's most violent and depraved murderers. In the book
you now hold, BLOOD WILL TELL, veteran true crime scribe
Carlton Smith takes a close look at a family that appeared to
have it all, and the brutal crime that tore them apart.

St. Martin's True Crime Library gives you the stories behind
the headlines. Our authors take you right to the scene of the
crime and into the minds of the most notorious murderers to
show you what really makes them tick. St. Martin's True Crime
Library paperbacks are better than the most terrifying thriller,
because it's all true! The next time you want a crackling good
read, make sure it's got the St. Martin's True Crime Library
logo on the spine—you'll be up all night!

Charles E. Spicer, Jr.
Executive Editor, St. Martin's True Crime Library

Ken seemed flat, almost as if he were talking about something he'd seen on television. Occasionally a deep sigh escaped as he looked down at his hands.

He told police Agent Denson how he had found Kristine at the bottom of the basement stairs, blood flowing from her head, how he'd run outside to get help, then back inside the house.

"And I—I looked to see if she was breathing," he said. "Her—back and chest were not going up and down at all." He was silent for a bit, then sighed again.

"So then I saw the black shoe . . ." he said. Suddenly he raised himself partly out of his seat and brought his two fists crashing down together on the desk.

"The GODDAMN BLACK SHOES!" he shouted.

Denson was taken aback by this outburst. Here was a man who had previously been so placid that he might have been describing a routine business transaction, now erupting with unexpected violence. Was that what had happened to Kristine, Denson wondered— had Ken Fitzhugh beaten his wife as viciously as he had just attacked the table top?

And was there something else here—maybe something a bit Freudian in his cursing of the shoes—*the shoes, the Goddamn black shoes*? Was Ken unconsciously pointing out to Denson the very evidence that seemed to suggest that Ken Fitzhugh himself had murdered his wife of thirty-three years—his *own* shoes?

The shoes, the shoes—both hers as well as his— here indeed was one of the keys to the puzzle, a psychological enigma if there ever was one.

St. Martin's Paperbacks True Crime Library Titles by Carlton Smith

Blood Money

Death of a Little Princess

Seeds of Evil

Dying for Daddy

Death in Texas

Murder at Yosemite

Bitter Medicine

Hunting Evil

Shadows of Evil

Death of a Doctor

Blood Will Tell

BLOOD
WILL TELL

Carlton Smith

St. Martin's Paperbacks

BLOOD WILL TELL

Copyright © 2003 by Carlton Smith.

Cover photograph of house by Palo Alto Police Department. Cover photograph of Kristine Fitzhugh courtesy California Department of Motor Vehicles.

ISBN: 0-312-97795-6

Printed in the United States of America

St. Martin's Paperbacks edition / February 2003

St. Martin's Paperbacks are published by St. Martin's Press, 175 Fifth Avenue, New York, NY 10010.

10 9 8 7 6 5 4 3 2 1

MULE CREEK

JUST outside of Ione, California, a small town nestled in the foothills of the old gold-mining country of the Sierra Nevada, atop a small rise, lies Mule Creek State Prison—a series of low buildings, an unattended guardhouse, a parking lot, an administration building, and, behind tall chain-link fences topped with barbed wire, three "yards," or cellblocks, each of them containing involuntary guests of the State of California.

A visitor to these precincts, which were erected in 1985 by then–California Governor George Deukmejian—a former State Attorney General and a law-and-order man of storied repute—must gain access through a closely scrutinized portal. No wallets may be taken through; no writing implements of any kind; no papers; no portable telephones, no tapes, no recorders, and of course, no weapons. Only a single key is permitted, and no more than thirty dollars, and that only in one-dollar bills—change machines on the left before you enter.

Shoes off before stepping through the magnetometer, followed by a wave of the wand to make sure one is *sans* metal. Then into the sally port through a rolling electronic gate. Wait until all is clear, then through a similar rolling barrier at the far end of the sally port.

Through the sunny interior courtyard to the "C" Yard, where a pass is checked by a guard in front of a sturdy, locked door. The pass is given to another guard, and after some delay, the man you have come to see finally emerges from the interior of the prison.

He is small, this man, and friendly. His once dark hair is now almost completely white. It looks as though he's lost weight, as he approaches, hand held out in greeting.

Sit down at table number 13 in the cacophonous visiting area, surrounded by other inmates with their children, wives and parents—all under the watchful eye of the guards.

How do you feel?—that's the question of the day.

"I feel cheated," says Kenneth Carroll Fitzhugh, Jr. "I'm not guilty and I'm in here."

THE HOUSE ON ESCOBITA AVENUE

MAY 5, the year of Our Lord, 2000. Cinco de Mayo, as some would have it. The 138th anniversary of the defeat of Emperor Maximilian by the peasant army of Benito Juarez. Puebla, Mexico, that was. A cause for celebration then, as now.

Time for a party.

A party, all right, but not for the victory of the fifth of May. Instead, a party for Gaelyn Mason's birthday, which wasn't on the fifth of May, but close enough to it so it didn't really matter. A party was a party, no matter what the occasion. And this would be a teachers' night out: the Big Casino. A craps table. Roulette wheel. The Wheel of Fortune. Bets in funny scrip. Gaiety. Shrieks of laughter. Chances taken, won and lost. A Saturday night's detour to the slightly risqué green felt jungle, a little harmless fun—all right there in staid, buttoned-down Palo Alto, home of "The Farm," Leland Stanford Junior University, one of the country's top ten institutions of higher learning, according to anyone's list.

Cinco de Mayo, the fifth of May. Time to go pick up the gambling apparati—might as well be literally precise—from the rental outfit in San Jose. Gaelyn waits in the little house she shares with her friend and roommate, Carol Piraino, not far from the Caltrain tracks that bisect the university town. Gaelyn is a fifth-grade teacher for the Palo Alto Unified School District, while Carol is an elementary school principal. Today, though, they're taking the day off—to get ready for the party. They're waiting for their friend, Ken Fitzhugh, Jr., to come in his Chevrolet Suburban truck—or is it a van?—with his two dogs, Boots the standard-bred poodle and tiny Reina the Pomeranian. So the five of them, Ken, Gaelyn, Carol and the two dogs, can drive to San Jose in the Suburban to pick up the gambling equipment for Gaelyn's birthday party on Saturday night, the sixth of May, which is nobody's national holiday, but it is a Saturday, thank God, no school.

One-thirty P.M., and there he is, right on time, just as expected, little Ken in his big truck, with dogs as promised, ready to be of service. Ken is always as punctual as he is helpful, Gaelyn knows. After all, he is an adult, she thinks, momentarily forgetting that she is an adult too, even if Ken is almost old enough to be her father. But Ken is—what's the word?—*responsible*, Galen thinks, which means if Ken says he'll do something, he will do it.

Ken pulls the Suburban to a stop at the curb a couple of doors away from the front of Gaelyn and Carol's house, not far from the abundant shade trees that make Palo Alto one of the leafiest cities in America. He gets out of the truck, dressed in black jeans, a plaid shirt, white sweat socks, leather loafers—*White socks and leather loafers!* Gaelyn thinks—his prematurely gray hair slightly too long, his eyes calm behind his large, wire-framed glasses. Gaelyn will remember for a long time how Ken looks this day, she just doesn't know it yet.

Ken comes up to her while she's putting an ice cooler into the front seat of her car.

"You'll never be able to drive with that thing in there," he advises her. That was typical of Ken: a fount of expert advice, at least to women, whether wanted or not. Ken's observation is so sensible it's almost irritating. Carol bites back the tart retort that bubbles up, and mildly tells Ken that it will be all right.

They head for the boxy blue Suburban, but not before Carol goes back into the house; she's forgotten something. Ken gets behind the wheel. Gaelyn gets in the front passenger seat. She has no way of knowing that any of this will be important later. They say nothing to each other for the few minutes that pass until Carol comes out of the house and locks the front door behind her. She'd forgotten her purse, Carol explains, as she gets into the second seat of the Suburban, behind Gaelyn, with the dogs.

Ken starts the truck.

Oh, by the way, he says, pulling away from the curb, do

they mind if they stop at the Fitzhugh house first? He wants to check on Kristine, his wife, and Gaelyn and Carol's friend, also a school teacher. He just had a call from the school district, Ken says, and it looks like Kristine missed her 12:50 P.M. class. A brief stop at the Fitzhugh house, some three minutes away, and then they will be on their way to get the gambling stuff for the party.

Ken guides the Suburban north on Alma, next to the tracks, on his way to the Fitzhugh home on Escobita Avenue. Gaelyn, Carol and Ken all try to remember what Kristine's class schedule is, but nobody can keep it straight because it always seems to be changing. Maybe Kristine just got confused and went to the wrong school, someone suggests. But it isn't really like Kristine, who is so organized as to be almost obsessive.

Ken turns left on Churchill Avenue, crosses the tracks, and makes another quick left to the small side street in the Southgate neighborhood of Palo Alto, Castilleja Avenue, then a quick right onto Manzanita, another left onto Escobita. The streets here are extremely narrow, so skinny that cars have to take turns to pass each other. Ken swerves the Suburban to a stop in front of the Fitzhugh house without bothering to park, shuts off the engine and heads for the front door, which appears to be partially open.

Gaelyn and Carol watch as Ken goes inside, leaving the front door open wider, and runs up the stairs to the second floor of the house. Both of them have been in the house many, many times over the years; they consider Kristine and Ken Fitzhugh among their very best friends.

A few seconds later they see Ken come down the stairs, then make a right turn to go down the hallway deeper into the house. Less than a minute passes, and suddenly Ken is coming out of the front door, yelling something.

"Come help me!" he says. For just an instant, Gaelyn thinks maybe Ken is playing a practical joke on her for her birthday. She thinks Ken and Kristine have planned this all out, and there's some sort of birthday surprise inside the house.

"Is he kidding?" Gaelyn asks Carol, but Carol doesn't

think he is; this is serious. They get out of the car, head for the front door. Ken has already disappeared back inside the house. They push open the front door in time to see Ken turn right into a doorway that leads to the basement landing. Gaelyn and Carol follow, and as they come onto the small landing, they look down and see Ken standing over Kristine, whose head is at the bottom landing of the stairs, feet trailing back up the steps toward them. She's face-down and isn't moving, and neither is Ken . . .

"Oh my God, there's blood everywhere," Ken says. "I can't get a pulse, call 911."

Gaelyn and Carol back out of the landing into the hallway, across the hallway and into the kitchen. Carol picks up the Fitzhughs' cordless phone and dials the emergency center while Gaelyn hovers nearby. It's almost exactly 1:40 P.M. The emergency operator wants to know the address and suddenly Carol's mind is a blank. She runs down the hallway to the front door, Gaelyn trailing behind her, to see the numbers of the outside of the Fitzhugh house. Carol tells the emergency operator the address, and says that someone has fallen, is badly hurt, and that help is needed in a hurry. The emergency operator tells Carol that help is on the way. The call is ended. Carol and Gaelyn go back inside the house, back to the landing. They look down the steps, and there is Ken, still standing near Kristine's head, and Kristine still hasn't moved, and neither has Ken.

"Call 911," Ken says, again, and Carol tells him she already has. "Do either of you know CPR?" Ken asks.

Gaelyn and Carol look at one another. They're supposed to know CPR; it's part of their training as teachers. But Gaelyn is afraid. She's never done CPR for real. What if she makes a mistake? Still, Ken is insisting, and the next thing she knows, she's come down the stairs near Kristine's feet. Ken is saying something about turning Kristine over so they can start the CPR, and before Gaelyn knows it she and Ken are turning Kristine over so she's face-up. Ken has pulled Kristine off the lower landing onto the cement floor. He is still talking and vaguely Gaelyn hears him saying something about Kristine not breathing, that she may be dead, but that they have to try. He tells Gaelyn to begin chest compressions while he tries to blow air into Kristine's lungs. A gurgling noise comes from Kristine's throat or chest, Gaelyn isn't sure which, and now she sees a pool of red; it's blood, oozing from the back of Kristine's head, a pool that seems to grow larger as Gaelyn begins the compressions.

In between breaths, Ken looks up at Gaelyn.

"Those shoes, those God damn shoes," Ken tells Gaelyn between breaths. "She must have fallen in those shoes. I told her to throw them away a thousand times."

He nods at the stairs behind them, and Gaelyn sees a black sandal lying on its side on the left side of one of the stairs. Ken says something more about the shoe on the stairs, that Kristine must have fallen while she was taking the dry-cleaning down into the basement. Gaelyn realizes that Kristine is lying atop a plastic dry-cleaning bag, that she must have been carrying the bag down the steps when she slipped and fell. Ken is saying that Kristine must have knocked herself out in the fall and suffocated on the plastic.

Carol appears again at the top of the stairs.

"They're coming," she says, and Gaelyn and Ken can hear sirens in the distance. They continue with the CPR. Between his breaths, Ken and Gaelyn try to figure out how long Kristine might have been lying there before they discovered her. Still Kristine doesn't move, or breathe.

The sirens are getting louder now, and the next thing Gaelyn is aware of is the firemen coming down into the basement with their resuscitation equipment. They tell Gaelyn and Ken to stop, they will take over, and as they begin to set up their equipment, Gaelyn notices that a large brass ship's bell is on the lower landing near the dry-cleaning, and in a place where it seems likely that Kristine may have fallen into it, striking her head when she slipped. One of the three firemen shoves the bell and the dry-cleaning away from Kristine so they can have more room to work.

"You did a good job," one of the firemen tells Ken as he unpacks his gear.

Gaelyn is backing away from Kristine now as the firemen insert a plastic intubation tube down her throat and cut away her clothing. As Gaelyn backs away, she sees it's too crowded to go back up the stairs. She sees Ken stepping around Kristine, and begin to climb anyway. He's holding his hands vertically, away from his body in a ninety-degree angle, almost as if he were a surgeon waiting to be gloved, and Gaelyn realizes his hands are dripping with blood, and so is his face and mouth. In fact, there is a large pool of blood now spreading from Kristine's head across the basement floor. Gaelyn is feeling trapped, stuck in a nightmare, but there's no exit. Then she remembers that there are two storm doors into the rear of the basement, so she goes to the doors, forces them open and emerges into the Fitzhugh back yard. The last thing she sees before leaving is Ken going up the stairs, bloody hands raised . . .

Palo Alto Police Officer Sascha Priess gets the call at the same time as the firemen, but the firemen beat him to the house on Escobita Avenue. Still, it's only a matter of seconds. At 1:47 P.M. on May 5, Priess is already out of his patrol car and heading into the Fitzhugh house, on the heels of the fire department. As he walks into the house through the open door, Priess sees Carol Piraino. Carol is still holding the Fitzhughs' cordless phone. Priess asks Carol where the victim was, and Carol nods toward the basement door.

Priess goes to the head of the basement stairs and walks partway down. He sees two firemen bending over Kristine, but no one else. He notices a large pool of blood beneath Kristine's head on the concrete basement floor. Some sort of communication—whether a raised eyebrow, a shake of the head or actual words, it later isn't clear—but some sort of signal passes between one of the firemen and Priess. Priess turns around and returns to the ground floor hallway, and asks Carol what's happened.

Carol explains that they have just found Kristine lying at the bottom of the stairs, that the front door was open, that Kristine's husband Ken was the one who found her. As he listens to Carol, Priess is facing down the hallway toward the basement landing, so he now sees Ken when he comes up from the basement, bloody hands raised at the ninety-degree angle.

Either Priess hasn't noticed him before or Ken was temporarily out of sight when Priess first went down. Ken doesn't say a word, but turns right and walks down the hallway, hands still raised in the vertical position. Priess watches as Ken disappears into another room at the end of the central hallway.

It's been less than two minutes since Priess' arrival just before 1:47 P.M. Priess sees a pair of paramedics go by, headed for the basement with their collapsible gurney. The next thing Priess knows, another Palo Alto police officer, Tom Pohl, is entering the house. It is 1:49 P.M. Priess tells Pohl the victim is in the basement. Pohl goes past Priess to the basement landing and disappears. As Priess talks to Carol, Ken emerges from the room at the end of the hallway and begins walking toward them. Pohl emerges from the door to the basement landing just as Ken begins to go back downstairs. Pohl stops him, and he and Ken come down the hallway toward Priess and Carol. Pohl is saying something to Ken, Priess isn't sure what. Priess takes the cordless telephone from Carol and walks past Ken and Pohl, looking into each of the rooms off the hallway. He realizes that the room Ken has just gone into and come out of is a bathroom, and that he has gone in there to wash the blood off his face and hands.

As he reaches the end of the hallway, Priess goes into another room, this one the Fitzhugh family room, and now that he's by himself, calls his station on his handheld radio. From his own observations, and from whatever passed between him and the firemen downstairs, Priess is pretty sure this is no accident. There's simply too much blood.

SOME of the smartest people in the world live in Palo Alto, California. There, in the reflected brainglow cast off by Stanford University, nearly 60,000 souls reside, the overwhelming majority of them white, wealthy, and extremely well-educated. Along its leafy narrow neighborhood streets, Mercedeses, BMWs, Audis and Lexuses abound, nestled securely in tidy driveways abutted by neatly edged lawns and carefully trimmed shrubs fronting shingled, two-story abodes symbolic of an earlier, saner era, when neighborhoods were sanctuaries, when everyone knew everyone else, when the idea of murder was something that only happened in the pages of delightful mystery novels, and even at that was almost always entirely fastidious.

Like a medieval village nestled up against the castle's walls, life in the town of Palo Alto revolves around its great center of existence, the University. Generation after generation of the nation's best and brightest have streamed through the University's quadrangles since its founding by California's one-time governor and railroad baron, Leland Stanford, back in the 19th Century. Over the years, Stanford's graduates have fanned out across the world, and have come to occupy some of the most important positions in government, business, the arts and academia. And like the retainers of royalty in another era, the townspeople of Palo Alto have come to have a pride of place at the foot of their great institution of learning. The ethos of the University diffuses itself throughout the town's streets and into its shops and residences, so there is a liberalism, but not too much; there is tolerance for differences, but only within acceptable limits; there is a sense of curiosity about others, but well within the bounds of good taste. Most of all there is a quiet satisfaction with life, a view that says, quietly and politely, but nevertheless insistently—*We are better*.

And so the good people of Palo Alto came out of their comfortable houses to gather on Escobita Avenue, where the fire engine idled in the middle of the pavement, along with the ambulance, the paramedics' van and a growing assortment of police cars, to gather in little knots and stare at the front of the house at 1545, where the battered body of their long-time neighbor, Kristine Fitzhugh, lay in a pool of her own blood at the bottom of the basement stairs, victim of a terrible accident, it seemed, because things like murder didn't take place in a town like Palo Alto, California.

At 1:40 P.M. on Friday, the fifth of May, 2000, Palo Alto police Agent Mike Denson was in his dress uniform, as were his immediate supervisors, Sergeant Scott Wong and Lieutenant Don Hartnett. All three men were on the freeway, near Stockton, California, having driven to Sacramento to attend the state's annual Peace Officers' Memorial ceremony. Just after 2 P.M., Denson's pager beeped. The department was calling. Denson extracted his cellular phone and called in. There was, Denson was informed, a suspicious, unattended death in Palo Alto. As the Palo Alto Police Department's only homicide detective, Denson's presence was immediately required at 1545 Escobita Avenue.

Unlike most other police departments, the Palo Alto force had an intermediate rank between officer and sergeant: agent. That rank denoted a combination of years of experience and specialized training that qualified the holder for either investigative or supervisory tasks. In the Palo Alto department, sergeants were the line administrators, while those filling the slots of lieutenant and above were management.

In the spring of the year 2000, Agent Denson was 39 years old. Married, father of an infant daughter, Denson was in his eighth year with the Palo Alto Police Department, after having worked as a reserve police officer for the Bay Area city of San Carlos in the late 1980s and early 1990s, following graduation from the College of San Mateo's criminal justice training program. Before that, Denson had worked as a water quality control officer for the city of Palo Alto.

Over his years as a police officer, Denson had taken over 2,000 hours in specialized training courses, ranging from traffic accident investigation to drug enforcement. In the late 1990s, Denson took a training course in homicide investigation from the state's Department of Justice, and, later, an advanced course in the methodology of murder investigation in Minnesota before becoming Palo Alto's primary homicide detective in June of 1997. As it happened, on Denson's first day on the job, the city had one of its rare murders, an event so unusual that people remarked about the coincidence of such a crime taking place on his first day. But over the next three years, Denson was required to use his specialty just three other times. It wasn't that Palo Alto had a lot of murders to investigate, but being prepared never hurt anyone. At least, that was the philosophy of the Palo Alto Police Department.

But crime in a college town is rarely the sort that one finds in big cities. Most of the problems confronted by the Palo Alto department were what one might expect with a large pool of young people on their own for perhaps the first time in their lives: underaged drinking, too-loud parties, bad driving behavior. True, there were the crimes that washed into town from those intent on victimizing the naive and gullible among the students, many of them rather well-to-do to begin with. And there were the other crimes the wealth of Palo Alto attracted: car prowls, residential burglaries, credit card scams and, not surprisingly for a college town, drugs.

Many of the eighty-two members of the Palo Alto Police Department actually lived in other, more affordable nearby cities, and commuted to work; this in turn led some in Palo Alto to consider the police and firemen that their taxes paid for to be, if not quite second-class citizens, at least the hired help.

Denson himself was just above medium height, and, although solidly built, was just beginning to encounter the middle-aged man's battle of the waistline. Although diffident in manner and frequently soft-spoken, he had a native shrewdness about people, particularly as to their peccadillos, great as well as small. He often hid his sense of humor behind a dry wit that seeped out of the corner of his mouth, almost as an afterthought, and the only way someone might realize that he was joking was by looking at his twinkling eyes. But Denson was peculiarly disciplined about his craft: having once learned the rules for investigating a murder, he methodically applied them, leaving nothing to chance, the same way a master carpenter builds a house: going step by step and cutting no corners. Not for Denson were any wild leaps of intuition, no sudden flash of inspiration to arrive at the solution by a great Inspector Morse–like leap of the imagination. Instead, Denson prided himself on his thoroughness, his patience, and the persistence of his logic, almost like a geometry student applying his compass, ruler, protractor and the theorems of cause and effect, to net his prey.

Denson, Wong and Hartnett reached Palo Alto about 2:45 P.M. on May 5, and after dropping Hartnett at the police station on Forest Avenue, went at once to 1545 Escobita Avenue. In front of the house, Palo Alto Police Agent Larry Buck, the acting watch commander, filled Denson and Wong in on the circumstances of the "unattended death," and both men used the rear storm doors to go into the basement and see for themselves.

There, sprawled on her back, a crimson pool of blood that was just beginning to coagulate oozing from her head, Kristine Fitzhugh lay as she had been left by the firemen who had attempted in vain to resuscitate her. Near her body lay a pile of what appeared to be dry-cleaning, still enclosed in its plastic coverings, and a scattering of school papers, some still wet with Kristine's blood. A large gray bell, like a Liberty Bell, was to the side, under the sheeted clothing. Up on the steps was a single right shoe, turned on its side.

Kristine's wounds, Denson soon learned, were far too severe to have been caused by a simple fall down the stairs. And the shoe: Denson thought its position on the stairs was peculiar. If Kristine had really slipped in her shoes, wouldn't the right shoe be on the *right* side of the stairs, instead of the left? And what on earth would a falling Kristine have been up to: carrying both dry-cleaning and school papers at the same time?

Why were the papers there, anyway? Surely she hadn't intended to grade them in the basement?

If Kristine had been murdered—and that was still an open question—the next issue was: had the murder occurred in the basement? That seemed possible, given the pool of blood on the floor. But Denson, Wong and others were bothered by what appeared to be a lack of blood spatter on the walls or stairs. If Kristine had been attacked by someone, and that someone had used some sort of object to hit her, there should be evidence of blood cast off from the object on the walls, floor and ceiling. This so-called "cast-off" is proof positive of an attack with a blunt object, and there didn't seem to be any visible anywhere on the walls near Kristine's body. Nor was there any obviously visible upstairs, Denson learned. But Denson was told that a fireman had spotted what he thought was a bloody sneaker print on the basement floor, and Denson himself thought he saw a similar shoe print on the door of the clothes wardrobe at the foot of the stairs.

Having seen enough to convince them that there were more questions than answers, Denson and Wong ascended the steps out of the rear of the basement. To their left as they exited was a brick patio; to the rear of the lot, a small back yard was fenced off from the neighbors by a green wooden fence. A small gate was cut into the planks to give access to the rear of the property on the other street.

Denson and Wong now entered the house through two doors that led from the patio area into the dining room. There they encountered Ken, Gaelyn and Carol. All three seemed subdued, almost numb. It seemed impossible to believe that Kristine Fitzhugh, a woman so full of life, a woman who was at the very center of their existence, was really dead.

FOR Gaelyn Mason, the timescale of the afternoon seemed warped, almost as if someone had taken the fabric of the day and twisted it into a barely recognizable semblance of normality. Some events were in slow motion, while others swept by her consciousness so quickly she later wasn't sure they had really happened. In short, she was in a state of shock.

After finding herself boxed in by the firemen, Gaelyn had picked her way over to the storm doors that led out of the basement. She shoved hard to open the doors, which she knew were rarely used. Up, up, out of the dark basement, over to the brick patio, then into the dining room, then the central hallway, where Carol, cellphone still in hand, was waiting. The house seemed to be filling up with men in uniforms—firemen, paramedics, police, all bustling around to no apparent purpose, at least to Gaelyn and Carol. At one point, weeping, Gaelyn found herself out on the front steps of the Fitzhugh house with Carol, where she tried to get her bearings and get her senses under control. But a policeman asked them to come back inside, and ushered them into the dining room.

The image of Kristine lying on the basement floor, unmoving, eyes unresponsive, had seared itself into Gaelyn's head. It didn't seem real; it couldn't possibly be real. Here was a woman who was Gaelyn's very close friend, her mentor, lying dead in a cluttered basement. And Gaelyn had been expecting a birthday present, or at least a fun party. It was impossible to sort it all out. Already the events were beginning to fade in and out of her awareness. Some things seemed sharp and vivid, while others barely registered. As the horrible afternoon progressed, Gaelyn would be asked what she saw and heard on several occasions, and by different people—worse, by people she had never before met until that moment; in other words, complete strangers. And the questions would keep coming for weeks afterward, although Gaelyn had no way of knowing that then.

Still later—much later—Gaelyn would describe her mental state quite vividly: "I have pictures that I see that just don't go away," she said. "I have sounds that I have . . ." The images in her mind would haunt her, some frozen in sharpness as if they were slides, others vague, even dreamlike.

She remembered being down in the basement with Ken. Ken asking her to help him with CPR. Her own reluctance. Carol coming to the top of the stairs, then going away. Ken pointing to the shoe on the stair, saying something about Kristine having fallen. Ken saying he didn't think CPR was of any use, that Kristine was already dead, but having to try anyway. The firemen arriving, Ken walking back up the stairs, hands raised like a surgeon, and the blood. Edging to the back of the basement, then out into the fresh air. Into the dining room, crying with Carol in the hallway, going outside, Carol trying to comfort her on the front stoop, the policeman asking (or was he telling?) them to go back in, into the dining room, because the police don't want people moving around inside the house. Gaelyn will recall seeing Ken coming down the hallway toward them as she and Carol go into the dining room, and then him joining them there, along with a police officer.

Inside the dining room there is a moment of quiet, as Ken, Gaelyn and Carol try to collect themselves. Gaelyn notices that there seems to be dried blood still visible in the cracks of the skin on Ken's hands, but for the most part he's washed it all off. Ken says he isn't sure what to do next. He's talking about who should be told, and how. He's concerned about his two sons, both away at college. He doesn't think they should be alone when they find out about their mother. At some point Ken gets up and goes into the kitchen to get a list of telephone numbers that the family keeps in a drawer. He brings it back into the dining room with him, along with his cellular phone.

Ken wants to make his first call to his oldest son, Justin, a senior at the University of the Pacific in Stockton, California. Ken wants to make sure that Justin has someone with him when he gives him the news. He thinks of Justin's college roommate, and decides to call him. But it appears that the roommate is in San Francisco. Ken dithers a few more minutes before finally deciding to call Justin directly. Ken asks if there is someone with him. Justin says he is alone. Ken asks him to find someone to be with him. Justin is impatient.

"What is it, what's going on?" he asks Ken. "Just tell me what's going on."

"You've got to tell him, Ken," Gaelyn says.

Ken finally tells Justin he's just come home and discovered that Kristine has fallen down the stairs. He tells Justin his mother is dead, that there was nothing anyone could do. Justin can't believe what he is hearing. He wants to come home immediately, but Ken tells him to wait for someone to drive him. He doesn't want Justin driving on the freeways by himself. Carol or Gaelyn takes the cell phone and calls Justin's fiancée, Angelina Whitesell, who is in her first year as a teacher in Concord and who has been living part-time at the Escobita house. Angelina agrees to go to Stockton to pick up Justin. Ken tells Gaelyn and Carol that he's sorry Kristine won't be able to go to Justin's graduation in two weeks. A bit later, Ken calls the second Fitzhugh son, John, who is attending college in Washington State, and arrangements are organized for him to fly home.

By then it is just after 2:30 P.M., less than an hour since Ken had arrived at Gaelyn and Carol's house with the Suburban to pick up the gambling equipment.

Ken is very thirsty. One of the police officers gets up and gets him a diet soft drink from the refrigerator in the kitchen. It is clear to Gaelyn and Carol that the police don't want any of them to leave the dining room. They continue making telephone calls to Kristine's friends, telling them what has happened. After some minutes, Carol remembers the dogs are still in the car. She asks the police if they can't get Boots and Reina out of the Suburban to put them in the back yard. Ken agrees that the dogs should be checked and removed from the truck. He takes his keys from his pocket, and goes outside with Palo Alto police Agent Larry Buck to let the dogs out of the Suburban. Ken opens a gate and puts the dogs into the patio area. Later they are let into the dining room to be with Ken, Gaelyn and Carol.

Now Ken tells Gaelyn and Carol they will have to find someone else to help them transport the party stuff, that he's sorry that he won't be able to help them now. Carol tells him to forget it; she says she's certainly not still going to have the party, not after what's happened.

"I'm sorry I got you involved in this," Ken tells Gaelyn and Carol.

WHEN Denson and Wong entered the dining room shortly before 4 P.M. on May 5, they saw a man they believed was a grieving husband, two distraught women, a large poodle, and a tiny Pomeranian, along with Officer Sascha Priess. Denson wasn't sure what was going on. He *was* pretty sure that Kristine Fitzhugh hadn't died from a fall down a flight of stairs, but even that was only a guess at that point. As he put it later, he hadn't had all that much experience with people who had fallen down stairs. Until the coroner came to take a look, they would all be working in the realm of speculation. Still, before going into the dining room, he'd told the officers in charge of the scene that until they found out different, they should be doing all the things they would do if a murder had occurred, not merely an accident. That meant minimizing the movements of people, officers and civilians alike, through the areas where evidence might exist.

Shortly after introducing himself, Denson asked Gaelyn to speak with him privately. They went down the hallway to the family room. Priess had already told Denson that Gaelyn was the second person down the basement stairs after Ken, and that Carol had never gone all the way down the stairs. In the family room, Gaelyn confirmed that information. She told Denson what had happened, from the time Ken came to pick them up to the time the firemen arrived.

After talking with Gaelyn, Denson was pretty clear on what he wanted to do next: he wanted to get everyone out of the house, and more importantly, separated, so he could get their independent versions of what had happened. He and Gaelyn went back to the dining room, and told Ken, Gaelyn and

Carol that he wanted them to come to the police station to be interviewed.

"There were a few reasons I wanted to do it in our police station," Denson said later. "Some of them being, I don't want to interview them together. I wanted independent recollections. We were controlling the environment, the house, at that time. It was a major incident scene, and we were investigating a death, and had already roped it off, and so I wanted to remove them from that, so the officers would have room to do what they needed to do."

But Ken didn't want to leave. He was worried that Justin and Angelina might show up while they were gone. Denson took Ken into the hallway and shut the dining room door. He explained that officials from the coroner's office would soon be arriving, and that they would be removing Kristine's body from the basement in a body bag, and that Ken didn't want to be around to see that.

"They're going to put your wife in a bag, and they're going to be taking her out of here," Denson said, "and it's not nice to see. I mean, that's their business, that's what they do, and I don't think someone should ever have to watch that sort of thing."

It took a little persuading, but eventually Ken agreed to go to the police station. As they were leaving, one of the police officers asked if he could move Ken's Suburban, which was still parked at an angle on the wrong side of the street where Ken had left it to run in and check on Kristine a little more than an hour earlier. Ken declined the offer, went to the truck, and re-parked it himself. Then he got into a patrol car with Agent Larry Buck, while Gaelyn and Carol got into the car driven by Denson and Wong, and everyone went off to the Palo Alto police station some five minutes away.

At the police station, Denson directed Gaelyn into one interview room, and Carol into another, and put Ken into a third. Denson wanted to get the details of everyone's story while they were still fresh. Most of all, he didn't want them contaminating each other's recollections of what had happened until he had everyone's version nailed down. Denson asked two other detectives to interview Gaelyn and Carol, while he prepared to talk to Ken.

Both Gaelyn and Carol were still in shock at the events. In their separate interviews, each told of the arrangements that had been made for Ken to pick them up in his Suburban, and his arrival at their house about 1:30 P.M. Then, as they had been pulling away, Ken's mention that he had gotten a telephone call from the Palo Alto school district asking about Kristine's whereabouts.

Each said Ken told them he'd tried to call Kristine, but had gotten no answer. They described how they had driven up to the house, noticed the open front door, and how Ken had checked the house, followed by his call for help, and then the attempt at CPR.

Both Gaelyn and Carol had known the Fitzhughs for years. They had met through the school district in the early 1990s, when all three women had taught at Cesar Chavez Academy in East Palo Alto, Palo Alto's heavily minority neighboring town. Over the ensuing years, Gaelyn, Carol and the whole Fitzhugh family had become quite close, often dining out, going on vacations together, and generally acting almost as an extended family. Both Gaelyn and Carol saw Kristine as more than a friend; in some ways, she was almost a parental figure, as was Ken. When Gaelyn and Carol decided to buy their own house in Palo Alto, Ken helped them with the real estate broker and mortgage lender. As the years unfolded, Gaelyn and Carol were there as both Justin and John grew from childhood into young adults. The Fitzhughs liked to refer to Gaelyn and Carol as "the Sadies"; it was sort of an in-joke between all of them, just as the Fitzhughs had their own nicknames for each other.

Ken and Kristine Fitzhugh had come to Palo Alto from the southern California city of San Diego in the early 1980s. Kristine was an accomplished pianist; so was Ken, although not quite as gifted as Kristine. Kristine had a teaching credential, and worked as a part-time music and singing teacher in Palo Alto–area elementary schools after having taught elementary school in both San Diego and East Palo Alto. While at Cesar Chavez Academy, Kristine had discovered a closet filled with unused musical instruments; she'd hit upon the idea of using Palo Alto music students to teach their younger counterparts in East Palo Alto, and with Ken's help, formed the Palo Alto/Ravenswood Collaborative Music Project, which provided scores of disadvantaged students with an opportunity to get involved in playing musical instruments. The cross-cultural music project was typical of Kristine, who took both her music and her teaching very seriously. For the past school year, Kristine had worked as a roving music teacher in the Palo Alto Unified School District, moving from school to school and classroom to classroom, teaching kids the rudiments of rhythms and singing. Although they were only elementary school students, Kristine was always meticulously prepared, and often agonized about her classes, worrying that her teaching skills were insufficient.

At five feet seven inches, the blond-haired Kristine was three inches taller than her husband, and among those who knew them, was seen as the primary social engine in the family, the person who made all the friends. It was Kristine who organized things, who was the more outgoing personality. She was extraordinarily meticulous about her appearance, and many saw her as a perfectionist. Ken, by contrast, was more of a tagger-along, or at least some thought: always present, but in a quiet, supportive way, for his vivacious wife. Later, even the Fitzhughs' closest friends weren't exactly sure what Ken did for a living, although they had the impression that he and Kristine were well-off, financially. There was talk that Ken had inherited quite a bit of money from his family in years past.

Although quiet, almost droll, in his personality, Ken was very smart. He had an undergraduate degree in electrical engineering and an MBA from Stanford. He had worked for almost a decade in the San Diego area as an executive for various housing development firms, and since moving to Palo Alto had worked for himself, primarily as a real estate consultant.

The boys were as different from one another as Kristine was from Ken. Justin, at 22, towered over his father, and was as outspoken as he was big-boned. John, 19, was more musically inclined, and much smaller in stature, even as he was quieter than his brother, much like Ken.

Now, as Gaelyn and Carol sat in their separate interview rooms, the Palo Alto police wanted to develop some of this background on the Fitzhugh family, even as they were listening for possible clues as to what might have happened.

Had either Gaelyn or Carol noticed any trouble between the Fitzhughs recently? Of course not, Gaelyn and Carol both replied. The idea was ridiculous. Ken loved Kristine, and Kristine loved Ken; they were devoted to one another. Any financial problems? No, no. The Fitzhughs were quite well-off, even by Palo Alto standards. Any secret love affairs? Now *that* was truly ridiculous. Kristine was just what she seemed: a lovely, beautiful woman who had tripped on her way down the stairs, the innocent victim of a horrible tragedy. What? Did the police believe this was more than just an accident?

It was too soon to say for sure, both Gaelyn and Carol were told, and that was just about the time they heard what sounded like a shout or a scream coming from down the hall. The detectives excused themselves, and rushed out to see what was wrong.

AT about 4:30 that afternoon, Agent Denson had settled into a chair in one of the Palo Alto Police Department interview rooms with Ken Fitzhugh. Ken sat across from him, a small table between them. The man Denson was looking at was 57 years old, with a full head of gray hair that was slightly too long, and wearing large wire-framed glasses that made his eyes seem larger, a short-sleeved blue striped shirt, black jeans, white socks and leather loafers. He slouched in his chair, either emotionally drained, Denson thought, or perhaps feigning an attitude of unconcern. He clasped his hands across his stomach, and twiddled his thumbs.

As Denson explained later, while he didn't know exactly what had happened to Kristine, he was aware that there were certain anomalies about the situation. For openers: even if she had taken a header down the steps, was it likely that Kristine could have hurt herself so badly? The firemen were convinced that the damage to Kristine's head far exceeded anything that might happen in a fall down a single flight of steps.

Denson's objective was straight from the investigator's manual: "I'm trying to get his account of what happened, right as fresh as I could get it," Denson said later. "And so, I'm not really making any judgment calls. I was collecting it all. I was being open-minded. And—it could be a fall. I mean, it could still be a fall. The medics had said they didn't think this was a fall down the stairs, but everyone falls different. And I didn't examine her myself. We don't touch the bodies. I had seen, of course, by the time I'm there, the blood all over the head, and on the floor. I know there's wounds there, but I don't know the extent of them."

So Denson approached Ken as he would any other griev-

ing spouse. But almost from the start, Denson noticed a pe-
culiarity in Ken's attitude about what had happened. He
seemed very detached, almost philosophical, Denson thought.

Denson began his interview almost diffidently, solicitous
of Ken's feelings. Because Ken was a primary witness, Denson had asked the department's technical people to turn on a
concealed video camera to record the interview.

After a few routine questions, as if he were simply trying
to get information needed to fill out a form, Denson began by
apologizing to Ken for asking him to come to the station.

"I'm very sorry about what happened," Denson told Ken.
"I know this is a very difficult time to be brought into a police
station."

"It's not—it's not an easy time, as you can see," Ken said.

"No, it's not," Denson agreed. "And I wanted to mention
that to you. I'm not going to compel you to make any statement. You're free to not make one at all. If you feel like you
can't, if you feel like you can't be here, I'll be glad to take
you home. But from my perspective, I think it's better to have
you here than to have you at home while the officers are
tramping in and out of your house and trying to do what
they're ultimately going to have to do. It's my experience that
it's best to not have other family members there while—"

"That's fine," Ken interrupted. "I'm probably better off
talking about this now."

Denson explained that because they needed to make a
complete investigation of what had happened, they would need
to know exactly what everyone had been doing up to the time
when the fire department arrived. And besides that, Denson
said, the police needed to search the Fitzhugh residence.
Would Ken mind them searching? Would he give his consent?

At that moment Ken's cellular phone rang. It was John,
who was just about to board a plane in Seattle to come home.
Ken encouraged his son to maintain his composure; it was
obvious to Denson that John had to be emotionally distraught
as he talked to his father. Ken told John that he, Justin and
Angelina would pick John up at the airport that evening.

While he had been talking to John, Ken had apparently
been thinking about Denson's request. When he hung up the

phone, Ken told Denson that it would be all right for the police to search the house. "I don't mind if they search the—they can tear the place apart," Ken said.

Denson hastened to assure Ken that the police wouldn't destroy anything. Then he read Ken the department's official consent-to-search form. By the time he was done reading, though, Ken apparently had second thoughts about the search.

"You know what," Ken said, "I don't want these guys just going through everything."

Denson tried to reassure Ken. "They really aren't going to go through everything," he said.

But even as Denson said it, one member of the Palo Alto Police Department was already doing just that.

Sometime between 4 and 4:30 P.M., after Denson, Wong, Gae-lyn, Carol and Ken had left the Escobita house for the trip to the police station, Palo Alto police Agent Gary Brooks, a twenty-year veteran of the department, noticed Kristine's car keys on the dining room table. He wanted to look at Kristine's silver BMW in the short driveway to see if anything special might be needed to search it, if and when that time came. The BMW was inside a strip of yellow crime scene tape that had been put up by that time, mostly to keep back neighbors and other curious onlookers who had gathered in front of the house.

Brooks noticed that there was a remote unlocking button on Kristine's keychain. As he approached the car, he pressed it. The BMW did nothing, but some few feet away Brooks heard a clicking noise. After a few more tries with the button, Brooks realized the clicking was coming from the blue Sub-urban, parked on the street where Ken had left it a few minutes earlier after re-parking it.

Brooks walked over to the Suburban, which was outside the yellow tape barrier, and opened the driver's-side door. When he opened it, he saw a pair of white running shoes protruding from underneath the driver's seat. Brooks remem-bered that he had seen those same shoes a few minutes earlier when he'd watched Ken re-park the truck.

Now Brooks did the wrong thing, as he later admitted.

"I bent down and looked at the shoes," he said, "and thought possibly I saw some bloodstains on one, and picked them up and saw what I thought were bloodstains on the shoes. I put them back as best I could, locked the car and called Sergeant Wong."

The bloodstains, if that's what they were, were tiny: about three spots altogether, more smears than anything else, all less than half-an-inch long, and on the inner front side of the right shoe.

Brooks hadn't been a police officer for more than two decades to proceed without knowing that his actions were problematic. For one thing, the Suburban was outside the yellow crime scene tape; for another, the shoes had been thrust under the seat, and therefore were not necessarily in plain view. Certainly the three spots on the upper right toe area of the shoes were hidden from casual observation. But Brooks was also percipient enough to realize that these blood spots might be extremely significant as the police tried to figure out what had happened to Kristine. Yet his actions in removing the shoes might put this critical evidence in jeopardy of being legally suppressed if someone were later to claim that Brooks' search was illegal.

Brooks decided to go into the station to tell Wong personally about his discovery.

Just as Brooks was explaining to Wong about the shoes, Denson was trying to convince Ken to give his consent for the search of the house, and the Fitzhugh cars as well, including the Suburban.

"I don't want to do that," Ken was saying. "I don't want—I don't want people that I don't know going through— we have valuable things. It's a very difficult time."

Denson nodded sympathetically, but he was thinking, *This guy is weird.* "He's flat-lining, as I call it," Denson said later. "Very calm. He just sits there talking to me. He was even grinning. Jovial. Unlike anyone I've ever dealt with before," when a death in a family had occurred. Now Ken was refusing to give his consent for a search. That was even more weird, to Denson.

"They're welcome to look in the basement," Ken added. "They're welcome to look on the basement stairs. And I don't want them anywhere else. No."

"Just in the basement?" Denson asked.

"Basement and stairs," Ken said.

"Okay," Denson said. "[I've got] to get some other things. I'm going to turn off the tape for a minute and go talk to my sergeant. It's ten till five. I'll be right back."

Outside the interview room, Denson encountered Wong.

"This guy's bizarre," Denson told Wong. "He's refusing to consent to the search of the house."

Wong said it didn't matter. That if Ken didn't consent to the search, they'd get a search warrant from a judge. Then he told Denson what Brooks had just told him—about the bloodstains on the shoes found in the Suburban. What was more, Wong added, it looked like the tread pattern of the shoe matched the bloody shoe prints seen in the basement.

Two minutes later, Denson was back in the interview room with Ken. The tone of his questioning sharpened subtly.

"Okay, Mr. Fitzhugh," Denson said, "what do you do for a living?"

"I'm a real estate consultant," Ken said.

"Your wife was a music teacher, you said?"

"Yes."

"And she's traveling—"

"Was."

"Was traveling?"

"Past tense," Ken corrected.

Denson was increasingly convinced that there was more to this than a fall down the stairs. Ken's demeanor seemed all wrong. Now he was correcting Denson on his grammar. Denson realized that Fitzhugh thought him stupid, that he believed himself smarter than all of the police put together.

"He was not the typical grieving widower or spouse I have always encountered," Denson said afterward. "Of course, you get a range of emotions, but he was very calm and methodical. His answers were thought out . . . very calm, he just sits there talking to me. And he wasn't like any grieving widower I'd ever seen." Denson told Ken that they needed to discuss everything that had happened that day, beginning from the time he and Kristine had first awakened.

Ken didn't seem to notice the slight difference in Denson's tone. He began describing everything he and Kristine had done that morning after rising.

He and Kristine had both awakened around six in the morning, Ken said, and they'd gone out jogging with the two dogs. Afterward, they'd returned home. Kristine had worked on the computer for a while, and then so had he.

Kristine had left the house around 10 A.M., Ken continued, to go to teach her first class. During that time, he had been going back and forth between his house and the next-door neighbor's, trying to help a lawyer who worked there with a computer problem.

"So I was there to tell her goodbye," Ken said. "And then at eleven o'clock, I put the dogs in the car and I drove to a real estate project." Ken suddenly was having trouble remembering where the project was. "Oh, man," he said. "I've been there a thousand times. My brain is not working."

"Okay," Denson said.

Ken said he'd try to remember where the project was, but they'd have to come back to that later.

"Okay," Denson said.

After going to view the property for the real estate project, Ken continued, he returned to Palo Alto for the 1:30 appointment with the Sadies, Gaelyn and Carol.

But as he was driving down the freeway, Ken said, he'd received a call from Phyllis Smith, who was the secretary for the school district's music program. Phyllis told him that Kristine had missed her 12:50 P.M. class at one of the elementary schools. That was very unusual, Ken said.

"That was a matter of concern," Ken said, "because Kristine never, ever missed a class. Hasn't missed a class the whole year."

When he'd arrived at Gaelyn and Carol's, Ken continued, he'd asked them if they had time to go by the house to check on Kristine.

"And we went over to my house to see what the hell was going on," Ken continued.

"And what happens when you get there?"

"Well, drove up in front and Kristine's car was in the driveway and the front door was open. That's very unusual ... so I pulled over and stopped and went in the house, [to] make sure everything was all right."

"And where did you go when you went in the house?"

"I went upstairs. I went upstairs and turned to the right, I expected to find her in the office. I didn't expect—I didn't know what to think, because she wasn't supposed to be there. But her car was there. I thought maybe her car hadn't started and she had gotten a ride with somebody or something ..."

Denson asked if he'd called out to Kristine when he'd entered the house, and Ken affirmed that he had.

"And she wasn't in the office," Ken continued. "I went into the master bedroom, the bathroom, she wasn't there. Went downstairs. And at this point I was looking for her. I was just looking around at this point. So I headed for the family room, and just as I passed the basement door, the door was open and the light was on. That's not the normal situation. So I went in there and I looked down—I looked down the stairs and she was lying there at the bottom of the stairs with her feet—her feet up and her face down, just lying there."

Ken still seemed flat, almost as if he were talking about something he'd seen on television. Occasionally a deep sigh escaped as he looked down at his hands.

"So I ran outside and Gaelyn or Carol saw me come," Ken continued, "and opened the door, and I yelled for help, to come help. I went running back in and down the stairs and she was not—she was face-down beside an old bell and there was a lot of blood, and her face was on a bunch of cleaning that we brought back from the cleaners and her face was on a plastic bag.

"And I—I looked to see if she was breathing. Her—back and chest were not going up and down at all." He was silent for a bit, then sighed again.

"So then I saw the black shoe ..." he said. Suddenly he raised himself partly out of his seat and began to yell:

"The GOD DAMN BLACK SHOES!" he shouted, grimacing, as he brought his two clenched fists crashing down on the desk. Then, recovering, he brought his hands back into his lap and interlaced them as before, as if nothing had happened.

Denson was taken aback by this outburst. Here was a man who had previously been so placid that he might have been describing a routine business transaction, who had erupted with sudden, unexpected violence. Was that what had happened to Kristine, Denson wondered—had Ken Fitzhugh beaten his wife as viciously as he had just attacked the table top?

The explosion was audible throughout the police station. Detectives interviewing Gaelyn and Carol excused themselves and rushed to look through the small dirty window into the Fitzhugh interview room. Some thought Ken and Denson had gotten into a fistfight. Denson saw them peering in. He spread his hands in a "who knows?" shrug.

Ken didn't seem to realize the impact of his outburst. He slumped back in his chair and continued, telling Denson that Kristine had owned a pair of black shoes that she had fallen in once before, giving Denson the history of the black shoes. Denson knew exactly what Ken was talking about, because he'd seen the single right black shoe on the steps, and had thought at the time that it was oddly placed.

"Okay," Denson said, to keep Ken going. But Denson's mind was whirling. Was there something else here—maybe something a bit Freudian in Ken's cursing of the shoes—*the shoes, the God damn black shoes*? Was Ken unconsciously pointing out to Denson the very evidence that seemed to suggest that Ken Fitzhugh himself had murdered his wife of thirty-three years—his *own* shoes?

Denson had already noticed that Ken was wearing black leather loafers with white athletic socks. *God damn black shoes, too*, Denson thought. Had Ken replaced his white running shoes—the ones found in the Suburban by Brooks, the ones with the bloodstains on them—with the black loafers?

The shoes, the shoes—both hers as well as his, worn and unworn—here indeed was one of the keys to the puzzle, a psychological enigma if there ever was one. Because if Ken Fitzhugh had really killed his wife, was he now subconsciously admitting his responsibility? And if he *had* killed his wife, why? Why in the world had he done it?

ALMOST a year later, when Denson was asked when he first began to think of Ken as his prime suspect in the murder of Kristine Fitzhugh, he didn't hesitate: "When I found out about the shoes," he said, meaning the white running shoes. Once he'd heard that a pair of bloodstained shoes had been found under the seat of Ken's Suburban, Denson was sure he knew who the killer was. But knowing who it was and proving it were two different things, and understanding why it had happened was another thing entirely. Nor could Denson have dreamed of what prosecutors would eventually offer to the jury as the reason for the murder—it was entirely too outlandish to imagine, at least on May 5, 2000.

Denson's strategy at this point was right out of the homicide investigator's manual: get Ken to commit to a story, then try to poke holes in it.

"I'm trying to get everything I can from him," Denson said later. "I want to lock him into a story, and I'll use whatever he's told me in the first one—I'll try to verify everything I can that he's told me, and then I'll refute it in later interviews." In short, Denson was working as a sort of human lie detector at that point.

Ken's explosion over "the God damn black shoes" nevertheless shocked Denson. The outburst seemed to come out of the blue, as Denson put it later. He realized that Ken was still talking about Kristine's shoes.

"She had a pair of black shoes," Ken was saying, "that she had fallen in before. She had fallen on the friend's sidewalk, the office sidewalk. Didn't have anything against the heel. And I told her after she—when she fell then, I caught her or she would have smashed her face on the sidewalk, and

I told her then how her—" Ken's voice trailed off, so Denson couldn't make out what he was saying.

"She didn't do it," Ken added. "And I must have told her—I must have told her six times to get rid of the black shoes. And then she bought some red ones just like them.

"She'd get dressed and she'd say, 'How do I look?' and I'd say, 'Well, fine, except I wouldn't wear those damn black shoes. You're going to fall.' And there they were, on the—one was on the stair and I don't know where the other one was."

"Okay," Denson said.

Ken continued his story: how he'd tried to resuscitate Kristine with Gaelyn's help.

"So I started mouth-to-mouth resuscitation. I got air in her lungs," Ken said, "but there was a gurgling sound and I thought, 'Oh my God.' And then I put my hand on her artery in her neck and couldn't find any pulse at all."

Ken said he told Gaelyn they should keep trying, even if it wasn't doing any good. "We kept at it until the paramedics came, 'cause I know you don't stop until the paramedics come."

It seemed like a long time before the fire department arrived, Ken added. "She gurgled when I breathed into her mouth. There wasn't any pulse. There wasn't anything. She was already gone. She was already gone."

Denson mumbled something sympathetic, and Ken went on.

"Now," he said, "the other thing that bothered me. The black shoes bothered me, the bell bothers me. The bell had been out in the yard. It's an old ship's bell. And it had been out in the yard for eighteen years. Last week I decided to bring it inside and see if I could sell it on eBay. So I took it down into the basement. I didn't put it away, really, it was heavy. By the time I got to the bottom of the stairs, I just kind of put it down. If I put it away—"

"Don't start blaming yourself," Denson said. But Denson was already thinking: Ken was trying to convince him that Kristine's death was an accident, that the combination of the black shoes, the plastic dry-cleaning and the bell were the culprits.

"If I had thrown her black shoes away," Ken continued. "If I threw—If I put the bell away—If I—I spent a lot of time in the home office. If I had been there, instead of away, then—"

But *was* Ken away? The white shoes, the bloody shoes found in the Suburban, seemed to show differently. If Ken had been wearing the white running shoes when the firemen arrived, that might explain the blood spots. But Ken was wearing his black leather loafers—black loafers with the white socks. Wasn't he? It was all about the damn shoes, Denson thought. How had the bloody shoes gotten into the Suburban? Denson was pretty sure that Ken had been under observation by Priess, the firemen and Pohl, to say nothing of Gaelyn and Carol, from the time they had all arrived at the house. When would he have had an opportunity to put the bloody running shoes into the Suburban?

Of course, Denson thought, it was always possible that the bloodstains had been on the shoe *before* Kristine had been killed, or that the blood had nothing to do with Kristine. Maybe Ken had bled on his own shoes in the recent past. Maybe Denson was making too much out of something that was perfectly explainable. Still, Ken's demeanor suggested that he was lying for some reason, Denson thought.

But Denson kept this internal dialog to himself. Now was not the time to confront Ken on a possible major inconsistency in his story. First Denson had to get as much detail as he could to lock Ken in, before he could even think about locking him up.

Back at the house on Escobita Avenue, Officers Priess and Pohl were examining the basement and the steps for evidence. They especially wanted to find blood evidence, including blood spatter, that might explain what happened to Kristine, and how she had come to have such severe wounds. Both officers had cameras. Priess began keeping a record of their photographs, and noting items they might wish to seize as evidence.

Priess photographed the single black shoe on the steps. It appeared to be a sandal-type shoe, sort of a mule. Priess looked around, and discovered the other shoe near Kristine's head at the bottom of the steps. Priess took photographs of the plastic-covered dry-cleaning and the brass bell, as well as the school papers. A small blue cabinet at the base of the stairs was partly open, and inside Priess could see other clothing hanging from white plastic hangers, along with a bent closet pole. On the floor of the basement, Priess discovered a portion of a woman's earring. Not far from that, Priess discovered a pair of women's eyeglasses with one of the lenses knocked out. Blood spatters were on the intact lens. A few feet away, Priess discovered the other lens; it was devoid of any blood.

Going upstairs, Priess noticed what appeared to be a bloodstain on the hallway floor, and a second one on the basement landing next to the hallway. Priess snapped pictures of those, and then began taking pictures of the kitchen and the dining room as well. Priess and Pohl continued to examine the house, still on the lookout for blood spatter, but besides the two spots they had already found, which looked more like drips than anything else, there were none. And even those spots weren't necessarily significant: with all the blood pooled downstairs, it was perfectly possible—perhaps even likely—that the spots had come off some fireman or policeman's shoes during all the earlier commotion.

The lifeless body of Kristine Fitzhugh still lay supine on the basement floor as the afternoon edged toward evening, and the Palo Alto police continued to go through the house.

Back at the police station, Denson invited Ken to theorize about what had happened to Kristine. This was another standard police interrogation technique: invite the subject to speculate on what happened. Often, during the course of a narrative, new facts will emerge.

"What do you think happened when you weren't there?" Denson asked. "What's your impression of what occurred?"

"Okay," Ken said. "We know that she was ready to go out, because beside her purse on the dining room table was her muffin and her water bottle. And that's the last thing she does before she goes out, is get those things together. I think she had loaded something in the car, come back in, hadn't shut the door, didn't matter 'cause the dogs weren't there. And then she went down into the basement for something, and I can't figure out what, unless it was the paper cutter. She goes into the basement seldom. At first, you know, when I saw the clothes there, that she was on top of the clothes, those clothes came back from the cleaners. They were winter clothes, she wanted to put them away, hadn't yet. And I figured that she had taken the clothes down to put them away."

The clothes were normally stored in the blue wardrobe at the bottom of the basement steps, Ken said. It was his guess, he said, that Kristine had decided to put the clothes away in the wardrobe when her foot came out of the shoe, causing her to trip on the stairs.

"Okay," Denson said. "So you presume that what happened is, [she's] loading stuff back and forth from the car, gets to the basement, for whatever reason, and trips on the stairs with her shoes and ultimately lands at the bell?"

"Yeah. I think she hit her head—was down beside the bell."

Denson asked if Ken had seen anything on the bell that would indicate that Kristine had hit it with her head, and Ken said he hadn't. But, he added, "I wasn't paying much attention."

Now Denson wanted to pin Ken down as to his whereabouts in the time before the murder. Ken said he'd left the house about 11 A.M. to view the real estate parcel, and that it took perhaps forty-five minutes to drive there. He'd taken the dogs with him, Ken said; before, he might have left the dogs at home, because the neighborhood had previously had a rash of burglaries, but since the burglary problem had abated in recent months, he had begun to take the dogs out with him more often.

Denson asked Ken what time it was when he left the place where he'd been viewing the real estate.

"Well," Ken said, "exactly forty-five minutes before 1:30."

Ken gave Denson a few details about the real estate project: the day before, a man had called to ask him about the parcel's ownership. He had previously done work on the same parcel for a business called Family Golf Centers, and the man who had called him wanted to put a church on the same ground. Ken said he went to the site to see whether a church could be built there.

"Okay," Denson said. "So you leave there at 12:45, because you have a 1:30 appointment with Carol and Gaelyn. You're called as you get close to town, about 1:15, you said?"

Ken agreed that he'd received the call from Phyllis Smith of the school district about that time, as he was heading south on the 101 freeway to pick up Gaelyn and Carol.

"Any reason you didn't go straight to your house before you went to Carol and Gaelyn's?"

Ken said he'd considered it, but thought he would pick them up first before going to his house, because they weren't very far away.

Denson asked Ken what time they got to his house.

"They took a couple of minutes wrestling something into their car," Ken said, referring to the cooler Gaelyn had moved. "So we probably left there at 1:35 and I was at my house at 1:40 or something, about twenty minutes to two."

"So you all three arrive, you got into the house, check the house, and ultimately you find her in the basement?" Denson asked.

Ken's cellular phone rang once more. He told Denson it might be one of his sons calling. It was John. Denson waited while Ken spoke into the phone. It sounded as if John's plane might have been delayed for some reason.

"Hello? Yes, John," Ken said. "That's all right. Oh, I'm sorry to hear that. Okay. Before we come to the airport we'll call and check so we know what time—No, just wait for us. Okay. Good. Yeah. Thanks for letting me know. Bye. Good luck to you."

Good luck to you? Again Denson was struck by the lack of emotion on Ken's part. Why was Ken wishing his son good luck? Or had John wished his father good luck, and Ken was simply returning the salutation? But 'good luck' on today of all days? Denson put that thought aside and returned to his questions.

"Okay," he said. "Ultimately you find your wife at the bottom of the stairs, you begin the CPR on her. I presume she was bleeding?"

"I don't know if she was still bleeding, but there was a lot of blood," Ken said as he put away his telephone.

"And you gave her CPR. I note that you don't have blood on you."

"Well," Ken said, "take a look."

"I see it on your hands," Denson now said.

"Take a look," Ken said again.

What was this? It sounded like Ken was being defensive about something, as if the absence of blood might somehow be incriminating. Or was Ken suggesting that the small amount of residue still visible was proof of his story?

"Did you change in any way?" Denson asked. "Have you changed clothing?"

Ken appeared to shake his head, no.

"No?" Denson asked. "That is exactly what you were wearing?"

"Yeah," Ken said.

Now he had Ken committed to the black leather loafers. Ken had just said those were the shoes that he was wearing when he'd found Kristine. If the blood on the running shoes found in the truck had come from Kristine, Denson knew, Ken would have some explaining to do. He decided to give Ken an opportunity to modify his answer.

"Okay," Denson said. "I expected more. So this is exactly what you were wearing when you got there, and you haven't changed at all. Okay."

Ken returned to the brass bell. He said that when the paramedics came, they moved the bell out of the way. He still seemed to be suggesting that the bell was the culprit. Denson decided to try to pin Ken down as to his movements immediately after he'd stopped his futile CPR on Kristine.

"When the paramedics take over," he asked, "where do you go?"

"I watched for—I watched for just a little bit," Ken said.

"And then I went up the stairs and into the bathroom upstairs. Washed off my face and hands. Then I went into the kitchen to the telephone there on the wall. I realized I couldn't call my boys yet. I ought to call them first and then a policeman came in and I talked to him and then I went back down the stairs and I washed up again because I still had blood on me. And finally my hands were dripping. I went back to the bathroom and dried my hands. They were wet. Went into the dining room."

It sounded as though Ken was saying he'd made two trips to the bathroom to wash his hands after leaving the scene in the basement. It also sounded as if Ken was saying he'd been in the basement twice. Denson knew that he could check those movements with the accounts of Priess, Pohl, the firemen and Gaelyn and Carol. He noticed that Ken said nothing about putting his running shoes under the front seat of the Suburban.

"Okay," Denson said. "Let's see if you told me everything. I know it's hard to relive, especially since it just happened a few hours ago. We like to talk to you right away so we can get what's fresh in your mind. Anything else you can tell me, offhand?"

"From an investigative point of view," Ken said, "it's a such a shame because she—The boys have gone off to college, she just found something she really loved to do, this music teaching. This is the first year she had it. It's such a terrible shame, because we were doing it together. I help her prepare stuff, and [she was] really enjoying herself again. Her older son graduates from college in a couple of weeks, so she wanted to get ready for that. Very sad time. Sorry to burden you with that."

Denson's mind was filled with a kaleidoscope of sudden, conflicting, fragmentary impressions. *From an investigative point of view . . .* What did *that* mean? *She was really enjoying herself again?* Did that mean Kristine hadn't been enjoying herself before that? *Very sad time.* What was sad about getting ready for her son's graduation? *Her older son?* What was this? Wasn't Justin *their* older son, not *her* older son?

"It's okay," Denson said, recovering. "You said 'her older son.' Is he not your son?"

"No," Ken said. "He's our son."

"Your son, okay," Denson said. He asked how long Ken and Kristine had been married.

"Thirty-three years," Ken said.

"Wow," Denson said. "How would you categorize your relationship? Did you guys have a close, good relationship?"

"As close as—" Ken's voice trailed off.

"No recent problems, no—"

"There were some difficult years when the boys were in high school," Ken said, "and their lives smoothed out when they went to college, and it's been very nice."

At the Escobita house, the efforts by Agent Buck, Officers Priess and Pohl, and others from the Palo Alto Police Department continued, even as Denson was finishing his interview with Ken. Sometime around 5:45 P.M., a civilian employee of the nearby Mountain View Police Department, Brad Flores, arrived with a video camera. Buck and Priess had decided that they needed a video record of the scene, and the Palo Alto Police Department's video camera was unavailable.

Flores at first believed that the Palo Alto people simply wanted to borrow his camera, but when he got to the house he learned that Brooks and Priess wanted him to actually make the tape. They told him they would tell him what to shoot. Flores began with an exterior shot of the house, surrounded by then with the yellow crime scene tape, and then moved up to and through the front door.

The house was larger than it appeared from the street. As one moved toward the large green front door, a large brass door knocker was visible, as was a pile of new mail on the lower right side of the stoop. A set of small windows bracketed the door on either side. Through the door into the entry foyer, a large living room was off to the right, and the dining room off to the left. The hardwood floor of the hallway ran straight back to the rear of the house, and the bathroom where Ken had washed the blood off his face and hands. On the right side of the hall, a fairly broad, carpeted staircase led up to the second floor of the house.

Following the directions of Priess and Buck, Flores and his camera moved down the hardwood hallway, past the dining room and past the kitchen, which was off to the left. At the entrance to the basement landing, on the right, Flores recorded what appeared to be a smeared blood spot, which Priess marked with a plastic measuring stick for scale. A second similar spot appeared at the top of the basement steps, and Priess moved the marking scale to this spot as Flores continued to record. Flores then entered the stairway, and about halfway down Kristine's right shoe still lay as it had been found, on the left side of the steps.

The basement was crowded with the oddments of a family's three decades of life in the house: an assortment of tools, filing cabinets, a set of exercise weights, stacks of cardboard boxes—all the usually unseen collectibles of an ordinary domestic environment probably duplicated in at least a million homes around the country. Flores' camera caught the image of a telephone on a post near the steps. Priess and Denson had noticed the telephone earlier, and wondered why Ken had come running back up the stairs to get Gaelyn or Carol to call 911, when he could have used this telephone himself and saved a few precious minutes.

Kristine still lay on her back, surrounded by the used life-saving equipment the firemen had scattered about as they tried to pump her life back into her. It was a frightening scene, with the blood having run across the floor. However she had died, it had happened with an incredible amount of violence. It was hard to believe that a few short hours before, Kristine had been eating a muffin and preparing to teach elementary school students the simple joys of music. But someone had decided, apparently, that she should die instead.

About six P.M., Denson, Wong, Ken, Gaelyn and Carol all returned to the house on Escobita. After having declined to agree to a full-scale search of the house, Ken had relented—but only if he could be present to keep an eye on the police. While in Denson's car in front of the house, Ken had finally signed the consent-to-search form after Denson assured him that he could be present. Gaelyn and Carol met two friends of Kristine's out in front, and because they were cold—all they had to wear was shorts and light shirts—they were allowed back into the house, where all four sat once more in the dining room while Ken gave Denson the walking tour.

In fact, Ken's presence was fine with Denson. "I needed him back in the house to tell me if anything has been stolen, if anything was out of place," Denson said later. "If any of the windows had been broken, if the house was locked. So I needed him back in the house. That was okay with me." It also gave Denson a chance to lock Ken further into his story, and the more details Denson had to work with, the more details he would have to check. Details, details—it's always the details that trip the liar up, Denson knew.

Denson had Ken take him through the house, room by room, on a search for missing items, and any evidence of a break-in. At first blush, there didn't seem to be anything missing. They checked china cabinets, all the sterling silver, all the places where valuable items might be kept. Nothing worth stealing had been taken. Nor was there any obvious evidence of a burglar—no jimmied doors, no broken windows. The search eventually led to the Fitzhugh bedroom upstairs. They checked to see if Kristine's jewelry was missing, but as far as Ken could tell, it was all there.

While Denson and Ken were inspecting the jewelry, two other detectives were busy at the Suburban. Now that he had Ken's consent for the search, the time was right to "find" the bloody shoes. Sometime around 6:15 or so, Palo Alto Police Agent Jean Bready opened the Suburban's driver's-side door and removed the white running shoes, but not before taking a series of Polaroid pictures of them. Flores was summoned, and he recorded the shoes on videotape.

In the meantime, another detective, Agent Sandra Brown, had opened the rear of the Suburban. There, wadded up in the back, was a reddish-stained, crumpled paper towel. Flores shot that, too.

By this time, Denson, Ken and Wong had finished up in the family room, back on the first floor. Now Denson was preparing to tighten the noose. He began by asking Ken about his footwear during the morning jog he had taken with Kristine. Ken said he'd been wearing his white running shoes.

"Where are the shoes now?" Denson asked. Ken said that after his run he'd put them in his closet upstairs.

"What size do you wear?" Denson asked him.

"Eight," Ken said. But his running shoes were eight-and-a-half, he added.

Now Wong produced a Polaroid photo of the white running shoes.

Those shoes *looked* like his, Ken admitted, but he wasn't sure if they really were his. Denson and Wong told Ken that the photograph had been taken of a pair of shoes found in the Suburban. Ken said he had no idea of how any shoes could have gotten into the Suburban.

"He said he was dumbfounded," Denson said later.

Since Ken declined to say that the shoes in the picture were his, Denson and Wong decided to bring the actual article in for Ken to identify. The shoes were placed in a clear plastic bag, brought into the family room and shown to Ken.

Those were his shoes, all right, Ken said. Denson and Wong said the shoes appeared to have blood on them, and Ken gave no reaction. Denson told Ken the police intended to test the red spots on the shoes to see if it was human blood. Still Ken said nothing.

Denson again asked Ken how his shoes wound up in the Suburban—which, by Ken's own account, he had with him at the time Kristine had likely died. Ken had no explanation. He was sure the shoes were in his closet upstairs, he said.

"Show me," Denson said.

Ken led them upstairs to the master bedroom once more.

"Where are they?" Denson asked. "What did you do with them after you went running?"

They were standing at the open closet door, and Denson could see that the closets were organized, with all the shoes lined up in pairs.

"Where would they be?" Denson asked. Ken pointed to the closet floor, and right in the middle of his row of shoes, there was a blank space.

Ken said that was where he'd left his running shoes that morning.

Now Denson asked Ken to show him his jogging suit. Ken opened a drawer and produced a black jogging outfit. Denson asked for the tee-shirt, socks and underwear Ken had worn during the run. Ken said they were in the laundry basket. Denson opened the laundry basket, and it was empty. Ken told him Kristine must have put the clothes into the washing machine.

"Let's go check the washing machine," Denson told Ken.

They went back downstairs and into the laundry room, which was next to the kitchen and the bathroom on the first floor. They opened the machine up, and Denson saw a load of wet laundry inside. Denson asked Priess and Pohl to collect the wet garments; he wanted to check them for blood residue. He, Ken and Wong returned to the family room.

Denson now asked Ken to reconstruct, if he could, his movements after the fire department rescue squad arrived at the house that afternoon. Ken said he remembered walking up the basement stairs to wash the blood from his hands and face. Because he didn't want to leave watery smears of blood on a green towel in the bathroom, he had gone into the kitchen to get a paper towel, and he'd used that to finish drying his hands and face. He dropped the used paper towel into the trash can in the bathroom, he said. Someone checked the bathroom, and found a crumpled paper towel there.

After he'd washed, Ken said, he recalled going out to the Suburban to check on the dogs.

Denson now produced the bloody paper towel that Agent Brown had found in the rear of the Suburban. Did Ken have any explanation for how *that* bloody paper towel got into the truck?

Ken said he had no idea.

"Could it have been," Denson asked Ken, "after you've done CPR, that you come up and you wash in the bathroom, and then you said you went to check on your dogs, could it be you were wiping your hands, and then, you threw it in the truck?"

Ken said that must have been it.

Denson was pleased. Sometimes, he would say later, "if you are not giving me anything, I will offer you something that I can disprove. Hand you an explanation. 'Oh yeah, that must be what happened.' Okay, good."

But Ken's acceptance of Denson's proffered explanation

for the bloody towel in the Suburban only intensified Denson's suspicions. "When I had talked to the officers earlier," he said later, "they had said that, upon their arrival, they had constant contact with or knowledge of where he was located at all times. He was with Agent Buck. So I was confident they knew exactly where he was, and that they would be able to tell me if he had paper towels in his hands [when he went out to the Suburban]." If Denson could prove that Ken hadn't put the bloody towel into the Suburban when he said he had, he would have evidence that Ken was lying.

Denson, Ken and Wong now went into the dining room, where Gaelyn, Carol and two of Kristine's friends were waiting. Ordinarily, Gaelyn and Carol shouldn't have been permitted back inside the house, but as Denson explained later, the police still weren't sure if they were dealing with a murder or an accident, and that limited their degree of control over the premises.

Not long after they joined the others in the dining room, Denson and Wong learned that Justin Fitzhugh had arrived at the house, and was outside the crime scene tape, asking to see Ken. Ken went outside to meet him, accompanied by Denson.

Justin was weeping. He and Ken hugged, but Denson thought Ken was still rather more unemotional than he would have expected.

Justin wanted Ken to tell him what had happened. Ken told him that it looked as if Kristine had tripped on her way down the stairs, and had suffered a severe head injury.

"I just can't believe it," Justin said. Ken said he couldn't, either.

Denson went back inside the house to talk to the officers there, again explaining that he wanted the scene handled as if a murder had occurred, even if they later discovered that it was an accident. When he went outside once more, someone told him that Ken, Justin and Angelina wanted to leave, to go to the airport to pick up John. They were in Angelina's car, since the police had taken possession of all the Fitzhugh vehicles. Denson asked Ken to wait a minute; he reminded Ken that he'd asked for Ken's clothing, and that Ken had agreed to give his clothes to him. Ken got out of the car and went back inside. Denson escorted Ken to the bedroom, where Ken removed all his clothes, item by item, and Denson placed each one in a separate plastic bag. Denson similarly inspected all the new clothes Ken intended to wear before handing them to him to put on.

Then Ken, Justin, Angelina and the Sadies drove off, to find something to eat before going to pick up John at the airport. Just as they left, a van from the Santa Clara County Medical Examiner's Office arrived.

As the on-scene investigator for the Santa Clara County Medical Examiner's Office, it was Andrea Wagner's job to make the initial call: accident or murder. Wagner arrived at the Escobita house at 7:50 P.M., about two hours after her office was notified by the Palo Alto police of the "unattended death." Ideally, medical investigators like Wagner should be summoned to the scene as soon as possible after the discovery of a victim, before a scene becomes too disturbed by evidence collectors to allow for accurate reconstruction, and also to most accurately assess the probable time of death. But the Escobita house was already disturbed, because the firemen had moved several items around to have more room to work, and the time of death was fairly clear: it had to have happened sometime between the end of Kristine's last class at 11 A.M. and the discovery of her body at 1:40 P.M.

After consulting with the police and learning that there was no sign of forced entry into the house, Wagner made her way to the basement to look at Kristine's body.

"The decedent is viewed supine on the cement floor to the right of the stairs," Wagner reported afterward. "She is cold to the touch . . . there is blood noted on her sweater (near the head and on the arms) and her pants (on the front legs). All her jewelry is cataloged, and left in place as her hands are bagged . . . there is a wound (possibly puncture-like) on the base of her left fifth finger (possibly from her ring). She has several (at least five) wounds to the top and back of the head."

It was her opinion, Wagner told Denson, that there was no way Kristine could have sustained the wounds to her head from a fall down the stairs. They were simply too severe. It seemed almost certain that Kristine had been attacked, probably with some sort of blunt object.

Had the attack taken place in the basement? The damage to Kristine's head appeared to have come from behind. Did that mean she was on her way down the stairs with dry-cleaning and school papers in hand, when she was hit from behind? How else could she have ended up face-down at the bottom of the stairs? But Denson was bothered by the position of Kristine's hands, at least as described by Ken and Gaelyn. He knew that if Kristine had fallen forward on the stairs, probably even if she had been the victim of a surprise attack, the chances were quite good that she would have dropped the plastic-enclosed dry-cleaning and school papers and put out her hands to break her fall. It was simply reflex action. Yet Kristine's body was on top of the dry-cleaning, and her hands were close to the plastic sheeting, rather than stretched out before her, as one might expect to see in a fall.

Now that the death had been tentatively designated a murder, Denson was on firmer legal ground. He went back to the police station to call a deputy district attorney to help him draft search warrants for the Fitzhugh house and all of the vehicles. About an hour later, Denson telephoned a judge in Santa Clara, and received authorization for the search warrants. And an hour after that, he placed a call to Ken Fitzhugh's cellular phone. Would Ken mind coming into the station to answer a few more questions?

Ken, having picked up John at the airport and had dinner at a nearby restaurant, told Denson he would be happy to come in.

"I couldn't sleep anyway," he told Denson. Denson thought Ken was trying to make a joke.

KEN arrived at the Palo Alto police station, accompanied by Justin and John, sometime after 10 P.M. Just why Ken agreed to this interview is a puzzler, however.

As Ken put it later, he had no reluctance to come forward because he knew he was innocent of any crime. In fact, Ken would say he still believed that Kristine had died in an accidental fall at that point.

But the events of the afternoon should have triggered Ken's suspicions about Denson's intent. After all, Denson had questioned him about the bloody running shoes and the bloody paper towel in the rear of the Suburban. He'd asked him to account for his whereabouts during the noon hour, when Kristine was presumably dying; he'd seized the Fitzhugh laundry from the washing machine, and had even taken the clothes Ken was wearing for closer examination. He'd asked Ken if he and Kristine had been having any recent problems in their marriage. Now Denson was asking him to come back to the police station in the middle of the night. All of this should have been a clear indication to Ken that Denson believed a crime had been committed, and that he, Ken, was the person who was most likely responsible for it.

Certainly the circumstances led Justin to believe that the police had their eye on his father. He told Ken that he needed to hire an attorney. And there seems to be little doubt that a competent legal advisor would have told him to forgo a late-night interview in the police station for the time being. Ken had been up for just short of eighteen hours, and had just been through a traumatic series of events. A lawyer would certainly have told Ken that this was hardly the best time to be answering more police questions.

But Ken decided to come in, just the same.

Later, Denson would conclude that Ken believed he could outwit Denson, that Denson was just a simple cop who would accept whatever Ken told him as gospel. It was, Denson thought, a part of Ken's tremendous hubris.

"Because he's still trying to convince me that it's an accident," Denson said later, "and that it was just a sad thing that happened. And I think that he thinks I'm going to believe whatever he tells me. That he's brighter than all the rest of us who are wandering around this world, and he just thinks he can tell me something, and that's the way it is."

All three Fitzhughs were led into the detectives' offices at the Palo Alto police station. While Denson and Wong intended to interview Ken, John and Justin would be separately interviewed by Agents Brown and Bready, who were assigned to find out how Ken and Kristine had been getting along. Both Justin and John thought the interviews would be over in a short time. They were wrong, because it would be nearly 1 A.M. before Ken's, at least, was finally over.

Denson began by asking Ken a series of routine questions "for my report paperwork," including some vital statistics. When Denson asked for the color of his eyes, Ken said gray.

"Gray?" Denson asked.

"Green," Ken said. He grinned. Denson thought Ken was practically being jovial.

Denson told Ken he appreciated his coming back to the police station for more questioning. "We understand this is the hardest time," Denson said, "and like I was telling you before, this is difficult, but we have time constraints to meet and we're just trying to do the best we can."

"I understand," Ken said.

Denson said the police had so far removed nothing from the house other than a few items from the basement, and that in any case, they would provide a receipt to Ken for the items they had taken.

But, Denson said, he wanted to go over the events of the day once again, this time in more detail.

Ken now began taking the detectives through his entire

day—what he did, where he went, and the approximate time of each activity. He and Kristine had taken the dogs for a run early in the morning [actually it was more of a walk, since Reina the Pomeranian could hardly keep up], then, following showers, he and Kristine had worked at their respective computers for about an hour. Around nine, Ken had gone to the house next door, where several attorneys had their offices. Ken occasionally did paralegal work for them. One of the lawyers, Thomas Moore, was having trouble with his printer. Ken assisted Moore with troubleshooting the printer. Because his computer was networked with Moore's computer, Ken decided to try to see if he could diagnose the problem from his own terminal. Throughout most of the two hours he had worked on the problem, Ken said, he'd been going back and forth between the two houses.

Sometime around 10, he continued, Kristine had left for her 10:20 A.M. class.

Wong wanted to know what Kristine had been wearing, and Ken said that she'd been wearing the same clothes that she had been found in a few hours later. Denson asked about the half-eaten muffin on the kitchen table. Had she taken that with her when she left at 10 A.M.? Ken said he didn't think so.

"I mean," he added, "if she had taken it, she would have left it in the car. Typically, on Friday after the 10:20, she would come back for an hour or so before she went out again, because—she had, what, a 12:40 and then a 2 o'clock [class], which lasted two hours . . . so she'd normally just run out for the hour, then run back [home]. So I'm not surprised she didn't take her lunch—her muffin as lunch. And the water is a new program. We just got a whole bunch of bottles of water a couple of nights ago. Wanting to drink more water . . ."

Ken said he wasn't sure which school Kristine would have gone to for the 10:20 class. He said he'd never tried to keep track of the individual schools, because they always seemed to be changing.

Around 11, Ken continued, he'd let the dogs out again, and then put them in his Suburban to look at a piece of real estate in San Bruno, about fifteen miles to the north. He'd been involved with the property, or at least guiding the owners of the property through the government permit process, for the past three years, Ken said. The owners of the property were Family Golf Centers, and they had leased the land from the San Bruno Park school district to build a driving range. He'd received a call the day before from someone who wanted to investigate the feasibility of building a church on the property, and had been referred to Ken by someone in the San Bruno city government.

"If it worked out," Ken said, "it could be an additional consulting job for me, because you would have to do processing for government information, and although I've been there many, many times, I had always thought of it in terms of the golf facility, and I really hadn't thought of it in [terms of] where a church would go, a place for a church. So I went to take a look at it."

Denson asked for the name of the person who had called Ken about the property, but Ken drew a blank. He told Denson he could check with the city of San Bruno for the name of the person.

After driving up to the property, Ken said, "I parked and walked around the property, and looked at it from various angles. Pretty much figured that there might be room for a church there. And I left about—I left about 12:45, 'cause I had to be back in Palo Alto at 1:30.

"And as I was traveling home," he continued, "I got a call about 1:15 from Phyllis Smith, who's the music secretary. Asking me if I knew where Kristine was, that she hadn't showed up for her 12:50 class. Which is highly unusual. I mean, she's never, ever missed a class."

"How would Phyllis know your number of your cell phone?" Denson asked.

Ken explained that Phyllis had called his home office number, which rang through to his cellular telephone if no one picked it up. Phyllis knew his home office number because he had often volunteered his help for the district's music program. Phyllis told him that she'd tried calling the Fitzhugh home number, and Kristine's cellular number, and that she'd gotten no answer. That's when she'd called him, Ken said. Because

Phyllis had the wrong number for Kristine's cellular, Ken said, he'd given her the right one, and had told her to call him back if she was able to locate Kristine.

"So Phyllis said she would call and I said I would call," Ken concluded. "Phyllis said she'd called the home number and left a message. I called the home number, got no answer, called the cell phone, got no answer."

"So when you called your house, did the answering machine kick in, or—?" Wong asked.

"Yes," Ken said.

Wong wanted to make sure he understood: Ken was saying that he called Kristine at both the home number and on her cellular telephone, and that both the Fitzhugh home telephone and Kristine's cellular phone had automatic answering equipment hooked up. Wong was already thinking that the equipment should have picked up Ken's two calls to Kristine if he was telling the truth about making the calls. That might be a way to verify Ken's approximate location at 1:15 P.M. He asked again whether the answering equipment had clicked on when Ken called.

"Yeah," Ken said.

Wong asked where Ken had been when he received the call from Phyllis Smith.

"Bayshore Freeway [U.S. 101], Redwood City somewhere," Ken said. Redwood City was a little more than halfway back to Palo Alto from San Bruno.

"What were you thinking at this point when you were driving back to Palo Alto?" asked Denson.

"I was thinking it was pretty strange she hadn't shown up."

"Very unlike her character?"

"Very unlike her character," Ken agreed. "It wasn't strange that she didn't answer the cellphone. She didn't have it on a lot. But it was very strange she wasn't where she was supposed to be. But I was supposed to—I was supposed to meet Carol Piraino and Gaelyn Mason at 1:30 to do some hauling with them and the dogs. And I went ahead and picked them up thinking that I kind of wanted to go home instead, but it's very close by and I was due there, so I just went ahead and picked them up."

Ken said it took Gaelyn and Carol about five minutes to get organized and into his truck. Then, he said, he told Gaelyn and Carol that Kristine had missed her 12:50 class, and that he wanted to check on her to see if she was all right.

"So then," Ken went on, "as I approached the house, I saw Kristine's car was there. And as we got closer, I saw that the front door was open. So I pulled over to the left and got into the car, went into the house. Called her name. There wasn't any answer. So I went upstairs, first into the office. She wasn't there. Then into the master bedroom, master bathroom, she wasn't there. So I went downstairs and headed down the hall toward the family room and I passed the basement door, the door was open and the light was on."

"Is that door usually open?"

"Never."

"It's usually closed?"

"Unless somebody's in the basement. Ah, jeez, Louise."

All three men were silent for a moment. Then Denson prodded Ken to continue.

Ken described seeing Kristine at the bottom of the steps, face down, feet trailing back up the stairs. "I knew I needed help," he said. "So I ran out the front door and Gaelyn and Carol saw me running out of the door and I yelled, 'Come help me.' "

He went back inside and down the steps, Ken continued, and noticed the large brass bell at the bottom of the stairs and "I immediately thought, *She's fallen and struck the bell.* So I looked to see if she was breathing, to see if her back was going up and down, and she was not."

Denson asked where the bell was when Ken first saw it. Ken said it was very close to the stairs.

"And you know," Ken added, "I'm really beating myself up over not [taking care of] the bell. And I brought it downstairs a week ago, it was heavy, and I just stopped there. So then I saw on the stairs one of the black shoes. And really triggered in my mind that it had come off, [while she] was trying to go down the stairs."

Ken said he had trouble getting Kristine into position for mouth-to-mouth resuscitation, but he was finally successful. Then he'd asked Gaelyn to help him with chest compressions.

Denson drew a diagram of the basement, and asked Ken to draw a stick figure representing Kristine. Ken showed the approximate position of Kristine on the steps, and how he had moved her to facilitate the resuscitation effort.

Denson asked what had happened after the firemen arrived. Ken said that the three fire rescuers pushed the bell and the dry-cleaning out of the way so they could get to work on Kristine.

"At that point I stood up and tried to get out of their way so they could do their job," Ken continued. " 'Cause there wasn't much room in there. There's a lot of them. I went upstairs. Went into the bathroom, washed my hands, mouth, nose." Ken's voice began to drop so that it was harder to hear him.

"There was blood everywhere . . . There was a big mess," he went on. "Went into the bathroom, cleaned up a little bit. Went in the kitchen to get a paper towel, 'cause I didn't want blood all over it [the green bath towel]."

"Do you remember using the towel?"

"No," Ken said. He added something about the blood being hard to wash away, but it wasn't clear. Then: "But it didn't come out. I washed it again . . . My recollection up until that point is pretty clear. After that point it's difficult."

"Certainly," Wong said, sympathetically. But Wong and Denson wanted to get this sequence down in the exact order it happened, in order to account for the paper towel and bloody running shoes that had been found in the Suburban, as well as the blood-streaked green towel and the paper towel in the bathroom. Which had come first, and when? They knew it was possible that some of the evidence had been left after the murder, but before the discovery of the body.

"It's more difficult," Ken continued. "And at that point, I went out—I went out to the car to check the dogs, 'cause we always make sure the dogs are safe, and everybody was running into the house. And they were—so I came back in, went down the stairs, I think I [talked to] a police officer. And I wasn't much interested in what he was doing there. I wasn't much interested in what he wanted. I was interested in what was going on in the basement. So I went down into the basement and they had stopped working on her."

Ken said his next clear recollection was going into the dining room and seeing Gaelyn and Carol. They began discussing how to tell the boys, he said.

Wong asked about the storm doors into the rear of the basement. Ken said he'd just rebuilt the doors two weeks before; until then, he said, it had been covered with a tarp. It had never been locked, he said.

In fact, until the past few years, the Fitzhughs had rarely locked any of their doors. It was only after the neighborhood began experiencing burglaries that they began to use their locks, Ken said. Before leaving to see the property in San Bruno, he added, he'd unlocked the gate into the side yard, so the gardener could come in. The gardener usually came every Friday afternoon between 1 and 5 P.M. Ken didn't think the gardener had come that afternoon before Kristine was discovered.

Denson returned to the issue of the Suburban. "You thought," he told Ken, "there was a possibility that you had gone twice to the Suburban. I want you to think about that again and refresh your memory in any way, about your trips to the Suburban after you had discovered your wife, at the time of settling down in the dining room."

"Okay," Ken said. "I went back, checked on the dogs. And then the next time I went back was to get the dog's collar. But I think that's after we were in the dining room." Ken said he wasn't completely sure.

"And you said you remembered an officer walking out with you one of those times, or conversing with an officer at some point?"

"No," Ken said.

"Do you remember him asking you questions about the dogs or dog?"

"No, I think they wanted us in just one room. So I talked to the officer about going out of the room to get the dog and that was okay." But Ken said he didn't remember talking about the dogs with any of the police officers.

One of the Palo Alto police officers had noticed Ken going through Kristine's purse as they all were sitting in the dining room. Ken said he'd looked through the purse to see if Kristine's personal phone book was there, so that he, Gaelyn and Carol could start calling people.

Denson now prepared to turn the interview in a different direction.

"How long had you and Kristine been married?"

"Thirty-three years."

"And you haven't had any difficulties, according to you. Is that correct, I mean recently?"

"No," Ken said. "It was difficult when the boys were in high school. Because we had one who didn't study and pretty much drove us both crazy, and we didn't know why. And there was—that was a tense time. Both boys are thriving in college. That concern is gone and life has been—life is pretty smooth. Particularly true this year, where my wife is so happy, she just loved what she was doing this year, and I was helping her with it and doing some music processing on the computer, to change [our] records to CDs."

"You folks have never had any kind of separation before?" Wong asked.

"We've never been separated before."

"Sounds like you spent most of your days together?"

"That's the way it's been. I had the office in the home now for several years. It used to be in the basement, have the desk there. It's still there because it's too heavy to move upstairs."

Both Wong and Denson noticed that Ken seemed to be veering away from the subject of his relationship with Kristine to material possessions. Denson decided to get back to the point.

"No disagreements about what to do with your life at this point, this is kind of your set routine, now?"

"Well, we don't— I think we were in agreement that we wanted to live somewhere else, that we don't need such a big house. We could sell it and buy properties in maybe two other places, and have money left over. And we were talking about maybe renting a house for a year and then renting somewhere else to see how we liked other places. We didn't have a disagreement about it. We had discussion about it, the exploration."

That sounded like perhaps Ken and Kristine might have disagreed over the issue of possibly selling the house, Ken's denial of any disagreements notwithstanding.

"But your question has two points," Ken went on. "One, was there disagreement? And the other, was life going to move—continue in the same direction? And I don't think life was continuing in the same direction, no. But we were kind of exploring together."

"Financially, were you okay?"

"Yeah."

"You felt comfortable?"

"Yeah," Ken said, "my business was good. She was working half-time. She cut down from full-time to half-time and I was [supportive of that]."

"What were you doing?" Wong asked.

Ken said he was a real estate consultant, that he had previously done some property management. He also did paralegal work for the law office next door, which included trying to get Tom Moore's printer working correctly.

"Okay," said Denson. "I'm just going to be real blunt with you. We have a few problems in this case, things we can't answer. The shoes are extremely disturbing to me. We did test them, we tested them for blood. The stains that we suspected are blood, are certainly blood, positively blood. We have a question of whose blood it would be, without DNA analysis, but we know we have shoes, which are your shoes, in your Suburban under your driver's seat . . . We are seeking to find out why, first off, I guess, the shoes are there. Secondly, why they had blood on them. And to test whose blood it would be.

"I asked you if those were your shoes, you confirmed they were your shoes, and you had last seen them, apparently, at eight this morning after going running, and presumably putting them in your closet. I don't know how we're going to get past this, but we need to try to figure out—we need you to really rack your brain and see if you can figure out why these shoes went from the closet into the Suburban."

Ken said the Suburban was normally kept locked, and that he was the main driver.

"Is there any reason she would have taken your shoes from the bedroom closet to the Suburban?"

"No."

"Is there any reason whatsoever you can think of that she'd move them?"

"I have no solution to that," Ken said.

"And still no recall of ever putting them in there?"

"No."

"Is there any reason," Denson asked, "why there would be blood on them, anything at all?"

"Well," said Ken, "we work in the garden and we were planting—we were planting together and pulling weeds, and she cut herself."

"When did this happen?" Denson demanded.

"This was last week."

"You don't remember where she cut herself?" Wong asked.

"Her hand," Ken said.

"Do you remember which hand?"

Ken said he thought Kristine had cut herself on her right hand. "There was some blood," he added.

"Okay," said Denson. Now he had another story from Ken he could use as a lie detector. He knew he would be attending the autopsy on Kristine's body the following day; if there was no cut on Kristine's hand, he would know Ken was fibbing about the origin of the blood on the shoes. Denson asked Ken to show where the cut was on a diagram of a hand that Denson made. Ken said Kristine had cut herself between the right thumb and index finger.

"So not a lot of blood," Denson continued, "but you stopped it with direct pressure?"

"Yes."

"And were you wearing those shoes?"

"Yes."

"Did she put a Band-Aid on it after that?"

"Yeah."

"Was she still wearing a Band-Aid to date?"

"I don't know."

"What kind of tool did she stab her hand with?"

"A trowel."

"A trowel? Is that kept in the basement?"

"In the basement."

Now Wong produced the Fitzhugh family telephone list, which the police had taken from the house that afternoon; they wanted to begin calling Kristine's friends on the list to check into the state of her marriage with Ken. Ken had no objection to the detectives making the calls, but he wanted to edit the list to remove such things as credit card numbers and the like so they wouldn't be misused by someone in the police department.

Wong now digressed into the joys of gardening; he apparently wanted to let Ken relax a bit before asking even harder questions. Then he swerved back with a new question: had Ken ever hurt himself gardening?

Ken's answer wasn't audible; apparently he was still thinking about the blood on his running shoes.

"How are your sons doing?" Wong asked, and again Ken made no audible response.

"Did you guys have a pretty close relationship with your kids?" Wong persisted.

"Yes," Ken said. "Yes. We loved doing all kinds of things together. Our friend even has a big boat and he told me, you know, probably fifteen years ago, he said that you still have that big boat, because that was what brought the family back together again. We kind of kept that in mind, so the activities everybody likes, which is skiing and boating, we went through and we'd be sure and bring everybody back together again."

Was this a key to what happened? Was Ken hinting that it was important for his family to stay together? That something was going on in his marriage with Kristine that threatened to pull the family apart? It wasn't clear.

"Do you have a boat, then?" Wong asked.

"Yeah."

"You do?" asked Denson.

"Just a little runabout," Ken said. "Nothing to water-ski behind. Everybody goes their separate ways and then . . . 'Kristine, let's take the boat out,' and all of a sudden the family will be . . ." Ken's voice trailed off.

Wong asked more questions about the family. Ken said that since both the boys had gone to college, it had been mostly him and Kristine at home. He said he and Kristine had gone to visit John at his college near Tacoma, Washington, three weeks before. Now they were getting ready for Justin's graduation from the University of the Pacific. Justin was already working on a job near San Jose, Ken said.

With that, someone came in and told Denson that he was wanted in the lobby. Wong suggested that they take a short break.

Out in the lobby of the police department, Justin and John were growing impatient. Wasn't this interview supposed to be routine? What was taking so long? Denson came out and explained that they had some more questions, that they just wanted to make sure they had all the information they needed. He told the boys to be patient, that their father would be out before long.

It was just after midnight, and the hardest questions of all were just coming up.

WHEN they resumed the interview, Wong and Denson asked Ken a number of questions about the big brass ship's bell. Ken said he'd acquired it years before in San Diego. It had been out in the back yard for years before Ken had rediscovered it. He decided to clean it up and put it up for auction on eBay; that was why he'd brought it into the house—to clean it up and take a photograph of it.

Now Denson veered back to the events of the afternoon.

"Mr. Fitzhugh," he said, "just a couple of things, and I might jump around. So, I'm not trying to confuse you, but my thought process is— I'll try to go back to when you first came inside the residence. How far was the front door open, if you recall?"

"Thirty degrees," Ken said.

"Unfortunately, I'm not good with geometry," Denson said. "Would that be big enough for someone to get through?"

Ken's answer was inaudible.

"When you noticed, or when you saw that, what went through your mind?"

"An abnormal . . . There was something abnormal about . . . There was something that was weird," Ken said.

Wong asked Ken to go over the events still one more time. Didn't Ken say he noticed that the light was on, that he'd gone downstairs?

"I didn't go down the stairs, I just looked down," Ken said.

"Then you came out and the two ladies, were they still in the car when you came back out and asked for help, or had they started to come up to the house?"

"They were opening the door. I went out the front door

running toward the car and they started to open the door."

"And that's when you went back inside?"

Ken didn't answer.

Wong asked about Ken's CPR experience. Ken said he'd taken a Red Cross course years before, and that he was familiar with CPR, because he'd been a Boy Scout master for his son's troop, and they had all practiced first aid.

"When you first saw her [from] the top of the stairs," Wong said, "I'm just curious as to why you didn't go down the stairs and check on her at that point, just out of curiosity. I'm just trying to think what was going through your mind."

"I think—we always trained the boys to do—to call for help, dial 911, and then see what we could do."

Wong now asked about the cut on Kristine's hand again, and this time Ken wasn't sure exactly when it had happened.

"I know Mike had talked to you," Wong said, "a little bit about our concerns with the shoes."

"Yes," Ken said.

"And I hope you understand, you know, why we are concerned about that. Taking into consideration, thinking about how the shoes got into the vehicle. Is there anything you can—any idea at all, or are you still pretty much dumbfounded in regards to what occurred?"

"I do not know how the shoes got in the car," Ken said. "It doesn't make sense."

"And you said, that's not normally the place where you would put them if you were to put them in your car?" asked Denson.

"No," Ken said. "Everything goes in the back."

Ken said he didn't remember seeing the shoes under the seat when he moved the truck just before coming to the police station. But, he said, "My brain wasn't functioning too well then."

Denson now wanted to clarify where everyone had been sitting in the Suburban, along with the positions of the two dogs. Then he and Wong returned to Ken's actions in moving Kristine's body when he had first discovered her, along with the relative positions of the dry-cleaning and the bell.

"Okay," said Wong. "And back to the paper towel again.

We did find one paper towel in the basket in the bathroom. But you think you remember that you may have washed your hands twice?"

"I did wash my hands twice."

"There were paper towels inside the car. You don't remember how those got there?"

"No."

Wong now asked Ken a series of questions about Kristine's medical history, and Ken said that Kristine had been seeing a psychologist over the prior year because she hadn't been able to sleep. Ken said he had a sleeping problem himself, with sleep apnea. He had to sleep with a mask on, he said, to pump air into his airway at night.

"Wow," Wong said.

Now Wong and Denson began working down a checklist of routine questions. Anyone in the family ever arrested before? No. Any juvenile problems? No. Any calls to the police before? Any break-ins? No. Unusual phone calls? No. Anything stolen? No. Any verbal arguments? No. Any firearms in the house? No.

"How about drinking alcohol, drugs, anything like that, did Kristine engage in that at all?"

Ken said he and Kristine enjoyed a glass of red wine most nights.

By now Ken was tired. "Are you about done?" he asked.

"We're almost done," Wong said. "What we have a concern about is, again, like Mike [Denson] was saying, was the blood. Okay? The blood on the shoes. We have another concern that we wanted to talk with you about, that we think is real significant. And that is that we found a footprint in the basement that appears to match the pattern of the tennis shoe. And the bottom of the tennis shoe appears to have blood on it as well.

"So," Wong continued, "we'd like to know from you if you can explain that in any way, or do you know—I mean, we can understand the potential of blood being on the shoe from an injury, but we're concerned about blood on the bottom of the shoe, and there was also a matching footprint in the basement. So we'd like to know from you if there's any explanation that you have for that."

"No," Ken said. "I didn't have those shoes on after we ran. It doesn't make any sense."

Wong now asked if anyone had seen him visit the property in San Bruno. Ken shook his head, no.

"And there's nothing you could think of so we could verify that you were there, or anyone we can talk with, you didn't get pulled over by anybody, didn't get a ticket?"

Ken shook his head, no.

"Do you or your wife have any enemies?" Denson asked.

"I don't think so," Ken said.

"Anything peculiar happen lately?" Denson asked.

"We get a lot of hang-up phone calls," Ken said.

"This is recently or something that's happened before?" Wong asked.

"This is ongoing," Ken said. "We didn't think too much about it, but every once in a while we talk about it."

"I have to ask you this," Denson said. "Any significant others on your part?"

"No."

"How about your wife?"

Ken didn't answer.

"Have you ever suspected it?" Denson asked.

Again Ken did not respond.

"Do you consider," Wong asked, "that you had a normal—normal might not be the right word. But can you tell me how you felt about your marriage . . . everything was fine?"

Ken said Kristine sometimes engaged in back-seat driving, but that was about the extent of their personal disagreements.

"I've got to tell you," Denson said, "we don't spend this great amount of time on every death investigation. There's a lot of things that are troubling us here. And that's why we're spending—"

"It's beginning to trouble me, too," Ken said.

"I would say you need to be troubled about it," Denson said. The shoes were a real problem, he said.

"At the time you find her, you're wearing your black shoes. I saw blood on those, and now you have blood on two pair of shoes. And the wounds themselves are not consistent with a bump, simply a fall."

"Well," Ken said, but his voice trailed off again.

"When somebody falls," Denson went on, "everything is done in patterns, and I'm sure you understand, you're an educated man. Everything is done in patterns, and things are expected to occur in particular fashion. Best example I can give you is a car accident. If the front of your car hits the side of another car, there are certain things that are going to happen, and we know that. We know that the front end of your car is going to get crunched up, so we know that the side of the other car is going to get crunched up, and that's what I'm talking about, in patterns.

"In this case, if we take it at face value, the way it looks is, your wife is going down the stairs and trips, however, on her shoes, and [she] falls down the stairs. Things are going to occur in a pattern, and they didn't occur that way. You know, if she fell down the stairs, she'd have certain types of wounds, and the wounds we're finding are not entirely consistent with having fallen down the stairs. And—"

Ken asked Denson what he thought had happened, in that case.

"We don't know," Denson admitted. "But we're forced to look at what your activity was, because of the shoes. We've got blood on the shoes and they're in your Suburban. And so, as you used earlier, it's dumbfounding, I guess."

Wong said the bloodstain on the shoe indicated that it had come from some sort of spatter, from close to where the original wound was inflicted. This was a stretch, because experts would later opine that the stains on the top of the shoe looked more like a transfer from some other article of clothing, or perhaps bloody hair, but there was no law against Wong trying to induce a confession by overstating his evidence, not at that early point.

"And our concern," Wong concluded, "is that, because of the trauma she sustained, and like Mike said, the shoes and your lack of explanation about how it came about, we do have some concern and I know—I think you do too, now."

"Yeah," Ken said.

Denson said if Ken wanted to ask whether someone had done something to Kristine, he would have to say that while they weren't completely sure, it was a distinct possibility. "And what we'd like to know from you," he finished, "is the truth about the shoes."

Denson explained that they would be checking Kristine's hand for evidence of the cut Ken said she had sustained.

"But what we want right now, because this is the best opportunity for you, is to find out the truth. That's what we want to find out."

"I don't know," Ken said.

"I don't believe that," Wong said. "Okay? I'll be honest with you. I've been a detective here for the last three to five years, and I've been a cop for eighteen years, okay? And I'm not going to lie to you, I'm not going to bullshit you . . . I have to look at facts. Based on everything you've told us in regard to the sequence of events . . . I've got some serious concerns. And 'I don't know' doesn't— I find that hard to believe, hard to fathom. I mean, you have a vehicle here that's under your care and control, okay, presumably during the whole day, according to what you've said. Your wife hasn't driven it because she wasn't with you, and these items show up in your vehicle. And they're there because I know one of our officers definitely saw it when you moved your truck. And by your own admission they're your shoes."

"They're my shoes," Ken said.

Wong asked if he and Kristine had gotten into an argument, but Ken shook his head, no.

"I can't— I don't believe that," Wong said.

"If there's something you're holding back, Mr. Fitzhugh," Denson said, "this is the time to tell us every detail. This isn't a chance you're going to have again, and there's so many things that don't add up on this, you've got to look at it."

"I don't know," Ken said. "I don't know what happened. And what you're telling me now, I don't know what happened."

Wong said they should go back to the injury to Kristine's hand. "Are we going to find an injury to her hand?" he asked. "Were you being truthful in regard to that?"

"Yeah," Ken said.

"So what happens when we do the autopsy and there's no injury to her hand?" Denson asked.

"You will find an injury to her hand," Ken said.

"You say you don't know what happened. You thought you knew what happened, but you don't know what happened?"

"If you're telling me that my tennis shoes were involved in this in some way—"

"Uh-huh," Denson said.

"I have no explanation," Ken said.

"Have you ever—" Wong started, but Ken interrupted.

"I have no explanation. I don't have . . . I don't understand."

"I'm just curious," Wong said. "When you get angry, how do you react?"

"I yell," Ken said. Ken said Denson had seen it earlier that day when he'd gotten mad about the damn shoes.

"You considered that a significant cause of death, that shoe?" Denson asked.

"It made sense," Ken said.

"Why didn't you tell your sons about the shoes?" Denson asked. After his brief contact with Justin and John, Denson decided that Ken hadn't said anything about the running shoes to either of them. That's what Agents Bready and Brown had told him, based on their interviews of Justin and John.

"I did," Ken said.

"They said you didn't."

"I don't know. By the time I talked to them, I'd talked to Carol, Gaelyn and your guys."

"*Did* you tell them about the shoes in the Suburban?" Wong asked.

"Yeah," Ken said.

"You did tell them about those?" Denson persisted.

Ken nodded.

"And that the police had found your shoes in there and you couldn't explain how they got in there?"

"I told them that there was some shoes with blood—with what looked like blood to you, and . . ." Ken's voice trailed off again. Justin had asked him, he said, why the police seemed so interested in the Suburban that afternoon.

Just in case Ken had missed the point, Denson told him the police would be sending the clothes he had worn into the lab for analysis, too.

"I want to tell you," Wong told Ken, "that I saw your reaction—and I heard your reaction—about [Kristine's black] shoes when you were in here with Mike earlier in the first interview. And you came out of nowhere. It was very surprising, it was very impulsive. And my perception was that it was pretty animated. You didn't just yell, you struck out at the table with both fists . . . Presumably you were talking about the shoes your wife was wearing at the time."

"That's the only thing," Ken said. "There are two things I think I could have done—there are three things I think I could have done to prevent this. I spent a lot of time in the home office. If I had been there . . . The bell was in a terrible place and we had had a conversation about [it] and at one point I thought about throwing it away . . . and it just dropped me."

Ken seemed oblivious to what Wong and Denson were implying. Wong decided to get the conversation back on track.

"Do you remember the last argument you ever had with your wife?" he asked.

"Last argument," Ken said. "The last argument would have been about my driving. She criticized my driving and I didn't think it had any basis, and told her to stop, it wasn't fair."

"Did you yell?"

"Did I yell?"

"Uh-huh," Wong said.

"Yeah."

"Have you ever struck her before?"

"No."

"Has she ever struck you?"

"No."

"Have you ever reacted in a way with an argument with your wife the way you reacted in regard to the shoes?"

"Years ago, about twenty-five years ago . . . so the answer is, no."

Wong now asked Ken to give them some reason to believe he was telling the truth, that he didn't know how Kristine had been injured so severely.

"I can't tell you," Ken said. "I don't know."

Wong asked if Ken was prone to memory lapses. Ken agreed that he'd experienced recent short-term memory losses, but that they seemed to be getting better.

"Any sleepwalking incidents?"

"No."

"How do you feel about this right now?" Wong asked.

"I feel horrible," Ken said. "I feel like— I feel like— I feel like I've been violated somehow. If you tell me— If you tell me there was—there was harm done, not by a fall but by someone doing something, I feel horribly violated in our home. It's just a whole 'nother dimension."

Wong said there were just too many unanswered questions about Kristine's death and Ken's own actions.

"Put yourself in my shoes, Mr. Fitzhugh," Wong said, in perhaps unconscious irony. "Okay. There's a lot of things here. Our job is to put together puzzles. And yeah, the only people who know what really happened are the people who were there, but the only people we can establish that were there at any particular time were you and your wife. Well, unfortunately your wife is no longer here, that's why we're talking with you. We want to find out from you what happened and we'd like the truth. I'll tell you that right now."

Ken said he'd already explained what happened.

"You did," Wong said. "And for me, for someone who's been married for this long and has two kids and so forth that you care about, I don't doubt that you love your wife. Okay. But I know that sometimes things happen when people argue. I've been there myself. I'll be honest with you. I'm a very quiet, docile person, just like I perceive you to be. Very introverted, when you think about what you say before you say things. But when I get angry, I get angry. I would probably react the way you did."

"That reaction hasn't happened to me in a long time," Ken said.

"I understand that," Wong said. "[But] It's not something

that's just going to vanish. And I know you're a smart person and you have your children here. And if we don't get to the truth—you've told us [that you told the boys] about the shoes and stuff, and we know that you haven't, so there is some dishonesty there."

"I told them about the shoes," Ken said.

"Okay," said Wong. "Well, maybe there's some miscommunication between us and them, and what we were questioning [you] about. But when we get done you're going to have to explain to them all the things that we talked about right now, and you're going to have to convince them—[and] you're not convincing me. I'm not going to be convinced. I'm not convinced until I hear the truth. That's all we want to know, is the truth."

"I'm trying to figure— I was trying to figure— Are you sure— Are you sure that somebody did something to her?" Ken asked.

"Yes," said Wong, "there's no doubt in my mind. There's absolutely no doubt."

"Are you sure that somebody [did something to her]?"

"Yes," Denson said. "And I know that your shoes were there after she was injured. And I believe that you were in your shoes, because they're now in your truck, which isn't where they should be."

"I wasn't in the shoes," Ken said. "And I was trying to figure out who—who would have wanted to do something like that."

"You presumably had your truck with you the entire time?"

"Who would want to do something to her?"

"You presumably had your truck the entire time, your shoes, you say, are in the closet?"

"Yes."

"We know that your shoes are in the blood—"

"Yes."

"—after your wife is injured," finished Denson.

"Yes."

"And we know they're in the truck when the police find

them, and you're in possession of the truck the entire time. You've got it up in San Bruno."

Ken didn't say anything.

Wong told Ken that the police would be able to use Ken's cellular telephone to discover where he was between 11 and 1:30—the cell phones left a geographic trail based on which antenna was being used.

"I told you everything I know about this," Ken insisted.

"I don't believe you," Wong said. "I don't think you're telling the truth. And I think that you would feel much better, being truthful about this whole incident."

"I told you what I know," Ken said again.

"I don't want to hear that," Wong said. "I'd like to hear the truth about what happened."

"I'd like to know too," Ken said.

"Okay," Wong said, "tell us."

"I don't know."

"You don't know or you don't remember?" asked Wong, trying to give Ken some wiggle room.

"I don't know," Ken said for the fifth or sixth time. "I don't know what happened."

Now Wong said that in addition to "the shoe problem," Ken had no alibi.

"I don't need an alibi," Ken said. "I don't need an alibi. I didn't do anything."

"You see the shoe problem?" Wong asked.

"Yes, I see the shoe problem," Ken said.

"How can you explain the shoe?"

"I cannot explain the shoe."

"I can't either," said Wong. He said that the police at first weren't sure if they should even mention the shoes to Ken, but when they saw the bloody shoe prints in the basement, and heard from the coroner's investigator that Kristine had been murdered, they felt obligated to confront him with the facts.

"Someone else was—was in those shoes," Ken said.

"Someone else was wearing your shoes?"

"Somebody else was in my shoes," Ken said again.

"Who?" Denson asked.

"I don't know," Ken said. "I don't know of anybody who would . . ." and his voice trailed off again.

"So you're saying that someone else was in the house and put those shoes on specifically to attack your wife?" Wong asked, incredulous.

"I don't know," Ken said again.

"And then they took the shoes off and presumably put them in the [truck]," Wong added. "Come on, Mr. Fitzhugh."

"I don't know."

"That's not believable. No one's going to believe that."

"It doesn't make any sense," Ken said.

"And I don't believe it," Wong agreed.

"It doesn't make any sense," Ken said again.

"You're coming up with different answers to some of the questions that we're trying to decipher, and your answers are going off on different tangents."

"I do not understand," Ken said.

Ken said he still thought Kristine had died in a fall.

Wong said that Kristine may have fallen, but that wasn't what had killed her. "The autopsy's going to show that it was trauma, blunt trauma," he said.

And even if it was a fall, Wong continued, Ken still had to find a way to explain how the blood had gotten on his running shoes. Suggesting that someone else had been wearing his shoes and then put them in the truck wasn't going to get it done, Wong said.

"I have no explanation," Ken said. "I'm grabbing at straws trying to figure out, just like you are, what in the world happened."

"Yeah," Wong said, "and the grabbing of straws is not believable."

"Aren't you trying to figure out what happened?" Ken asked.

"Yeah," Wong said.

"I want to know what happened, too," Ken said.

"Then tell us what happened," Wong insisted. He added that he didn't believe Ken when he said he'd been gone for an hour or two when Kristine had died.

"Two-and-a-half hours," Ken corrected.

Wong now gave a lengthy recapitulation of all the facts—that Ken hadn't gone straight to the house to check on Kristine, that he hadn't immediately tried to help her, that a pair of bloody shoes belonging to him was found in his truck, that Ken kept insisting that Kristine had fallen in her own shoes.

"You keep alluding to the shoes," Wong said. "The shoes she was wearing. Directing us to the shoes. You had what I would consider to be a violent reaction in regard to those shoes."

"I was upset by those shoes," Ken said.

But, said Wong, the medical examiner's investigator had concluded that Kristine could not have died in such a fall. Wong pointed out that Ken still had indications of blood on his hands.

"Doesn't it bother you that you have your wife's blood on your hands?" Wong asked. "How come you haven't washed your hands, just out of curiosity?"

"I washed them," Ken said.

"And that's the best it would come off?" Wong asked.

Wong said he was also bothered by Ken's seeming lack of emotion. He had to question Ken's concern about his wife's death, he said.

"Figure out who else might have— I've told you everything," Ken said.

"I need to know the truth," Wong said.

Wong said if Ken wasn't able to convince him, he certainly wasn't going to be able to convince Justin and John. In fact, Wong added, he didn't think Ken was even able to convince himself.

Ken said he was struggling, all right, to figure out how his shoes had gotten into the truck, and how they could have matched a bloody shoe print in the basement.

"We did some comparisons," Wong said.

"I don't think so," Ken said.

"I could show you the photos," said Wong. "So we'll be able to compare it definitively, and we'll be able to compare the blood definitively, and we'll do that because we don't want to make any mistakes . . . and if I'm wrong, I will tell you, 'I apologize, the blood was not your wife's, it was something else.' I will apologize. I will admit when I am wrong. But right now, based on everything I see, I can't admit that."

"Well, you're on the wrong track," Ken said.

"I don't believe I am," said Wong. "I mean, if you put yourself in my shoes, Mr. Fitzhugh. Put yourself in my shoes. You're an educated man. You have a lot of common sense. What would you think, in my shoes? What would you be thinking?"

Wong's repetition of the word "shoes" seemed calculated to trigger an outburst from Ken.

"I would think," Ken said, "that you need to figure out, if she didn't fall, who did this to her."

"How about the shoes?" Wong asked. "You think that would be— Do you think you would be a little concerned about the shoes?"

"Oh, yes," Ken said. "It's so strange."

"It's unexplainable," Wong agreed.

"Right," Ken said.

Wong asked if Ken were in his place, would he believe that someone else had sneaked out of the house under the very noses of the police to plant the shoes in Ken's truck?

"I believe it," Ken said.

"Convince me," Wong said.

"I don't know," Ken said for the last time.

The hour was growing late, and outside in the lobby the boys were growing more and more concerned. Wong decided to sketch in a scenario that might let Ken take responsibility for what had happened to Kristine and still save face—anything to get beyond "I don't know," he thought.

"If there was an accident," Wong told Ken, "and she fell down the stairs and she got hurt, and you were down there, and you thought, oh, something—you know, catastrophic, maybe you felt that you may have pushed her, maybe you were arguing and she got pushed by accident, I don't know; and then you decided that no one would ever believe you, and so you needed to change your shoes and your clothes and trying, you know, to protect yourself, because you didn't think anybody would believe that it was an accident. And then put the shoes inside your truck and forgot about them . . . not thinking that we would look. And then found your wife the way you did, by having people there with you while you found her. Then I could possibly believe that. I probably could believe that, if that were the truth. But I have to hear it from you, because you were the only one who was there."

This was the moment of truth, all right—the time for Ken to break down and admit that he and Kristine had had an argument, that Kristine had fallen or was pushed or somehow hurt, and then that he had panicked, and tried to cover it all up. It was a story that Wong was offering to Ken, a believable story, and if it was true, it might make all the difference— between an intentional murder charge and manslaughter or, given the right circumstances, self-defense. From this point forward, there would be two pathways for Ken Fitzhugh, Jr.— one that would lead inexorably to being charged with murder, or the other, to a possible quiet, if tragic, resolution to the events of the fifth of May, 2000, to an ending in which most people would never have heard of Kenneth C. Fitzhugh, Jr., an ending without all the notoriety that was still to come.

Ken said something, but it wasn't clear what it was. He may have said he'd like to talk, but . . . Or perhaps he said only that he was tired, and wanted to go home.

"Then tell me what happened," Wong said.

Ken told Wong that it sounded like Wong was sure Kristine's injuries couldn't be accounted for by falling into the bell.

"That's what I'm telling you," Wong agreed.

Ken said something so soft that it couldn't be picked up by anyone but Wong, who responded by demanding, once more, that Ken explain about the bloody shoes.

"We've been over that many times now," Ken said. "I don't think we need to . . ." and his voice trailed off once more.

At that point they took another short break; outside in the lobby Justin and John were growing insistent on being allowed to talk to their father.

"They want to know an explanation," Wong told Ken when they resumed. "I don't have any problems telling them what our beliefs are. I'll let *you* tell them, if you'd like. And I want you to know that I'm not lying to you. Now, we haven't done confirming tests, DNA stuff, but we will do that. But we'd like to get your blood to compare it, and I hope that you will be cooperative with that."

"Okay," Ken said. He said he wanted to be the one who told the boys about Wong's questions.

"You can tell them," Wong said, "and I'd like to think that you could tell them the truth. Would you mind if I sat in there with you when you did? All I want is the truth."

"I think I'd rather just be with my family," Ken said.

Now Wong told Ken about the search warrant for the house.

"If what you're telling us is the truth," he said, "and you did not harm your wife—okay. [But] we have a job to do."

"Now you're getting on the right track," Ken said.

Wong said Ken's continued willingness to answer questions would be considered evidence of possible innocence.

"How can I get you fellows on the track to finding out who harmed her?" Ken asked.

"We'll do our damnedest," Wong replied. "Right now, we have almost all the detectives working on the case. You go to another department, like the City of Oakland or another agency, you have one homicide detective working twelve, thirteen, fourteen, fifteen homicides. We have twelve, thirteen, fourteen, fifteen officers working one homicide."

"Good," Ken said. "Good."

Denson now added that Ken's Suburban was to be towed to the county crime lab for intensive examination.

"Again," said Denson, "in the interest of being thorough, as an investigative technique, that's an avenue we have to take. So your Suburban will be processed at the crime lab and then returned to you. You don't look too pleased about that."

"I'm not too pleased about my car being towed," Ken agreed.

Denson explained that if the blood on the shoes matched Kristine's, that had to mean that the killer also had contact with the Suburban, since that's where the shoes were found.

"Let there be no doubt in your mind," Denson said,

"we're going to find out whose foot was in that shoe.

"Unfortunately," he added, "you're going to have to find some place to stay, probably, tonight."

"Yeah," Ken said.

Shortly after that, the interview ended, and soon Ken, Justin and John were driving away from the police station to stay with family friends for the rest of the night.

And as they drove away, sometime around 1:30 A.M.—a little less than twelve hours after Kristine's body had been found in the basement—Denson himself left the station and returned to the Escobita Avenue house. He wanted to make sure that the police had the place under guard during the rest of the night, however little of it was left.

By the next morning, most of the people of Palo Alto were learning of the death of Kristine Fitzhugh from the pages of the local newspaper, the *Palo Alto Daily News*:

Music teacher dies in an apparent accident

A Palo Alto school district music teacher died yesterday after apparently falling down a flight of stairs and hitting her head, police said.

Kristine Pedersen Fitzhugh, 53, died at her home at 1545 Escobita Ave. in the Southgate area of Palo Alto yesterday, police Agent Jim Coffman said. Fitzhugh's husband, Kenneth, and two family friends went to look for her after she failed to make a 12:45 p.m. appointment, Coffman said.

The three found Fitzhugh at the bottom of the basement stairs at 1:40 p.m., Coffman said. She was pronounced dead at the scene by paramedics, Coffman said. Foul play isn't suspected, he said.

Whether this was a deliberate fib on the part of the police depends, of course, on what the meaning of the word "is" was. It *was* true that foul play was not suspected, oh, for about a minute or so after the fire department arrived on the scene; but from that point forward, about the only thing that wasn't suspected was that this was some form of "play"—as if Kristine had been hurt in some sort of innocent romp. Whoever had murdered Kristine Fitzhugh hadn't been playing, that was for sure.

That was also the conclusion of Dr. Diane Vertes, the assistant medical examiner, who began her autopsy on Kristine's remains just after 10 that same morning.

Dr. Vertes' examination of Kristine's head disclosed twenty separate bruises on her face, ranging from her upper left forehead to her lower right jaw. Most of them were on the left side of the face, and suggested to Vertes that Kristine had been struck repeatedly by a right-handed fist as she faced her attacker. Dr. Vertes also found two areas of white pressure marks on both sides of Kristine's neck, which indicated that Kristine had been strangled by someone's hands, a finding that was supported by deep hemorrhaging in the strap muscles of the neck, and bruising of the tongue.

The rear of Kristine's head told an even more fearsome story: Vertes found seven separate lacerations—tearing—of the skin, with surrounding bruises, including one area of the left rear head that covered a "palpable" skull fracture, meaning that the bones of the skull could be moved by Vertes' fingers.

It was possible that *some* of the bruising to Kristine's face might have occurred as a result of a face-first fall down the stairs, but not *all* of it. And it was impossible that Kristine should have so many injuries to the rear of her skull, particularly the one at the left rear of the head that had the underlying fracture. The multiple blows to the head, Vertes found, had caused Kristine's brain to hemorrhage from being bounced from one side of the skull to the other in a so-called "contrecoup" effect. A person falling face forward would hardly have seven different injuries to the rear of the skull, Vertes reasoned. It was far more likely that Kristine had been struck from behind by some sort of club, or possibly that someone had smashed the back of her head into a hard surface, such as a table, wall or floor.

And even all that hadn't been enough to kill her, at least instantly. Vertes observed several bruises on Kristine's left forearm, another bruise on the left hand, several more bruises on the left ring finger, as well as a narrow cut on the finger, where Kristine's ring had been driven deeply into her flesh. She had been wearing two rings, one with a clear stone, probably a diamond, and a second plain gold band. The diamond ring was the one that had done this damage.

In contrast, the webbing between the thumb and forefinger of Kristine's right hand—where Ken had said Kristine had cut herself while gardening—was unscratched.

"The death of this 52-year-old female," Vertes wrote in

her subsequent report, "is attributed to multiple blunt force head injuries and manual strangulation. Discrete injuries are present on both sides of the face and both sides of the back of the head, consistent with separate blows. Injuries on the left hand are consistent with defensive-type posturing."

In other words, Kristine had tried to ward off the rain of blows that had so savagely claimed her life.

That same morning, Ken Fitzhugh arose and began to consider his options. It was plain to him, as it had been to Justin even earlier, that the Palo Alto police thought that he had murdered Kristine. Justin had told him that he needed a lawyer, and now Ken decided to take Justin's advice. He called three lawyers he knew who specialized in real estate, and asked them who they would suggest for a criminal lawyer. All of them, he said later, recommended the same person: Tom Nolan, a well-known defense attorney in Palo Alto who was experienced in homicide cases.

Nolan had been a lawyer since 1971, after graduating from law school at the University of California at Davis, near Sacramento. He also taught criminal procedures at Stanford Law School. He was widely regarded as an aggressive practitioner, a ferocious defender of a defendant's legal rights, and quite willing to attack law enforcement authorities when he believed those authorities had made mistakes in judgment.

In signing Nolan to represent him, Ken had taken the first step toward recognizing his own legal jeopardy. For the next year-and-a-half, Nolan would zealously defend Ken against all comers, and insist that the police had made, and were continuing to make, a series of unforgivable errors in targeting the 57-year-old Ken as their prime suspect.

One thing was sure: whatever his convictions, Nolan did not come cheap. By the time the whole thing was over, it would be rumored that Ken paid Tom Nolan as much as $500,000 to defend him, a sum which might or might not have included tens of thousands of dollars that expert witnesses would later admit they had received. Ken himself would refuse to say how much he gave Nolan, saying the figure was "between Tom Nolan and me."

But one thing was evident on the morning of May 6, 2000, and that was that Ken Fitzhugh did not intend to go down quietly.

• • •

Denson got word of this development sometime on the afternoon of the same Saturday, when someone from Nolan's Palo Alto office called him, told him that Ken was being represented by Nolan, and inviting him and Wong to Nolan's office to discuss the matter further with both Nolan and Ken. Denson spent part of the day tracking down some of Kristine's friends, using the telephone list that Ken had let him copy the night before. No one seemed to think that Ken and Kristine had been at each other's throats in the days before Kristine's death. But most described Ken and Kristine as less than self-revelatory personalities; neither was the type who would tell friends their innermost secrets.

While Denson was telephoning, several Palo Alto police officers were maintaining a watch at the Escobita Avenue house, which was still sealed off behind the yellow crime scene tape. At that point, the police were taking a visual inventory of the house's layout and contents, preparatory to a more detailed search that was planned for the following day.

About eight that night, Denson and Wong arrived at Nolan's office in downtown Palo Alto, not far from the Stanford campus. Denson asked if he could record the discussion, and Nolan said it was okay with him.

Nolan said he'd been hired by Ken, and that Ken had told him the police wanted to talk to him a third time. Nolan said he'd called the police to tell them that a third talk "would be no problem." Nolan wanted to make sure that it was on record that Ken was cooperating with the police.

"I understand that you need, in a homicide case, to get moving quickly," Nolan said. "He [Ken] wants to cooperate in every way possible. And I'm just here to assist."

Wong admitted that Ken had so far been very cooperative.

"I requested representation," Ken now said, "because I was very tired the other night, and I've been through a great deal, and I want to cooperate with you in every way—but I think I need some help."

Denson said he'd attended Kristine's autopsy that morning, and now he had some new questions, along with some old ones:

"Since having had some rest and some time [to think]," Denson asked, "did anything come back into your memory, any recall on how the shoes could have gotten into the Suburban?"

"No," Ken said.

Nolan said it was his understanding that Ken had moved the Suburban while he was still wearing the clothes he'd been wearing while he'd performed CPR on Kristine. Nolan's implication was that it was possible that the blood on the shoes had transferred to the shoes from Ken's black jeans or from some other surface. Then Nolan quickly reversed his direction, and suggested it was also his understanding that neither Gaelyn nor Carol had seen the shoes in the truck that afternoon, and neither had Ken; now Nolan seemed to be suggesting that someone *else* had put the shoes in the truck after Ken had begun the resuscitation efforts.

Ken was confused, Nolan added, and Denson said, "Yes, that's a confusing point for us, as well."

Now Wong introduced a new wrinkle: he said he was told by other police officers that when Ken went out to move the truck to a better parking spot, that—

"You unlocked the car," Wong said, "and said, 'Oh, there's shoes on the floor board.' "

"So these shoes had blood on the top of them," Nolan said. "And the question is, did they have blood on the bottom [as well]?"

"Yes," Denson said. "We assume so."

"Yeah, well, in other words," said Nolan, "a lot?"

Wong said they hadn't done all their tests yet, but there was enough blood on the bottom of the shoe for the police to be concerned about it.

"One of the things obviously is, that the blood on the top could have come from his pants and [black leather] shoes that, you know—it depends on the nature of it. Is it a splatter—"

"Exactly," Wong said.

"—or is it a rub?" Nolan concluded. The blood on the running shoes could have been transferred there from Ken's jeans, Nolan said. And as for any blood on the bottoms of the shoes, one had to believe there would also be blood tracked from the house to the car.

"There's a whole bunch of variables," Wong agreed.

"It's a very strange situation," Nolan said.

Nolan said he talked the situation over with Ken, as well as Gaelyn and Carol that afternoon. "We simply don't have any real idea [of how the blood got on the running shoe]," Nolan said. "I mean any real idea at all."

This was a pre-emptive strike on Nolan's part to shut down further questions about the shoes. If Ken, Gaelyn and Carol all agreed that "we" simply had no idea, what was the point of pursuing that line of questioning any further?

Denson now pulled out his hole card.

"When we discussed the shoes," he told Ken, "you told me that the only possible source of blood you could remember would have been from your wife when she was gardening about a week ago, and cut her hand with a gardening tool. Do you remember that?"

"Yes," Ken said, "but it was about two weeks ago."

"I think he also said it was unlikely," Nolan jumped in, "because it looked like—what he was shown [on the shoes] didn't look like two-week-old blood." Here Nolan was trying to remove the onus of possible deception from Ken: by reminding the investigators that Ken himself had said the blood on the shoes didn't look like it had really come from Kristine's "cut," Nolan could portray Ken as being cooperative rather than deceitful.

There now ensued a short, mild dispute between Nolan and Denson about the properties of dried blood. Denson realized that Nolan was leading him into a thicket of definitions, which was Nolan's home turf. Denson decided to get out before he got lost.

"At any rate," Denson said to Ken, "you told me Ms. Fitzhugh sustained the injury to this portion of her left hand. [Actually Ken had told Denson it was the right hand that had been cut, not the left.]" Denson reminded Ken that they had drawn a diagram of the hand together.

"That's correct," Ken said.

"I can tell you now," said Denson, doubtless feeling a bit like the magician ready to pull the rabbit from the hat, "I went to the autopsy today, [and] there are no injuries to that portion of her hand. I told the doctors to specifically examine for that. They can find no evidence of injury, either two-week-old or new. The doctor said there was no injury there."

"I presume . . ." Ken began to say, and once more his

voice trailed off as he suggested that whatever cut Kristine had, it had healed by this time.

"Well, you know," Nolan said, "again, this is speculation. He's asked to speculate on what it *could* be. He remembers an incident where she hurts herself. I don't think *he* thinks the blood came from that, because, I mean he's asked to speculate. And . . . it's unlikely that it was there [before Ken moved the truck], because he might have noticed it wearing the shoes."

"If I may refresh your memory," Ken added, "that was the only thing I could think of that could account for the blood, as far as I know."

Wong said Ken had agreed that the cut required a bandage, and that it had taken direct pressure to stop the bleeding.

"We didn't talk about a bandage," Ken said, "we talked about a Band-Aid. And we didn't talk about a big wound. But yes, I put pressure on [it] and that's what happened."

"Okay," Denson said, "you didn't answer the question. It doesn't surprise you that there's no evidence of any injury to the hand?"

Nolan: "Well, that's a speculation. How would he have looked—there'd be no reason for him to look at the hand prior to this incident and say, 'How is your hand doing today?' It wasn't that type of injury, apparently . . . Would it surprise *you*? I mean, I don't know what a doctor would say about how long it takes. It depends on the nature of the wound and the healing process of the person. I mean, you know, it's like you ask him to speculate how possibly could blood—the only thing he thinks about blood is that a particular thing happened. He doesn't even say the blood went on his shoe at that point. He says, 'All I remember, blood-wise, is I remember I put my finger on it, and we put a bandage on it."

Both Denson and Wong now realized why Nolan got the big money. They had come in with what they believed were significant holes in Ken's story, only to hear Nolan fuzz them up with quibbles about definitions.

If this was a taste of what they were in for, Denson and Wong now realized, proving Ken Fitzhugh was his wife's killer wasn't going to be easy.

• • •

Denson, Wong, Nolan and Ken now spent most of the remainder of the interview wrangling about the healing rates of various wounds, and how the running shoes might have gotten into the Suburban. One thing was clear: this wasn't the same Ken of the night before, the person who had said he was "dumbfounded" about the shoes being found in his truck. This Ken was combative, quick to contradict. When Denson asked again if Ken knew whose blood was on his running shoes, Ken said, "I don't *know* that there's blood," and when Wong suggested that the Suburban had been under only Ken's control throughout the day, Ken said that wasn't entirely true: there were several periods when it had been unlocked and unattended.

Denson and Wong turned to Ken's alibi, his trip to the Family Golf Center driving range in San Bruno. Ken sketched a rough drawing of the property, and showed where he had parked, where he had walked. But Ken admitted that he hadn't talked to anyone, not even the manager of the property, Carol Gossett. Still, Ken insisted, he was there.

"The first thing I always do at the start of a real estate project," he said, "is go look at it. I wanted to look at it, see if it was still in the same condition as I remembered it six months ago. And my plan, which was interrupted by this accident," had been, he continued, to telephone the man who had solicited him as a consultant.

Now there unfolded a brief discussion between the detectives and Nolan about a possible polygraph test. Denson asked if Ken would be willing to take one, and Ken said he would be. Nolan said when the police were ready, to let them know.

"Fine with us," Denson said. "Let me kind of tell you where we're at with this matter. I'm sorry to report to you that it's been deemed a homicide. The coroner did the autopsy today and the—"

"How do I know you're telling me the truth?" Ken demanded. "Because you told me you lied. I would like to know what happened. I guess you can just lie."

"We can lie," Wong admitted.

"What's the basis of them deciding it's a homicide?" Nolan asked.

"The wounds are not consistent with a fall," said Denson.

"And how's that so?" Nolan asked.

"It was from the pathologist," Denson said, "and they looked at the wounds and said the wounds that she sustained are not consistent with having fallen down the stairs."

Wong now asked Ken for permission to inspect the Fitzhugh cellular phone records, both his and Kristine's, for the prior three months, along with their credit card statements. "I think we understand," Wong said, "that in a homicide involving a spouse or a significant other, the first person they suspect is the significant other or spouse."

Wong suggested that if Kristine's credit card billings showed her frequenting places that were unfamiliar to Ken, such as restaurants or hotels, that might be an indication that she had been having an affair. The same would be true of Ken's charges, and also, all the telephone records. If there *was* evidence of an affair, that would widen the field of possible suspects, Wong indicated. Ken said he was familiar with all the places where Kristine spent money, because they paid the credit card bills together. That seemed to indicate that Ken was prepared to rule out the secret lover scenario.

Denson said the police still needed to do a more thorough search of the house. He told Ken that he thought it was possible that he and the boys could go home late Sunday night. He asked for Ken's ring; the authorities wanted to inspect it to see if any of Kristine's DNA might be found in its cracks and crevices. Ken gave them the ring.

"Understand," Wong said, "this is a difficult investigation. Because of the possible inconsistencies with regard to the shoes. We're going to have to do our analysis in that regard. I have already talked to you about this, if we thought we had enough to place you under arrest, we would do so. We're still perfecting an ongoing investigation . . . so we have to look at the possibility of your involvement, and look at the possibility of someone else's involvement. And we appreciate the fact that you're going to be working together with us in that regard. Your willingness to do so says a lot."

But after they left Nolan's office, both Wong and Denson agreed: Ken's decision to lawyer-up was, if anything, going to make things a lot more difficult.

THE next morning saw a number of police officers at the Escobita house, among them Sascha Priess, who had been assigned, as the responding officer, to an evidence team under the supervision of Palo Alto Police Sergeant Curtis Chan. On the Friday of the murder, Priess and Pohl had taken numerous items of evidence from the house, including Kristine's shoes, her glasses, the bloody school papers and dry-cleaning, the brass ship's bell, Ken's shoes, Ken's clothes. Now that the official determination of murder had been made, it was decided to take still more evidence.

On this Sunday morning, Priess recovered the bloody paper towel from inside the downstairs bathroom, a soap bottle from the same bathroom, and a paper Peet's Coffee cup from the kitchen table. It appeared that Kristine had been drinking the coffee in the minutes prior to the attack. Priess also recovered some school papers from the kitchen table that looked like they might be part of those that had been found in the basement.

At one point, Priess noticed a diary in the dining room. Scanning it, he saw that it was in handwriting that appeared to be Kristine's. Upstairs, the searchers had also discovered two books on Kristine's bedside table: *The Language of Letting Go*, by Melody Beattie, and a second book, *Breaking Free: A Recovery Workbook for Facing Codependence*, by Pia Mellody and Andrea Wells Miller. Both books consisted of meditations and exercises for people grappling with codependency issues. It appeared that the diary represented Kristine's attempt to put some of these affirmations into practice.

What did that suggest about the Fitzhugh marriage? Some thought it indicated that Kristine and Ken had been having recent marital troubles, and wondered if Kristine had been planning on separating from Ken. What had Ken been saying during the midnight interview? *Keep the family together* ... Was this a possible factor in the murderous attack? Or did it have anything to do with Ken and Kristine at all? Denson knew that he would need the help of the Fitzhugh family friends to see whether any of this was significant.

Sometime that same Sunday morning, Sergeant Chan asked for the help of Agent Cornelius Maloney, the Palo Alto Police Department's resident blood spatter expert. Maloney, who normally was assigned to the traffic detail, was asked to look over the scene in the basement so he could offer an opinion on whether the murder had occurred there.

Maloney spent about a half-hour looking through the basement for evidence of blood spatter. "Any time you have a victim who's been beaten and bludgeoned like that," Maloney said later, "there's going to be blood transfer." Blood transfer could include "cast-off" from a moving weapon, blood drips from a wound, and transfer from one bloody object to another, previously unbloody object. Analysis of the blood patterns could provide the basis for a reconstruction of an attack.

There was a lot of blood in the basement, Maloney soon observed, but most of it appeared to have come from Kristine's head, primarily the pool that formed during the fruitless resuscitation efforts. Maloney inspected the surfaces of the walls and other upright objects in the basement, but didn't find a single drop on the basement walls. True, there was some dried blood on the leading edges of the stairs, but none on the side of the stairwell.

While Maloney was inspecting the basement, the Santa Clara County Medical Examiner, Dr. Gregory Schmunk, arrived at the house, along with Dr. Vertes. They had been asked to come by Denson. Denson had recalled that Schmunk had once told him that if he ever wanted help with a crime scene, to simply ask, and Schmunk would come to give him the benefit of his opinion. So on Saturday Denson had called Schmunk, who in turn invited Vertes. "I called Schmunk and I said, 'Look I want you to check this out, and see if there's any way possible that these wounds could have occurred from these stairs,' " Denson recalled.

After finishing his inspection, Maloney went outside and contacted Sergeant Chan. Maloney said he didn't think Kristine had been killed in the basement. He told Chan that the police should back up, and begin a search for blood throughout the entire house. Chan now told Maloney that Schmunk had seen what he thought might be bloodstains in the kitchen.

After looking through the basement with Vertes and Denson, and, like Maloney, finding no evidence of what he thought should be blood spatter for a person to have been attacked there, Schmunk ascended the stairs. He'd already noticed the pair of blood drops that had been marked by the police on the basement landing and the central hallway. Now, for some reason, Schmunk decided to go into the kitchen. There, he was to say later, he found what appeared to be evidence of bloodstains on the kitchen floor, underneath the kitchen table, and on the legs of the chairs next to the kitchen table. Some of the tiny spots looked as though they might have been diluted with water, Schmunk thought, leading him to believe that someone had tried to clean them up at some point. Schmunk took several photographs of the spots he had discovered, and then called them to the attention of the police.

Chan, Maloney and Denson now joined Schmunk and Vertes in the kitchen area. Schmunk pointed out what he thought were the bloodstains, and suggested that some might have been residue left after wiping.

Schmunk's discovery suggested a substantially new way of looking at Kristine's murder. If there were bloodstains in the kitchen, did that mean it was possible that she had actually been attacked in that room, rather than the basement? And if so, did that mean the killer had moved her body to the basement? Had the killer then positioned the body in such a way as to make it appear to have been an accidental fall? And if that were true, who, of all people, would have the strongest interest in making a murder look like an unfortunate tragedy? In whose interest would it be to "stage" the awful scene? Who would have taken the time to clean up the kitchen after such a murderous assault?

Certainly a burglar would not. A burglar picking a house at random to rob, having encountered a homeowner, would be unlikely to commit murder in any event, and without any doubt would never take the time to clean up after himself and stage his victim on a flight of stairs.

The one person who seemingly had the most to gain from such a clean-up and staging was none other than the victim's husband, Kenneth C. Fitzhugh, Jr.

It all fit, Denson was now sure: Ken had surprised his wife, attacked her in the kitchen, dragged her body to the basement stairs, cleaned up most of the blood left from the attack, then had rushed off to pick up Gaelyn and Carol to help him "find" the body, in the process getting a small smudge of blood on his running shoes. Was that why Ken had been wearing his black leather loafers with the white athletic socks—because he hadn't had time to clean the white running shoes? *The shoes, the damn shoes*, thought Denson.

At this point, Chan, Maloney, Denson, Wong, Schmunk and Vertes left the Escobita house and returned to the police station, there to lay plans as to how this potentially vital blood evidence might best be handled. The chances of Ken being able to return to the house that same night had just plunged to absolute zero.

At the police station, Maloney wrote down a brief outline of how the police should proceed on their search, and presented it to Chan. The discovery of the possible bloodstains in the kitchen had changed everything. Now Maloney wanted to take everything from the top—start the whole search over beginning on Monday morning—just to make sure that nothing had been overlooked.

"I didn't want to have to leave to chance what anybody who had been there before had done," Maloney would say later. "I wanted to make sure we did everything correctly."

Maloney's plan required the assembly of a team of seven searchers. One member of the team would be assigned the job of "recorder," which required noting down everything that was discovered and seized, by whom, where and when. Each time something of possible significance was recovered in the house, it would be reported to the recorder, logged onto a laptop computer, packaged in protective covering, and labeled with an evidence number produced by the computer. By the time the search was over, the police would collect hundreds of different items, and have a massive collection of photographs to document their efforts.

WHILE the police had hoped to buy themselves a little time by putting out the story that Kristine had died in a fall, it was impossible to keep this dissemblance up for long. Denson and Wong had warned Ken that the cause of his wife's death would soon become known to the news media, and that he would have to expect a considerable amount of public attention. They were right. Even as the searchers worked on Sunday, a full complement of television cameras, reporters and photographers had gathered at the Escobita house, apparently after they learned about the results of the autopsy from either the medical examiner's office or the police. The next morning the *Palo Alto Daily News* had the story:

Teacher's death a homicide

The death of a popular Palo Alto music teacher found at the foot of her basement stairs has turned into a whodunit, prompting homicide investigators to spend the weekend sorting through clues.

Police originally classified the Friday death as an accident but upgraded the case to a homicide Saturday after results from an autopsy provided new evidence, Palo Alto police Agent Jim Coffman said. . . .

Coffman wouldn't say whether the home was burglarized, if there was a sign of struggle or whether a weapon was used in the homicide. . . .

The news that Kristine Fitzhugh had actually been murdered unnerved some people in the neighborhood, the paper also reported. Some also noted that the killing had come after a number of residential burglaries in the area, and wondered whether Kristine had been killed by a burglar—and whether they were at risk, too. But Coffman said the police hadn't decided on a theory of the crime yet.

"We're not at a point yet to say how this happened," he said. "This is a very fluid situation."

Fluid was exactly what Maloney was looking for when he and his search team returned to the house early Monday afternoon. Wearing protective coveralls, booties and latex gloves, the team members looked like some sort of decontamination squad from a science fiction movie. They opened the front door, and immediately began a hands-and-knees search of the entry area using magnifying glasses. Maloney knew that there had already been a horde of people to go through the area, what with the firemen, the paramedics, the police, Ken, Gaelyn and Carol, but he didn't want to take the chance of any further disturbance if something was still there.

After scouring the entryway, the team did the same for the dining room. Maloney wanted to clear a space where he could set up the department's laptop computer with its portable printer. Keeping track of each item by establishing a computerized database would be Priess' job. Once the dining room was secured, Maloney's men worked their way down the central hall to the entry to the kitchen. Eventually, the team would explore the entire house on hands and knees, from the basement to the attic. As the team explored, if something that warranted further examination was discovered, a small three-by-five card was folded over it, and the number recorded in the computer.

By late afternoon, Maloney and the team had identified seventy-two separate possible bloodstains, each of them marked with a separate, folded three-by-five card; interestingly, Maloney believed he had found several possible bloodstains on the bannister of the stairs going up to the second floor of the house. If Ken had been telling the truth about his movements on Friday afternoon, those stains shouldn't have been there—at least, not from Ken, not after he had found Kristine's body. He hadn't gone upstairs during the entire time, from the discovery of the body to the time he had left the house. Of course that didn't rule out the possibility that Ken had gone upstairs after killing Kristine but *before* picking up Gaelyn and Carol—perhaps when he had changed into his leather loafers.

Maloney and his searchers left the house under guard that night at 7:20 P.M., and returned the next morning, Tuesday, May 9, at 8. This time Maloney's men began photographing each of the folded cards, and took measurements to show how far each of the suspected stains was from nearby walls or doorways. With seventy-two cards, this was time-consuming, to say the least; but Maloney knew that the documentation had to be accurate if the possible stains were to be used as evidence.

On the following day, Maloney and his team returned to the house once more, this time armed with packaged kits containing sealed vials of distilled water and two sterile swabs— Q-tips, in fact. Then they began the laborious process of dipping one of each pair of swabs into the distilled water, rubbing the suspected stain to moisten it, then putting the reddened swab aside to dry for later testing. This was called the "sample swab." In some cases, the suspected stain was so tiny, it was virtually rubbed out by the swab. But that wasn't the end of it. Each time Maloney took a sample from a stain, he had to do the same with a "control swab"—a moistened Q-tip rubbed in a nearby area that didn't appear to have any stain.

By the time this was all finished, it was almost 1 A.M. Altogether, Maloney had recovered 144 swabs, counting both samples and controls. Now each of the sample swabs would have to be tested—first to determine whether the stuff was blood, and after that tested again to determine *whose* blood. Eventually Maloney, using copies of the blueprints of the house found for him by Denson, would devise a diagram of the floor plan of the house which showed a little red circle for every drop of Kristine's blood that had been found.

On the same Wednesday that Maloney and his team were beginning the arduous process of taking their swabs, criminalist Katie Ryan was looking over the 1999 blue Chevrolet Suburban that had been towed into the Santa Clara County Crime

Lab early on Monday morning. Katie, who held a master's degree in biology from San Jose State University, was an expert in identifying and typing bodily fluids, among them bloodstains.

The truck was covered by a blue tarp placed there by the Palo Alto police. After having a technician photograph the truck, Katie opened the driver's side door, and soon thereafter looked underneath the driver's seat. There, she found what looked to be a wadded-up bundle of green fabric. After asking for more pictures, Katie pulled the fabric out from under the seat, unfolded it, and discovered it was a green, short-sleeved Brooks Brothers polo shirt, with a breast pocket and two small white buttons at the neck. On the front of the shirt, approximately at the midsection and just below the pocket, was a reddish damp spot that Katie knew was probably blood.

To be sure, she tested the stain with the criminalists' presumptive test for blood—treatment with a chemical called orthotolidine. This involved taking a piece of filter paper, rubbing the paper over the suspected stain, then subjecting it to a few drops of the chemical. If the rubbed-on spot of the filter paper turned blue-green, it was considered "presumptive"— that is, presumed, barring some other explanation—for the presence of blood.

The paper from the green shirt reacted almost immediately. Katie had photographs taken of the shirt, then had it placed in a bag, and had the bag put into the crime lab's freezer. Then she returned to a further examination of the Suburban. She found no more bloodstains.

That same day, an officer from the Palo Alto Police Department delivered a sealed brown paper bag to the laboratory. The bag contained Ken's white running shoes, for further blood and DNA testing.

The authorities weren't the only ones doing tests that same Wednesday, it would turn out. One of Nolan's first moves after learning that the police suspected Ken was Kristine's murderer was to hire his own pathologist to examine Kristine's body. True, the medical examiner's office had already determined that Kristine had been killed by "blunt trauma," but Nolan

knew it would be better if he had his own, independent review
of Dr. Vertes' autopsy. Because the body had been released
to a funeral home, Nolan was able to send Dr. Thomas W.
Rogers, also a forensic pathologist, there for a new look. Rogers noted all the same injuries that Vertes had seen, but when
it came to offering a cause of death, Rogers demurred. "De-
ferred," he wrote in a report he would submit to Nolan. It
appeared that Nolan wanted to keep his options open—maybe,
just maybe, it wasn't possible to say Kristine had died in a
fall, but Nolan didn't want his *own* expert to put a formal,
written kibosh on that idea. At least just yet.

And there was yet one more test to be performed on that day—
or night, actually. Around 7:30 P.M., Chan, Denson, criminalist
David Chun, crime lab photographer Jonathan Baldwin, and
Santa Clara County Deputy District Attorney Michael Fletcher
arrived at the Escobita house, where Maloney and his people
were still at work with their swabs. The plan was to spray a
chemical called luminol over the various floors and walls of
the house in order to verify the presence of blood, and more
importantly, its patterns.

  Basically, the luminol test was another so-called "presumptive" test. That meant that it couldn't positively prove the
presence of blood residue, but that it could effectively exclude
it if it wasn't there. Even more significantly, it could show the
traces of efforts made to wipe up blood. That's what Denson
and the others hoped to see on this particular night. There was
a downside to luminol, however: it reacted to a variety of non-
blood substances as well as blood, such as some metals, fruit
juices and a variety of cleaning agents.

  The test involves mixing three different chemicals together with water, then placing the mixture in a squeegee bottle. The concoction is then sprayed over the area to be tested,
but in complete darkness. If blood—or any of the other substances—has been present on the surface the mixture will lu-
minesce, that is, glow in the dark. But the glowing isn't the
most important result. Instead, one can see the edges of the
reacting substance, particularly if it's been swiped as part of
an effort to clean up. The edges represent a photographic rec-

ord of long-past actions which wouldn't ordinarily be observable.

"You decide what the area is that you want to spray," Chun said later. "And what we do is, you take a picture, a photograph of the area that we're going to process before spraying it. The camera is on a tripod, so it has to be still. So you take a picture, shut the lights off, close the windows, and make sure it's pitch dark before you spray. And if there is blood present, even if it's been cleaned up or diluted, it will glow in the dark. It's a pretty obvious glow, because it's pitch black."

After arriving at the Escobita house with Baldwin, Chun first tested the mixture he had brought with him by spraying some on some small squares of paper that he had previously marked with X's of diluted blood. Chun told the others to turn off the lights and block the windows. He sprayed from his squeegee bottle. There in the darkness everyone could see Chun's test markings glow on the paper.

Then Chun went to work on one of the kitchen chairs, the place where Maloney believed Kristine had been sitting when she was attacked. Spots on the chair gave off an eerie bluish-green glow; one could see where some sort of reacting substance had dripped down the legs and cross pieces at one point. Next Chun tried the lower east wall of the kitchen, and one could see the faint glow of small circular spots near the doorway, presumably cast-off blood.

Chun now sprayed the area of the kitchen floor between the hallway and the table, an area about four feet by four feet, and the results were astounding. There, in the bluish-green glow, one could see several apparent shoe prints that looked to everyone as if they had been made by a rubber-soled running shoe, along with some small animal paw prints, perhaps made by a small dog or cat. Also visible was a large X-shaped wipe mark.

Out in the hallway, the luminol showed still more tiny circular spots, some additional possible shoe prints, and more small animal prints. Then, inside the landing to the basement stairs, one could see a T-shaped area of luminescence, where some apparently large object had been deposited at one time.

The evidence was dramatic. There in the darkness, Denson believed he had his whole case: Kristine had been killed in the kitchen, dragged to the basement landing, then down the stairs, to be left face-down, as if she had tripped and fallen. And at some point, one of the Fitzhugh cats, or perhaps little Reina the Pomeranian, had walked through the blood, the only innocent witness to the savagery that had claimed Kristine's life.

And there was more: Fletcher, for one, was convinced by the demonstration that the killer had to be Ken.

"Because once we understood that the murder occurred in the kitchen," Fletcher said later, "a number of things flowed from it. One, why was she moved? And second, therefore the body was staged, and there was a clean-up. And if there's a clean-up, it answers the obvious question of: who's in the best position to do that?"

And who else but Ken would want to?

BY the next day, Thursday, May 11, the worriers in the Fitzhugh neighborhood were in full cry: did the police believe there was a marauding, murdering burglar loose in their back yards, or not?

> Residents of Palo Alto's South Gate neighborhood said yesterday they were troubled that a string of daytime home burglaries had gone unsolved and asked police whether murdered music teacher Kristine Fitzhugh might have interrupted an intruder.

So reported the *Palo Alto Daily News*, even as Katie Ryan was finding the bloody Brooks Brothers shirt in Ken's truck. The paper reported that at a meeting held Tuesday evening by nearly 100 of Ken and Kristine's neighbors at the school district's office, just down the street from the Fitzhugh home, Palo Alto Police Lieutenant Torin Fischer tried to assuage the anxieties by telling residents it was too soon to connect Kristine's death with any event, let alone the previous rash of burglaries. The paper reported:

> One woman asked whether she should let her teenage daughter walk home from Palo Alto High School to have lunch alone. Fischer said he wouldn't discourage his own daughter from walking home alone.
> "I don't want you to think you can't walk into your own house," Fischer told the audience. "I do want people to leave here a little bit more concerned but not paranoid."

Some residents, the paper reported, criticized the police for not increasing patrols in the neighborhood after a number of residences were burglarized the previous summer. Even after six reported burglaries in a little over a year and a half, the police didn't seem to take the problem seriously, some said.

Others pressed for more information about the attack on Kristine, but police didn't offer much.

"If you get the feeling we are trying to be evasive, you're right," Coffman said. "In a case like this we are very tight-lipped. We don't want to jeopardize the investigation, or God forbid, an arrest or trial."

Some of the town's more discerning readers, however, probably guessed what the police were suspicioning. On the day of the neighborhood meeting, the *Daily News* reported that Ken had hired Nolan to represent him, and identified the lawyer as a "well-known criminal defense attorney." The paper said Nolan wouldn't return its telephone calls. But the paper also quoted Coffman as saying that Ken was "cooperating with the police," and that they had no suspects. The police search warrant for the house was sealed by a judge, the paper said, after Denson had sworn that release of the information could jeopardize his investigation. But a confidential source told the paper that the police still hadn't found a murder weapon.

On one of their explorations of the house, the searchers had noticed a large wood Spanish-style chest that appeared to be locked. Fletcher, among others, was curious: what did the locked chest contain? It was, of course, possible that the missing murder weapon might be concealed inside. Eventually one of the police officers got it open, and Fletcher realized that it only contained a rather extensive sterling silver service, one that looked to be as ornate as it was antique. Fletcher ordered the chest shut and re-locked, and the police went on their way.

By Friday, May 12, all the searching was over, and Ken, John and the dogs were finally allowed back into the house. Likewise, Ken's Suburban was returned to him. Wong wanted to interview Justin and John again, but they referred him to Nolan. At that point Wong told the boys that they really needed to get a separate lawyer for themselves—Nolan couldn't represent both Ken and them at the same time. The boys checked with Nolan, and Nolan decided to bring in Alan Lagod, another attorney, to represent the boys' interest. The whole thing was turning into a first class stinker, everyone agreed.

On Saturday, May 13, 2000, more than 500 people turned up at the Roller & Hapgood & Tinney funeral home in Palo Alto to remember Kristine Fitzhugh. Ken and the boys were there, of course, along with Gaelyn, Carol, Angelina and all of Kristine's closest friends. Ken had taken pains to arrange the music. He'd contacted professional organist James Welch, and asked him to play the same music that had been played for the Fitzhugh marriage in 1966: Henry Smart's March in G, a happy, nearly bouncy tune. Welch—who taught at Santa Clara University and who had once given organ lessons to Ken, almost seven years before—thought the selection an odd choice. "It's a very obscure piece," Welch would recall. "Very upbeat, almost jolly." That was how Ken seemed to Welch, as well: very chipper, considering that Kristine had just been murdered. Literally across the street from the funeral home was Addison Elementary School, where Kristine was to have taught the 12:50 class that her murder had caused her to miss.

A number of Kristine's friends and acquaintances spoke, including Palo Alto Mayor Liz Kniss, school district officials, and members of the city council. Many recalled Kristine's willingness to do for others, how she had extended her gift for music to so many children, how she had become a friend and confidante for so many young women in the neighborhood, and how the Fitzhugh house was the center of so many festive activities during the holidays.

Then Angelina, a gifted soprano, sang Carol King's "Now and Forever," accompanied by an acoustic guitar, and many in the overflow crowd wept.

When the services were over, Ken, Angelina and the boys went out the side door to avoid the news media.

But even as the last strains of music were dying away at the funeral home, an effort to tie Ken to the murder scientifically was under way at the county's crime lab. There, supervising criminalist Cyndi Hall went into the lab's walk-in freezer and removed the sealed brown paper bag containing Ken's running shoes. Looking at the shoes, Cyndi could see "numerous red stains on tops and toe areas, and laces of both shoes," as she reported later, and "a few stains also on sides and back and bottoms."

Cyndi, who held a master's in molecular biology, now tested several of the red spots with orthotolidine, the so-called "o-tol" test, and the stains turned bluish-green on the filter paper. Next, she tried the test on the spots she saw on the bottoms of the shoes, and two of those reacted positively for blood as well.

Now Cyndi took three of the swabs and set them aside for DNA analysis, and then turned her attention to the green Brooks Brothers polo shirt her colleague Katie Ryan had found under the seat of the Suburban. Like Katie, Cyndi discovered that the large, almost round spot just below the front pocket was presumptively positive for blood, as were two other smaller spots, one on the right arm, and another near the white buttons of the neck. Cyndi then cut a small section of the shirt out for DNA testing, and then returned both the shirt and the shoes to the freezer for continued preservation.

As the second week after Kristine Fitzhugh's murder began, Denson, Wong and their fellow detectives at the Palo Alto Police Department found themselves facing an altogether strange sort of jigsaw puzzle—one in which most of the borders were complete, but which still had a gaping hole in its center.

After the luminol test, Denson was certain he knew *what* had happened, and approximately when: Ken, Denson was convinced, had clobbered Kristine in the kitchen with some sort of blunt object, such as a two-by-four, and had then dragged Kristine's body to the landing, perhaps leaving it there temporarily while he rushed around the kitchen and hallway mopping up. Then he had fetched the dry-cleaning from the wardrobe at the bottom of the basement stairs, put the plastic sheathing between his body and Kristine's bleeding head, and had dragged her to the bottom of the steps, where he'd left her, head down, feet up, face pressing into the plastic. Ken had then taken the blunt object, whatever it was, along with the stuff he'd used to clean up all the blood, and put this in a garbage bag or something similar to dump it somewhere. At that point, perhaps, Ken had noticed the bloodstains on his shirt and his shoes, but then, running out of time, he had quickly changed into a clean shirt, put on the leather loafers, jammed the bloody shirt and shoes under the seat of the Suburban, and then driven off to pick up Gaelyn and Carol, probably throwing the garbage sack in a Dumpster along the way. This accounted for all the known facts: the moving of the body, the clean-up, the odd shoes and the apparent absence of the weapon. All this had taken place sometime between 11 A.M.

and 1:30 P.M., Denson reasoned. So much for the borders of the puzzle.

What was missing, however, was the heart of the matter: *why* had this happened?

By this point, the Palo Alto detectives had talked to scores of people who knew the Fitzhughs, and there was literally no one who had anything bad to say about either Ken or Kristine. True, Ken himself had told the detectives that there was a $48,000 life insurance policy on Kristine—with a double indemnity clause—but that hardly seemed a realistic motive for murder. People kept telling the detectives that Ken and Kristine were devoted to each other. Some called them the "Ozzie and Harriet" of Palo Alto, not only for their well-known love of music, but mostly for their sheer geniality. Ken was the former scoutmaster of Palo Alto Troop 57, and a Mason; Kristine had a wide circle of friends and admirers throughout the community, and was almost universally seen as someone who was simply great with children. The neighbors kept telling the detectives about the parties the Fitzhughs had had over the years at the Escobita house, and how often they would hear either Kristine or Ken softly playing the grand piano that dominated the living room as the evenings fell. It seemed impossible for many to believe that she was actually dead—worse, that she was killed in her own house. The very idea that Ken might be responsible seemed to many to be absurd.

But Denson and Wong knew they had to keep trying.

In the meantime, there was still some work to be done on the borders of the puzzle: like Ken's alibi. An investigator was sent to San Bruno to talk to the manager at Family Golf Center, the place where Ken had said he was when his wife was being killed. The manager, Carol Gossett, told the investigator that she knew Ken Fitzhugh well, that Ken had worked on turning the property into a golf driving range in 1998 and 1999. But no, Gossett said, she hadn't seen Ken for months, and certainly not on May 5—that was the day after Family Golf Centers' New York headquarters had declared bankruptcy, Gossett remembered. She pointed out that the window of her office looked directly out onto the undeveloped portion of the property. If Ken had been out there walking around for the better part of an hour, she said, she surely would have seen him.

And there was another edge to the border that could be locked in place: the paper coffee cup that had been on the kitchen table, along with the half-eaten muffin. The lid was still on the coffee, which made it seem as though Kristine had just picked it up when she was killed.

The nearest Peet's Coffee outlet was in the Town and Country Shopping Center less than three minutes from the Escobita house. Agent Jean Bready visited the store and discovered that Kristine was a frequent customer. The assistant manager of the store, Emily Nessi, recalled that Kristine had come in on Friday morning, May 5, around 11:45 A.M. Emily remembered that Kristine had complained that by the time she usually arrived, the muffins she liked were almost always sold out. Emily agreed to order more of the muffins, and Kristine bought another kind of muffin and her usual latte, and left.

That pushed Kristine's arrival at home back to between 11:45 and noon, the detectives believed.

And the police got another break: a canvass of the Fitzhugh neighbors turned up the information that a driver for Federal Express had delivered a package around noon to a nearby house. Investigators checked with the FedEx people, who in turn identified the FedEx driver as James Selby. Selby had been at 1555 Escobita Avenue at 12:08 P.M., the records showed. That was the house next door to the Fitzhugh house.

A detective was sent to interview Selby, who now provided an unexpected bonus: he had taken a photograph of his delivery address because he admired its landscaping. When he had taken the picture shortly after 12:08 P.M., there were no cars in the driveway of the Fitzhugh house—nor any, apparently, parked on the street. Where was the film? Selby said he would look for it. But if Selby was right—and he seemed quite certain—that meant two things: Kristine hadn't yet arrived home from Peet's at 12:08 P.M., and Ken's Suburban was missing at the same time.

Then, a further canvass of the neighborhood turned up another possible witness: resident Tracy Wang, who lived on the street behind Escobita, Castilleja Avenue. Tracy told detectives that she had noticed a blue Suburban-like vehicle parked on her street around 10 A.M. on the day of the murder, and that it had been gone the next time she looked, around 2 P.M. The blue vehicle had been parked on the west side of Castilleja in front of the house at 1550—as it happened, the house directly behind the Fitzhughs'. That led Denson and Wong to a theory: perhaps Ken had moved the blue truck to the street behind the Fitzhugh house that morning, parked it there, and then had reentered his own property through the gate that was cut into his rear fence. Then, Denson reasoned, Ken might have reentered his own house through the basement storm doors, and waited in the basement for Kristine to come home . . .

If that were the case, it would be evidence of premeditation: that not only had Ken intended to murder Kristine—that seemed apparent from the wounds—but that he had actually *planned* to do it, that he lay in wait in the basement. Then, after the deed was done, and the clean-up finished, Ken would have left his own house the same way he had entered, gone back through the gate into the rear neighbors' yard, then out to the Suburban to drive away to pick up Gaelyn and Carol.

Detectives also interviewed lawyer Thomas Moore, who had been working with Ken on the printer problem next door—according to Ken, between 9 and 11 A.M. Moore said he hadn't arrived at work until shortly after ten. When he came in, he met Ken, Moore said. They worked on the printer problem together until perhaps 11:15 or 11:30, and then Ken left. Moore had rebooted his computer at about 11:30, he said, just after Ken had left. Ken had not been wearing a green Brooks Brothers polo shirt that morning, Moore said; and he thought Ken had been wearing the black leather loafers with the black jeans, although he wasn't sure.

What did this mean? For Denson, this was still more evidence of premeditation. If Moore was right about Ken's clothes—and if Ken had killed Kristine—that seemed to suggest that Ken had worn one set of clothes to work with Moore, then changed into clothes for the murder, then changed back into the clothes he had previously worn to go pick up Gaelyn and Carol. Why would Ken make these clothing changes if he hadn't planned the murder ahead of time? Bizarre as it seemed, it was the only explanation that fit with Ken having committed the murder—that is, if the blood on the shirt and shoes had come from Kristine.

Finally, efforts were made to collect the records of the various Fitzhugh telephones. There were several lines running into the Escobita house, and both Kristine and Ken had cellular telephones. A check of the answering machine on the Fitzhugh home telephone showed that Phyllis Smith of the school district had indeed called at 1:15 on Friday and left a message for Kristine, noting that she'd missed the 12:50 class and asking her to call in.

And Phyllis confirmed that she'd then called Ken's office telephone, which rang through to Ken's cellular. Ken had answered about 1:16, according to both Phyllis and the phone records. That was when Ken had told Phyllis he was heading south on Highway 101 through Redwood City. But was he really? The detectives knew that if Ken had been using his cellular telephone to take the call from Phyllis, there would be a record of the antenna which had broadcast the call when Ken picked it up.

If Ken were telling the truth about where he was when he talked to Phyllis, the records should show an antenna closer to Redwood City than Palo Alto. But if Ken were lying—if the whole supposed trip to San Bruno was nothing more than an elaborate attempt to manufacture an alibi, and Ken was actually at home when he took Phyllis' call—then he was cooked. One thing was for sure: there were no messages on the answering machine from Ken to Kristine—at all—although he had told Denson and Wong, as well as Gaelyn and Carol, that he'd tried to call her after hearing from Phyllis.

Denson now had a tentative timeline for the murder:

9–11 A.M.	Ken works with Moore on computer printer problem
10 A.M.	Kristine goes to teach her class

11:30 A.M.	Ken leaves Moore's office, changes clothes, parks the Suburban on the street behind the Fitzhugh house, reenters via the back gate, waits for Kristine to come home
11:45 A.M.	Kristine buys coffee, muffins from Peet's
12:08 P.M.	Selby delivers the Federal Express package to the house next to the Fitzhughs'
12:15–12:45 P.M.	Ken kills Kristine in the kitchen while she sits at the table with her coffee and muffin
12:45–1:15 P.M.	Ken cleans up the blood, places Kristine's body on the stairs
1:15 P.M.	Phyllis Smith calls first Kristine, then Ken, alerts him to Kristine's disappearance
1:15–1:30 P.M.	Ken leaves the house, exits through the rear gate, gets in the Suburban and drives to the Mason/Piraino house, ditching evidence along the way

In turn, this possible timeline raised another question: where was Kristine between 11:45 and 12:15 or so? Selby insisted that Kristine's silver BMW hadn't been in the driveway when he'd made his delivery at 12:08. Had Kristine made another, unknown stop between Peet's, five minutes away at most, and home? If so, where was it? And if so, had Kristine therefore come home later than Ken had anticipated? Was that why the shirt and shoes were under the seat of the Suburban—because Ken's murder plan had been thrown off schedule by Kristine's unanticipated delay between 11:45 and 12:15? It was something to think about.

Meanwhile, the check of Ken's cellular records seemed to

show, based on the antenna that routed the call, that Ken—or at least his telephone—was in the immediate vicinity of the Escobita house when he'd taken the call from Phyllis Smith, not miles away as he'd claimed. The records seemed to show that Ken had lied about his alibi.

Following Kristine's funeral, Denson and Wong began to notice a subtle change in the attitudes of many of Kristine's friends. Where, until the time of the funeral, many steadfastly insisted that Ken and Kristine were a devoted couple, after the service it seemed that people became a little less guarded in their assessment of the relationship. Perhaps it was just because the shock had worn off, or maybe it was because people had begun to think a bit more critically, but as time went on, the detectives picked up on a sort of trend: Kristine, it appeared, had been the primary social engine in the Fitzhugh household, while Ken was—well, Ken was just *there* . . . It was hard for many people to explain.

Gaelyn and Carol, meanwhile, continued to believe that Kristine had died in a terrible accident, and when it became apparent to them that the police believed Ken had murdered their friend, Gaelyn and Carol wouldn't hear of it—at least at first.

Still, checking the telephone list Ken had given them, Denson and Wong realized that almost all of the names on the list were people who felt they had known Kristine, but not Ken. Oh, they knew *of* Ken, they knew Ken was Kristine's husband, but they didn't really know Ken himself. He was always in the background, rarely front and center. He was shy, some said; others thought he was so reserved as to be almost condescending. He didn't seem to have any close friends of his own, the detectives thought—everyone who knew him thought of themselves as Kristine's friend, not Ken's.

Kristine's friends used words like "intelligent," "extroverted," and "personable" to describe her. She was a physical fitness buff, worked out at a gym on a regular basis, and was extremely careful of her diet. Most saw her as a generous, caring person. Over the past few years she had been seeing a psychotherapist. Several people thought that, in the days before her death, she had been "radiant," and very happy.

Ken, on the other hand, was seen as a far more introverted personality. Several friends said that Kristine had said she was frustrated by some of Ken's habits, such as his eating preferences, his excess weight, and a supposed reluctance to exercise. Many saw them as completely different personalities, with Kristine being described as warm and outgoing, while Ken was reserved to the point of coolness. And while Kristine enjoyed taking trips—sometimes without Ken—Ken was pretty much a homebody.

Neither partner, however, seemed to have confided in anyone about the state of their marriage. No one could ever remember seeing them argue, let alone act violently toward one another. Still, some thought that Ken and Kristine were *too* physically undemonstrative toward each other; some told the detectives they believed the marriage was more platonic than anything else.

And as the interviews progressed, Denson and Wong began to pick up a whiff of something more . . . something that suggested that perhaps Ken was suspicious of Kristine, or jealous, or something . . .

Several people told the detectives how they might be at a restaurant with Kristine when suddenly, who should appear but Ken. It was as if Ken was checking up on Kristine, perhaps following her. Kristine seemed to take this in stride, however, as if it was no big deal.

But as the detectives worked outward from the Palo Alto people, using the telephone list that Ken had provided, eventually they began to talk to friends from the Fitzhughs' days in San Diego, and it was here that a rather different story began to emerge, although it would take some weeks before the true dimensions would be discovered. And even then, the whole story had yet to be told.

ON Tuesday, May 16, 2000, supervising criminalist Cyndi Hall obtained several of the swabbed blood samples she had taken from the shoes and shirt, and subjected them to a relatively new form of DNA testing called "STR," which stood for "Short Tandem Repeats." In this kind of test, small amounts of cellular DNA are first amplified—that is, they are induced to replicate themselves—then joined to known sequences of molecules, then run through a chemical analyzer.

Cyndi began this process by first extracting the DNA from all the samples—that is, the bloodstains on the shirt and shoes, and reference samples of blood taken from Ken and Kristine. Using chemicals, the blood cells are "broken" open, and the nuclear material is removed. The stuff is then placed into individual containers, like test tubes, and mixed with a "primer"—a short piece of known DNA—and an enzyme which will later cause the DNA strands to stretch, which allows them to be copied repeatedly. The mixture is then heated to near boiling in a computerized oven known as a "thermal cycler." The heat separates the two intertwined strands of DNA—the famous helix—into individual strands. Then the temperature is lowered to a bit over 125 degrees—hot enough to prevent the reattachment of the twin strands to each other, but not so hot that the "primer" doesn't slip in to take their place. The mixture is then reheated, this time to about 180 degrees, which causes the new compound to stretch under the influence of the enzyme. The entire process is repeated twenty-eight times, and by the end of the day, the DNA expert has an ample supply of DNA that mirrors the material of the original samples.

Cyndi began this amplification process on May 18. But as the process of repeatedly heating, cooling and reheating was under way, the crime lab suffered a power failure; one of the "rolling blackouts" that were just beginning to afflict California that summer struck without warning.

Denson, meanwhile, had been expecting to hear about the DNA results from Cyndi that same day. He called her, and learned that the power failure had ruined the first experiment. At first Denson was worried, thinking that the evidence had been destroyed, but when Cyndi explained that they still had plenty of DNA left over from her original "breaking open" process, and that they would merely have to restart the amplification routine, he relaxed. It only meant that he would have to put the arrest of Ken off for one day, he realized—that is, if the DNA on Ken's shirt and shoes matched the DNA taken from Kristine's blood.

But the day's delay was to have some unfortunate consequences.

Friday, May 19, 2000, was to have been a big day in the Fitzhugh family—the day of Justin's long-awaited graduation from the University of the Pacific. Both Ken and Kristine were enormously proud of Justin. From the days when they had worried—and occasionally argued—over his high school performance, Justin had blossomed. He had become interested in computer technology, and had excelled in it while at the university—to the point where he already had a job waiting for him at a Silicon Valley technology company. Now the day both Ken and Kristine had looked forward to had finally arrived, but Kristine would not be there to see it.

As Ken, John and the two dogs pulled away from the Escobita house, a team of Palo Alto police began to shadow him.

"I had put a surveillance team on him very early that morning," Denson said later, "on his entire neighborhood. We had probably, I'd guess six to ten detectives out there. So I told them, 'You stay on him all day until I get my DNA results back'. That's what they were doing. They were staying on him. Wherever he went they were gonna go."

Although Denson believed he had probable cause to support Ken's arrest almost from the beginning, he wanted to wait until the DNA results came back from the crime lab.

"Because that's pretty much a dead-bang cinch," Denson said later. "I had probable cause to arrest—and we discussed it a lot. We didn't feel that he was necessarily a danger to the public; he was a danger to who he killed. And so, we were kind of keeping track of him."

As the cars moved off toward the freeway, Denson was waiting in the Santa Clara County courthouse with a complaint for murder, along with an affidavit of probable cause in support of Ken's arrest. He had the paperwork in his hands when he called Cyndi Hall at the crime lab, who now had the results of the DNA tests on Ken's shirt and shoes.

After spending Thursday morning re-amplifying the various samples of DNA following the power outage, Cyndi began the process of actually testing the expanded samples. This was accomplished by placing all the samples in a computerized machine, a PerkinElmer ABI Prism 310 Genetic Analyzer. Each of the samples was in its own tube, and the machine had a tray that could hold up to forty-eight samples. Once the machine began its work, it inserted a small tube called a capillary and a tiny electrode into the now-viscous genetic material. A tiny electric current was applied for thirty minutes, which drew the negatively charged DNA material past a laser coupling. As the material passed the coupling, the laser fired, and a visual profile of the genetic component was recorded. Eventually, each sample would have thirteen different places on the DNA strand which would be "shot."

Because every person has a different sequence of the molecular material available at the same thirteen places on the genetic strand, each person's DNA is therefore different and, except in the case of identical twins, unique.

Thus, late on Thursday afternoon, Cyndi was able to say authoritatively that the blood found on Ken's shoes and shirt had come from only one person in 190,000,000,000,000,000 people—more human beings than have ever existed since they had begun to walk upright. That person was Kristine Pedersen Fitzhugh.

• • •

Denson got this news from Cyndi over the telephone while he was at the Santa Clara County District Attorney's Office in San Jose, where he had gone to get Fletcher to approve his complaint and arrest warrant. Denson now called Wong, and told him that the DNA results showed that the blood on Ken's shirt and shoes had come from Kristine. Then Denson drove back to Palo Alto, perhaps thirty minutes away, and pulled into the branch court there. He took the complaint and warrant to Judge Charles W. Hayden, and explained what was going on. After listening to Denson and reading his complaint and affidavit, Hayden signed the arrest warrant. Denson thanked the judge, went outside into the hallway, and called the surveillance team on his cellular telephone.

"The arrest warrant's in my hands, arrest him," Denson told the team trailing Ken.

The team then called the California Highway Patrol, and informed them that they wanted to serve an arrest warrant on a murder suspect. The CHP radioed its own officers, and the freeway traffic was soon blocked off—in case Ken decided to make some sort of break for it, however unlikely that seemed. At that point the Palo Alto police moved in behind Ken's blue Suburban, flashed their red lights, and pulled Ken over. Shocked, he realized that some of the police had their guns drawn.

Ken was now told that he was under arrest for murder.

KEN said nothing to the police officers who had arrested him, either before or after they read him his Miranda rights. John, of course, was left to drive the Suburban off the freeway, accompanied by Boots and Reina. Now Justin would have to attend his graduation without either of his parents.

Somehow, one of the local television stations had tumbled to the surveillance, and was on hand for the arrest. Ken suspected that the police had tipped them off, which was like adding the insult of ignominy to the injury of arrest—and on this day, of all days.

The police officers transported Ken back to the police station in Palo Alto. Still Ken said nothing. Doubtless he had been drilled by Nolan on what to do if this day ever came. Denson called Nolan's office to inform him that Ken had been arrested. Nolan was out of town, but one of his associates came right over to be with Ken. After visiting with the associate, Ken was taken to the county's main jail in San Jose to be booked. It was a place he would stay for most of the next eighteen months.

Husband arrested in murder of popular teacher, the *Palo Alto Daily News* headlined the next day, Saturday, May 20.

> Police yesterday arrested real estate developer Kenneth Fitzhugh on charges of strangling and beating his school-teacher wife in their Palo Alto kitchen and then moving her body to make her death look like an accident. . . .
>
> Deputy District Attorney Michael Fletcher said Fitzhugh denies any role in his wife's killing, as he has from

the beginning of the investigation. He declined to give a motive for the murder. . . .

Kristine Fitzhugh, 52, was a beloved music teacher who taught in several Palo Alto and East Palo Alto schools. Friends yesterday remembered her as someone who had an ability to motivate the children she taught. . . .

"We are confident that the killer of Kristine Fitzhugh is in custody," said Palo Alto police Agent Jim Coffman. . . .

Shortly after the murder, Fitzhugh hired criminal defense attorney Thomas Nolan of Palo Alto. Nolan didn't return telephone calls from the Daily News yesterday. . . .

The paper went on to paraphrase Denson's affidavit in support of the arrest, and said that the luminol test performed in the kitchen had shown "a blood bath."

Monday's story began:

A spatter of blood as large as a basketball marred the wallpaper of the kitchen . . .

That was certainly an overstatement, even if it made for lurid reading; there was actually no blood in that particular stain, which appeared to be a reaction to some sort of household cleaner. But the paper had given an accurate synopsis of the rest of the evidence cited by Denson: wounds inconsistent with a fall down a flight of stairs, Kristine's blood on Ken's shirt and shoes, the unverified San Bruno alibi, and the fact that police had been unable to find any record of the calls Ken claimed he had made to the Fitzhugh answering machine after hearing from Phyllis Smith.

"I don't know why he did it," Fletcher told the newspaper when it pressed him for Ken's supposed motive. "You'll have to ask the perpetrator why he did it . . . sex or money is usually the motive . . ."

On the following Monday, after spending the weekend in the madhouse that was the Santa Clara County Jail, Ken was driven to Palo Alto for his arraignment on the murder charge before Judge Hayden.

Apparently at the request of the defense, the hearing was moved out of the courtroom normally used for such proceedings to one on the ground floor which had a private entrance. That prevented the television people from videotaping Ken's arrival, which ordinarily would have been made down a publicly accessible corridor. Then, two bailiffs were stationed in front of the courtroom doors to prevent anyone taking pictures from outside the courtroom. It was a sort of privacy rarely afforded an indigent defendant, the *Daily News* pointed out to its readers the next day.

When everything was set, the judge asked for Ken's plea to the charge. "I am innocent," he declared.

Hayden shook his head. Ken had to say either "Guilty" or "Not guilty," not "I am innocent."

"Not guilty, Your Honor," Ken said. The judge ordered the court's Office of Pretrial Services to prepare a report on Ken's suitability for bail, and with that, the whole thing was over.

On the way out of the courthouse, other bailiffs strung up a barrier of gray blankets to prevent the photographers from taking Ken's picture as he left the facility. For a man of comparable anonymity, Ken had been thrust into the public eye with astonishing rapidity, and it had to be a bit unnerving.

Outside the courtroom, Nolan's partner Daniel Barton, standing in for Nolan in his absence, said the Palo Alto police had gotten the wrong man—that Ken loved Kristine, and had no reason whatsoever for wanting to see her dead. "No one," Barton said, "has suggested a motive for killing his wife. There is none."

That was a lack that was troubling Denson and Fletcher as well, although not nearly as much as Barton probably thought. As Fletcher observed later, they didn't really *need* a motive— the physical evidence was simply overwhelming.

And, apart from the life insurance policy, it wasn't entirely true that they were bereft of ideas about motive: Kristine had been beaten so savagely that it literally cried out that the crime was one of intense, highly personal anger—not at all the sort of thing a stranger would do. Only someone who knew his victim intimately would have that much rage, all the experts said.

There was something in Ken and Kristine's background that would shed light on what happened that day in the Escobita house, Fletcher was sure, and he was right. Because even as Ken was declaring his innocence, Denson was learning something that might begin to explain it, or at least most of it.

Almost from the beginning, Denson and Wong had wondered whether this highly personal and savage beating had occurred because of a love triangle. Among the Fitzhughs' Palo Alto friends, the idea that either Kristine or Ken had been having an affair was ridiculous. Still, Denson and Wong kept asking, even when it tended to make people upset. To the detectives, the violence of the attack seemed to make sexual jealousy the leading contender in the motive derby.

"What was unfortunate," Fletcher said later, "is that you need to ask questions that suggest to people that you— When you ask somebody whether Kristine's having an affair, you can't help but suggest to some people that you think that's a possibility. And that's very unfortunate. I don't know how to do it without offending some people, but I think part of what the investigators have to do is, try to ask difficult questions of people, who were very close to this family, who didn't see this coming, who were very protective, first of both of them, and then always of Kristine."

The fact that Kristine had a number of gay and lesbian friends sparked the same inquiries, and a number of people were quite offended, Fletcher recalled.

"You're asking whether there was a gay affair, if there's *any* affair, and none of that's going on," Fletcher said, "and some people here, that struck them as particularly offensive. People asking if some people were gay, and so forth, and it was just like, 'You're on the wrong track.' I totally understand that point of view, [but] if they [Denson, Wong and the other detectives] hadn't asked, I would have said, 'You've got to go back and ask.' Because we need to ask these questions."

Eventually, however, Denson made telephone contact with Dr. Thomas Schaide in San Diego, a long-time friend of both Kristine and Ken's. It took some tactful persistence on Denson's part, but in the end, Schaide told Denson the truth: years before, when the couple were still living in the San Diego area, it was a matter of common belief in their social circle that Kristine had had a long-running affair with a close personal friend of both Kristine and Ken.

And Schaide added: it was likewise a matter of common talk that the lover was actually the father of Justin Fitzhugh—not Ken.

Who was this? Denson asked.

And at that point, Schaide provided the name of Robert Kenneth Brown.

LATER, Denson would explain just how he had located the man Schaide had identified as Kristine's former lover, Robert Kenneth Brown: he asked the state's Department of Motor Vehicles for Brown's address, and thereafter had very little trouble finding him. Of course, it wasn't quite so simple as that: there were a number of Robert Kenneth Browns in the motor vehicle department's drivers' license database, and how was one to know which was the right Robert Kenneth Brown?

But Denson had a few other clues from Schaide: he knew Brown's approximate age, and he knew that he lived somewhere near Placerville, California, a small town in the foothills of the Sierra Nevada Mountains.

And Denson knew one other thing: Robert Kenneth Brown was a disbarred lawyer.

So, having established a likely address for the Robert Kenneth Brown he hoped to talk to, Denson asked the El Dorado County Sheriff's Department to drive up to Brown's house in the woods southeast of Placerville, and leave a Sheriff's Department business card with Denson's number on it, asking Brown to call Denson right away.

On June 8, 2000, Robert Kenneth Brown called Denson to ask what he wanted; Denson was out. When he returned to the office later that morning, Denson found a note from Brown with a return telephone number.

After identifying himself, Denson said he was investigating the murder of Kristine Fitzhugh.

"Yes," Brown said.

"And I understand that you knew her."

"Yes, I did, sir."

"Okay," said Denson. "How did you know her?"

"Oh," Brown said, "I've known the family for over twenty years. We went on vacations together. We did a lot of things together. We were partners on a small sailboat for years before I got really ill."

"Uh-huh," Denson said.

"Other than that we were good friends."

But, Brown said, he hadn't seen or heard from either Ken or Kristine for almost four years—not since 1996.

"I'm going to get right to it," Denson said. "Kristine was killed in her home on May fifth. I don't know if you knew that or not."

"I just got that news about ten days ago," Brown said.

"And since then," Denson added, "Kenneth Fitzhugh has been arrested for the murder."

"*He has?*"

"Yeah," Denson said, "and—"

"That comes as a shock," Brown said.

"Yeah," Denson continued, "and in doing our investigation we have discovered that you had an affair with Kristine. It was reported to us that you did, and we're kind of calling to, kind of confirm that, and see if we can get any information from you about anything she might have told you, or what was going on in her life at that time."

There was a pause on the other end of the line. Denson realized that if his news about Ken having been arrested was a shock, the fact that police were claiming to know that Brown had had an affair with Kristine must have been a stunner.

"I was fishing," Denson said later. He wasn't sure that what he'd heard from Schaide and a few others in the San Diego group was really valid. What if Brown told him that it simply wasn't true, or worse, told him to get lost?

Brown mumbled something unintelligible. Denson took that as a yes.

"You did?" he asked.

"Years ago," Brown said.

Now Denson asked whether Ken had known about the affair. Brown wasn't sure. It began, he said, after Ken had invited him home for dinner with Kristine. He and Ken worked at the same place, Ryan Aeronautical in San Diego, in the late 1960s.

"It just developed," Brown said of the relationship with Kristine. It had continued for six or seven years, and then Brown had moved away.

Now Denson wanted to determine whether Brown could possibly have been Justin's biological father. He knew Justin was born in 1978, so he asked Brown if the relationship with Kristine might have possibly gone on as long as eight years.

"Possibly, yes," Brown said. "You see, my memory isn't what it used to be."

After getting some additional background, Denson asked about the boys.

"Okay," he said, "were those children his children?"

"I don't know," Brown said.

"Did you guys ever discuss that?"

"We discussed it, but I don't know."

"Okay, was there ever any speculation as to whether you were their father?"

"Between her and I?"

"Yeah."

"She thought that I was, but I don't know that for a fact."

"She thought they were your children?"

"She did. Or she said that she thought one of them was."

"And which one would that have been?"

"The oldest one, I think."

"Okay, and what made her believe that?"

"His general build is closer to mine than close to Ken's."

After he hung up, Denson wondered whether Ken had known all this—it seemed hard to believe that Kristine could have had an affair for six to eight years without Ken having realized it—especially if, as Schaide had said, the relationship between Brown and Kristine was common knowledge in their social circle in San Diego. Was one of the children really fathered by Brown, not Ken? And had Ken known that? Was this possibly part of the long-sought motive for the murder?

Denson and Wong decided they had to interview Brown again, so they made plans to drive to the Placerville area to see him personally.

. . .

The next day was June 9, and even as Denson and Wong were preparing to go to Somerset and meet Brown face-to-face, Nolan was trying to get bail for Ken. Nolan wanted the court to grant it, Fletcher did not. Hayden said he'd hear from Nolan first. The lack of an apparent motive would figure prominently in Nolan's argument.

The court had to grant Ken bail, Nolan said, because the law only permitted the judge to consider two factors: whether Ken was a danger to the community, and whether he was likely to flee to avoid trial.

No one had provided any evidence that Ken was a danger to the community, Nolan said. "The court must find by clear and convincing evidence there is a substantial likelihood that the person released would result [sic] in great bodily harm to others," he said. "That's what needs to be found in order to deny Mr. Fitzhugh bail." The Santa Clara County District Attorney's Office hadn't met that burden, Nolan said, so the court had no choice but to set a bail amount.

The only thing the D.A.'s office had said, Nolan added, is that if convicted, Ken would be facing a substantial amount of prison time. That was like saying if you're arrested, you must be guilty, Nolan said.

"In this particular case, there is no one entitled to bail more than Mr. Fitzhugh," Nolan continued. He had utterly no motive to murder Kristine. Ken had cooperated with the police from the start, and had never refused to talk to them. When they'd asked to review his financial records, he agreed. When they wanted to search, he'd given his consent.

"All of these things are done because that's what an innocent person does," Nolan said. The D.A.'s office had failed to come up with any motive other than the $48,000 insurance policy, he said—and that Ken had already signed over to Justin and John. "If that were ever a motive in Palo Alto, you would want to get life insurance substantially more than $48,000," he said. "The idea of $48,000 being some kind of motive, that he's going to flee, he runs off to try to get that money, is absurd."

Ken's primary asset, Nolan said, was the Escobita house,

valued at $2 million, and he intended to sell it. With a
$450,000 first mortgage, that left $1.5 million or so, and Ken
was entitled to half of that. "He would therefore be able to
post a $375,000 property bond," Nolan said. If and when the
house was sold, Nolan added, Ken would be willing to put up
even more money for bail.

Ken was entitled to a presumption of innocence, Nolan
continued, which meant that he was entitled to be out on bail.
Keeping Ken in jail would make it far harder for him to have
a fair trial. The only reason the D.A.'s office wanted to keep
Ken in jail was to "satisfy the community, to get the community relaxing—like, 'We caught the person.' "

Even Denson's affidavit in support of Ken's arrest was
calculated to poison the community against Ken through the
news media, Nolan added.

"The only reason I can see that he filed that particular
document [the affidavit in support of the arrest] is that it's
designed for one thing and one thing only—that's the media.
I'm not talking to the media."

Nolan was getting wound up, excited; his argument was
beginning to jump around spasmodically as he tried to convince Hayden to let Ken out on bail.

"Motive," said Nolan, "no prior behavior of any kind that
would indicate he is responsible for this—none. A community
that's concerned, yes. They [the police] have got that on their
hands. They have to do something about that."

The luminol test—Nolan said it was ridiculous. "I chal-
lenge them to go to ten kitchens [and] do the same luminol,
the same test—you will get the same picture. His face was put
on the front page of the San Jose *Mercury News* so huge that
it would make Mother Teresa look like a crook."

Ken's assets were completely tied up, Nolan went on. "He
has nowhere to go. He has no place to go, no resources to go
there, and has no interest in going there. He has two sons to
take care of."

Nolan was beginning to wind down after his rambling
outburst.

"Your Honor, I am sorry that I got [off] to kind of an
aggressive start," he said. "It's hard when you see what happens in the media, and you realize that there is no way in

today's age that you can get a fair trial in the media . . . it's unfortunate that Palo Alto has a rag instead of a responsible newspaper, because I think we deserve better than that, quite frankly. I think the community . . . does not feel good about the way the press has handled this matter . . ."

So far, Nolan said, he hadn't seen a single police report on the murder, but from where he sat, he couldn't think of a single thing that Ken could have done to warrant the treatment he'd received at the hands of the police.

"They go out when they decide they want to arrest him at gunpoint on the freeway. They make a felony stop on the freeway with his son in his car on the way to his graduation. You know, there are sick things that police departments get involved in. They are sick. They're like—"

Nolan was starting to go off again, but Hayden jerked him back. "Let's refocus on the bail issue," he said.

"The fact of the matter is," Nolan said, "their job is to do an impartial investigation into this particular case. They were too anxious to satisfy the community . . . 'You don't have to worry, we've now caught the person.' "

The police had offered to give Ken a polygraph, Nolan said, but since they'd made that offer he hadn't heard a single other word about it. He'd had to find his own expert on polygraphs, Nolan added.

Hayden finally cut Nolan off. He said he wanted to hear Fletcher's side of the story.

Fletcher had been thinking about Nolan's argument.

"Let's for a moment adopt his position, that the defendant had no motive," Fletcher said. "Where does that put us, then? For no reason whatsoever he kills his wife, the mother of his children, and there are literally thousands of people he has no reason to want to kill." In that case, Fletcher said, "they're at equal risk." In other words, if Ken had no motive for killing Kristine, but did anyway, then everyone else he had no motive to kill could also be killed.

It was a ridiculous argument, but it pointed up the fallacy of Nolan's contention.

Fletcher said he wasn't prepared to argue the merits of bail at that particular point. "Your Honor," he said, "I don't think bail is appropriate. If you're going to set bail, it ought to be very substantial, and we ought to have a source-of-bail hearing." Fletcher meant that if Hayden was going to grant bail, Fletcher wanted to know where the money would be coming from.

Nolan said that Fletcher's argument was ridiculous. Ken was entitled to bail because he wasn't a threat to anybody, and he had a right to defend himself without the stigma of being incarcerated, especially when he had cooperated with the police from the very beginning. Nolan wanted Alan Lagod, representing Justin and John, to speak to Hayden.

"Very briefly," said Lagod, "their position is, they would like their father released." While it was true that Ken was not entitled to use money from Kristine's half of the estate, Lagod said, if it were possible to do so, they were willing to let Ken have that money for his defense as well, "that's how strongly they feel." Lagod said Justin and John were willing to speak to the judge on their father's behalf; he wanted it done in the judge's chambers, however. He didn't want the news media reporting John and Justin's words.

"Well," said Hayden, "I share the concern of both counsel. I do not want this matter tried in the press or public sectors, that's not where it belongs," thereby unilaterally jettisoning the First and Sixth Amendments to the Constitution. "I have taken pains to try to avoid that the best I can."

Hayden asked if Fletcher and Nolan were done, and they said they were.

"I don't believe he is entitled to bail. I'm going to set bail. I do consider—I don't know if I consider him to be a threat to others." The noise in the courtroom was of several hundred heads sustaining severe whiplash as Hayden contradicted himself twice in three sentences.

"Mr. Fletcher used the analogy, if there's no motive, then he is a threat to everybody. I don't think that's correct, but I am very concerned about the flight risk. I find the risk he is facing—he is facing the most horrific charges to be placed against a person. I think that bail will be appropriate. I am going to set bail at this time in the amount of $10 million.

That's a hefty sum. He may or may not be able to make that at this time."

Nolan said that was the same as no bail. It would require a $1 million premium. For that amount someone would have to have $20 million on hand.

Hayden said he had no idea of how much money Ken had. And, he said, if Ken sold the Escobita house, he would have to put the proceeds in Nolan's trust account. Ken would have to surrender his passport.

Nolan asked that Hayden make his ruling without prejudice, meaning that it could be raised again later. He said he would sit down with Fletcher and iron out just how much money Ken had available, so the flight risk issue could be put to rest. Hayden agreed that Nolan could raise the bail issue again. Nolan would do so repeatedly throughout the next eight months, to no avail.

But the issue of the motive was about to gain some new clarity.

Denson and Wong met Bob Brown in person three days later after the bail hearing. Brown was lying in a hospital bed that had been set up in the living room of his house, which itself was up a long winding road from the tiny crossroads of Somerset, southeast of Placerville. Having been injured in a motorcycle wreck just over a month earlier, Brown could barely walk. Not only that, Wong and Denson soon learned that Brown was under the influence of a significant amount of pain medication, which had the effect of blunting both his thinking and his memory.

"Okay," Denson said. "We want to talk to you about some history you've had . . , and get your perspective on things."

"Just so I can clarify something," Brown said. "I can't . . . I don't need an attorney for anything?"

"No, you—" Denson began, but Brown interrupted him.

"I can't even walk," he said.

By this point, the police had run a check on Brown's past. They had discovered that not only had Brown been disbarred as an attorney, he had a prior conviction for receiving stolen property. And only the year before, Brown had been arrested again, this time for taking a motor vehicle without the owner's permission, and possession of stolen property—a Rototiller, to be exact—for which he was still awaiting trial, and would subsequently plead *nolo contendere*. And they knew, or had reason to believe, that Brown had a fairly extensive history of illicit drug abuse. So Brown's question did not surprise them. They wondered whether Brown was worried that somehow the police were going to try to pin Kristine's death on *him*.

"You're not in the least bit of trouble," Denson reassured him.

"I know I'm not in trouble," Brown said. "I'm just devastated by this."

Denson said they only wanted to talk to Brown because he had been so close to the Fitzhughs.

Brown agreed with that assessment.

"I thought it was strange," he said, "that Ken called me ten minutes before the memorial service, to tell me that this had happened."

Ken, Brown now related, had called him just before the service for Kristine to let him know that she was dead. Brown said he'd already heard about it from his aunt, Janet Moore, and had called John Fitzhugh to ask him to have Ken call him. He hadn't heard anything for several days, and then Ken had called just before the memorial service, so Brown was unable to attend.

"I said, if he would have let me know . . ." Brown said. "Sorry, I have a tendency to wander."

Denson said it was okay. He wanted Brown to give him the short history of his affair with Kristine. He asked when Brown had first met the Fitzhughs.

It was, Brown said, in 1970 . . .

But the circumstances that led to the intertwining of the lives of Ken, Kristine and Robert Brown actually went back much further than that.

THE CASTLE

WHO can say when anything truly begins? Is it in the moment of conception, or is it in the hidden tide that runs through human existence, the sinews of relationships that bind the present to the past as well as future? Just as our parents were what their parents made of them, we are what our parents have made of us—as our children will be what we make of them. This is the endless cycle of living, and in one way or another, goes far to explain much of what otherwise may seem inexplicable. In this manner, the fates of Kenneth Carroll Fitzhugh, Jr., Anna Kristine Pedersen Fitzhugh and Robert Kenneth Brown were the product of their respective pasts.

"I grew up in the small town of Del Mar, California," Ken was eventually to tell his jury, "[a] town of three hundred people in San Diego County. I was an only child, in an intact family. My parents were married for forty years. I think I had a fairly normal childhood. I was a good student. My interests were playing the piano."

This was true enough, if somewhat abridged; in reality, Ken's entire life was the indirect but inevitable result of the actions of two different men, both born in Michigan in 1854: his grandfather, Frank Fitzhugh; and one of his uncles, a rather extraordinary man named David Eugene Thompson.

Both men, before they died, came to reside in the San Diego area—Frank in the city of San Diego, and Thompson in the exclusive San Diego resort community of Del Mar to the north, site of the present day Del Mar Racecourse.

The place that was to become Del Mar was originally a broad, high, sparsely treed bluff whose rocky base was lashed by the waves of the Pacific, some twenty-two miles outside of San

Diego. The cliffs of the bluff rose abruptly from the beach, and were cut by a number of narrow ravines that ran down to the shore. As early as 1889, an attempt was made to take advantage of the spectacular setting by the construction of a first-class hotel, but after the hotel burned to the foundations in 1890, the small hamlet became a near ghost town. All of that began to change fifteen years later, mostly because of a man named Ed Fletcher, a San Diego produce merchant.

Perhaps tiring of a career in carrots and cucumbers, Fletcher became interested in water—a commodity in short supply in turn-of-the-last-century San Diego. Sometime in 1905 Fletcher hooked up with four wealthy and powerful Los Angeles men, including Henry E. Huntington, the developer of southern California's storied Pacific Electric Railroad, the so-called Red Car Line. In those days, owning a streetcar line was one of the surest ways to sell residential real estate. Huntington and his partners in the South Coast Land Company envisioned extending the Pacific Electric service from Santa Ana, southeast of Los Angeles, all the way to San Diego. They hoped to steal most of the train traffic from the only existing Los Angeles–San Diego connection, the Santa Fe Railroad, and develop the oceanfront real estate and the nearby fresh water resources, all the way from the city of Oceanside to Del Mar, which would in turn be connected to San Diego by the first stage of the electric line to Los Angeles. Huntington had three partners in this enterprise, including a man named William G. Kerckhoff, a Los Angeles millionaire partner of Huntington in the Pacific Electric.

After becoming a minority investor and general manager in Huntington and Kerckhoff's South Coast Land Company, Fletcher began to buy up options for the purchase of land and water rights along the coast, and up the San Dieguito River Valley, which ran up into the mountains north of San Diego. Early in 1905, Fletcher obtained an option on a large chunk of the bluff of Del Mar, and then reported to Kerckhoff. Kerckhoff told him he didn't want the Del Mar bluff, so Fletcher offered it to the Santa Fe instead. At that point, Kerckhoff and Huntington came to look at the real estate personally. They decided it was wiser to own the land than let it go to their competitors, so they bought it after all.

After looking the land over, Kerckhoff decided he'd been wrong about its possibilities. Almost immediately the PE began grading a new rail line from San Diego to Del Mar, and the South Coast Land Company set about constructing a new first-class hotel with a 1,000-foot pier, along with a garage for those new-fangled machines called automobiles and a huge indoor swimming pool of heated seawater. Then, after constructing a depot for the PE extension, the South Coast Land Company began to sell residential building lots to all comers—provided, however, that the purchasers agreed to spend a minimum of $2,500 to build a home, a considerable sum in 1905. Absolutely no commercial uses would be permitted, except a store owned by the land company itself, of course—Kerckhoff wanted his Del Mar to be a bucolic retreat for the well-to-do, and any spending by the newly arrived rich he wanted to go into his pocket, not someone else's.

To design the classy hotel, Kerckhoff brought in Los Angeles architect John C. Austin. Austin was an admirer of William Shakespeare, and had a partiality to the English half-timber style. The three-story hotel he designed would, in fact, be called the Stratford Inn—after the Bard's own hometown, of course. Thus, the new resort would be graced by a gigantic piece of English architecture plunked down in the middle of what was essentially a seaside desert.

The hotel opened in 1909, and almost from the first it attracted a distinguished clientele, including the newspaper man E. C. Scripps, the Los Angeles lawyer H. O. O'Melveny, Charles Sedgwick Allen, the San Francisco editor of the fashionable tourism icon, *Sunset* magazine, and a wide variety of other prominent, wealthy people. Many bought the lots put up for sale by the land company. Three years later, the land company tooted its own horn by publishing a sales brochure in the form of a book:

Groves of indigenous pine trees of rare variety and thousands of eucalyptus and acacias planted years ago by the far-sighted pioneers [meaning the original hotel developer, who had planted most of the trees a little more than twenty years before] *lend their beauty to the landscape . . .*

The gentleness of the climate, if one may use the phrase, is not only agreeable, but it is responsible for a wonderfully varied flora, and botanists who have traveled widely are ever ready to say that for variety and brilliancy of coloring no part of the world can surpass this section of San Diego County in its flowering herbaceous plants. A walk of one-half mile brought to the [flower] *press and case of one young scientist 243 varieties of pretty blossoms . . .*

The book hastened to assure prospective property purchasers that no matter how attractive the location, the land company would always make sure that no cheap gimcrackery would be allowed—not like other beach resorts, it said. "Del Mar is planned for the exclusive," the company maintained.

As a sales job, this rhapsodic paean to the growing village seems to have done the trick. Between 1912 and 1920, the population grew apace, until by the beginning of the 1920s, Del Mar was considered one of the "in" spots of the country, the West Coast version of Newport, Rhode Island.

It was sometime in 1923 that Ken's uncle-to-be, David Eugene Thompson, arrived in Del Mar. Thompson, among the wealthiest of the new Del Mar residents, promptly purchased a Del Mar landmark for his home. This was the "Sunken Gardens," a four-acre estate lying athwart one of the canyons that had been the showplace of architect William English Hyer. Hyer surrounded the cottage he built with spectacular, dense tropical foliage, and installed a system of pools and waterfalls that ran down the length of the entire canyon. When Thompson bought the place in 1923, he built a new "cottage" farther down the canyon, and used the original dwelling as a guest house. Years later, the entire property would be subdivided, and all that would remain of the house built by Thompson—"Casa de Canyoncito"—would be the house itself, a monument to a most unusual man.

• • •

Born in Bethel, Michigan, on the last day of February of 1854, David Thompson—or D.E., as he would come to be known— was the son of a farmer; his formal schooling ended at 13, when he became a watchmaker's apprentice. At 18 David Thompson became a laborer on the Burlington Railway in Nebraska, soon rising to the positions of truckman, then brakeman. Thompson must have had a tremendous amount of ability and drive, because by 1881 he was named superintendent of the railroad, a singular achievement for someone only 28 years old, especially someone with only a grammar school education. Thompson was the railroad's superintendent for nine years, until 1890, when, according to the National Cyclopedia of American Biography, he resigned to "take the management of various industrial enterprises." In 1902 he became president of the Lincoln *Daily Star* newspaper, as well as the Columbia Fire Insurance Company.

A staunch Republican, in the same year D.E. was named Minister Plenipotentiary to Brazil by President Theodore Roosevelt, and made a full ambassador in 1905. The following year, Roosevelt appointed him Ambassador to Mexico, then in the waning years of the dictatorship of Porfirio Diaz. "During a three years' incumbency of this important post he distinguished himself by a remarkable activity in the interest of his country," the Cyclopedia reports.

In 1910, D.E. managed to get control of the Pan-American Railway, the only rail line running the length of Mexico from the United States to central America, for the payment of $10 million in gold. After he secured ownership of the railroad, D.E. resigned as ambassador to tend to his interests in Mexico and the United States, which by now included extensive real estate holdings in Los Angeles, as well as significant timber holdings on the Olympic Peninsula in Washington State. In short, by his middle years, D.E. was as wealthy as he was accomplished.

D.E. Thompson was married five times. According to his will, on file in San Diego County, his first two wives died, leaving one daughter. A third marriage, to Nora Trousdale of Los Angeles—daughter of a prominent real estate family—

resulted in a son, David Eugene Thompson, Jr., of Los Angeles and Washington State; this marriage ended in a divorce.

After arriving in Del Mar with his fourth wife, Gladys Garber Thompson, D.E. soon became popular throughout the town, at least among the younger set: it was his practice to give every child in the town and its outlying areas a present of a silver dollar for Christmas. It was all quite well organized, as several of the beneficiaries were to recall. Thompson's manager, E. C. Batchelder, had made a list of every child in the area, from ages 1 to 12, then checked it twice. Each of the children, even babies in the arms of their mothers, lined up at the post office, where Batchelder solemnly gave each one his dollar, then checked the name off the list.

It appears that at some point in the 1920s, D.E. and Gladys were divorced, because on August 23, 1929, in Del Mar, California, D.E. married Helen Fitzhugh, one of six children of Frank and Susie Amanda Edson Fitzhugh. D.E. was then 75 years old; Helen, one of four daughters of Frank and Susie Fitzhugh, was 38.

Just how D.E. came to woo and wed Helen Fitzhugh isn't at all clear. Ken, who knew his Aunt Helen fairly well, recalls that she worked as a secretary in the Newport, Rhode Island, area before coming to California. In fact, according to Ken, all of his father's family resided in Newport before coming to San Diego in the 1920s. Whether Helen knew D.E. Thompson while in Newport—then, as now, a playground for the rich, just as Del Mar, California, was and is—is unknown. It is possible, of course, that Helen worked for D.E. as a secretary before becoming his wife.

Comparatively little is known of Frank Fitzhugh, except that he was likely rather small in stature, as was Ken, two generations hence. Whether he knew of David Eugene Thompson while both lived as boys in Michigan isn't certain. Ken himself knew almost nothing of his grandfather—what he did for a living, for example, or why he came to reside in the San Diego area in the 1920s. "I was given to understand they were of modest means," Ken was to say later, of his grandfather and his family.

But if Ken is correct, it appears that while D.E. went west and south in his younger years, Frank Fitzhugh went east. As noted, he married Susie Edson, a native of Massachusetts, and then apparently returned to Michigan, because most of the six Fitzhugh children—Harriet, Frank, Ruth (1886), Helen (1891), Susie (1893) and Kenneth Carroll Fitzhugh, Sr. (1897)—were all born in Michigan. Then, if Ken is right, the Fitzhughs moved to Newport.

All of the Fitzhugh daughters were small, slim and, according to contemporary accounts, quite beautiful, as well as artistically inclined. While the family was still in the Newport area, daughter Ruth married a man named Marston Harding, who was some four years younger than Ruth. A native of Cambridge, Massachusetts, Marston, with his brother Lawrence, held substantial interests in textile mills in the Boston area, and was quite well off. Harriet, apparently the eldest daughter, eventually married a successful dentist, a Dr. Lane, and moved to the Washington, D.C., area, where she would live until the 1960s after her husband's death.

The youngest daughter, Susie, also married well. Her husband was Harvey Wave Miller; Ken's recollection is that Miller was a psychiatrist for the U.S. Navy, and that the Millers traveled extensively in South America before returning to live in the San Diego area in the years before World War II. Like both Helen and Ruth, the younger Susie married past the age of 30, in Susie's case when she was 34.

Based on death certificates for both Frank and Susie Amanda Edson Fitzhugh on file in San Diego, it appears that Frank and his wife arrived in San Diego about 1919. However, Ken recalled being told that Ruth and Marston Harding came first, driving an automobile across country, and finishing up in Del Mar. There, according to Ken, Ruth and Marston drove to the top of the highest point overlooking the growing resort community, and there and then decided to build a fabulous house on that very spot. "She'd always said she'd wanted to live in a castle," Ken was to recall.

So Marston decided to build one for her.

MANY years later, after all of the Fitzhughs had left Del Mar for good, it wasn't at all hard to find The Castle, as Marston Harding's grand achievement came to be called. All one had to do was ask; everyone in town knew exactly what The Castle was, and how to get there.

Built in 1926 for the then-staggering sum of either $150,000 or $300,000, depending on whom one chooses to believe, The Castle's profile was made distinctive by its round, crenelated white tower. Sited on three acres at the very top of the ridge behind the town, the fabulous dwelling was patterned after Mediterranean-style castles seen by the architect, Richard S. Requa, in Spain and Italy. Ruth made The Castle's stained glass windows herself, according to the legend. There were five bedrooms, six fireplaces, a large living room with double-height vaulted ceilings and a balcony, a large formal dining room, a spiral staircase up the tower, and a room at the top which gave a 360-degree view of the surrounding countryside. The grounds had a number of pools, terraces and fountains. The periphery of the property had two separate houses, one for The Castle's staff, the other for guests. Marston furnished the house with an array of antiques—among them valuable Persian carpets, paintings, an enormous carved dining room table that took ten men to lift, and a beautiful Spanish-style wooden chest that contained at least a complete sterling silver service, including two dozen place settings, each of them marked with a number so that none might become lost, strayed or stolen.

Telephoning The Castle was simple, according to Ken Jr.: one simply called the operator and asked for Del Mar 1.

Thus by the end of the 1920s, at least two of the four

Fitzhugh sisters, Helen and Ruth, were living in Del Mar, and both had married very well, indeed.

As for the two sons of Frank Fitzhugh, the older, Frank Hallett Fitzhugh, had moved to the Los Angeles area. Kenneth—the man who would be the father of Ken Jr.—followed his two older sisters to Del Mar, but not to marry.

Instead, Kenneth—"Kenny" to everyone who knew him in Del Mar, and there were many—went to work at the Stratford Hotel's garage. In 1927, the Stratford was renamed the Hotel Del Mar. In addition to working in the garage, Kenny also had the job of picking up the mail from the train depot and bringing it to the town post office.

Years later, many people in Del Mar would recall Kenny as a quiet, almost meek man; some recalled that he may have had suffered some sort of back injury that limited his ability to move freely. But all remembered him with great fondness, even if he wasn't the most talkative man in town. It seems possible that Kenny also lived at The Castle, at least for a time, in the late 1920s and early 1930s.

When Kenny was 31 years old in 1928, his father Frank died at the age of 71. Ken Jr. remembers being told that, up until the time of his death, his grandfather and grandmother, Susie, had lived on Front Street in San Diego, but that for his last illness, Frank and Susie had also lived at The Castle. It appears that Grandma Susie continued to live there until she herself died in 1945 at the age of 87.

In 1937, Kenny took over the management of the Hotel Del Mar garage; two years later, the garage owners, the Kerckhoff family, sold it to another man, who leased it to Union Oil. The oil company in turn hired Kenny to continue as manager. At some point in either the late 1930s or the early 1940s, Kenny acquired his own modest little house just down the street from the garage, and it was there that he continued to reside alone, a "confirmed bachelor," according to Ken Jr., with his beloved dog Brownie, at least until the coming of World War II.

But by then, a lot of other things were changing.

The 1930s were not kind to Marston Harding and his wife

Ruth. "The only depression-related casualty noted was that Marston Harding lost his cotton mills in Boston," wrote Nancy Hanks Ewing, in the Del Mar Historical Society's hardcover history of the town, *Del Mar—Looking Back*, published in 1988.

But it wasn't only the cotton mills that were lost, according to Don Terwilliger, a life-long resident and president of the society. Terwilliger's own father had invested money in a Harding scheme to operate a silkworm farm in Chula Vista, south of San Diego, and when the Depression came, the silkworms went. There just wasn't much of a market for silk shirts in those lean times. Similarly, money invested by Marston in the Aqua Caliente racetrack in Mexico was also lost. The Bank of America foreclosed on The Castle, and Marston and Ruth had to move out—into The Castle's guesthouse, which Marston had managed to save from the wreckage. This may have been when Kenny bought his own house down the street from the garage. As for The Castle itself, Don Terwilliger recalled that during the war, the bank made the sumptuous house available as living quarters to ranking naval officers and their families. One can only imagine how Marston, Ruth and the rest of the Fitzhughs must have felt at seeing the service interlopers living in Ruth's dream house.

By the first year of the war, Kenny had surprised everyone by falling in love: according to Ken Jr., his father met his mother at Del Mar's premier hangout joint, Del Mar Drugs, on Coast Highway. The drug store had a lunch counter, where locals mixed with celebrities drawn to the racetrack which had been built in 1936 at the county fairgrounds just north of the town— a track frequented by such Hollywood stars as Bing Crosby and Jimmy Durante. Crosby, in fact, was one of the driving forces in getting the track built (Marston Harding must have gnashed his teeth at the success of the enterprise he had first envisioned, albeit in a different location). So Del Mar Drugs became sort of the Schwab's of the South by the time 1941 arrived. It was at Del Mar Drugs that Kenny, now the manager of the garage, made a practice of having lunch every day, which was when he met Pauline Stoops, a native of Iowa by way of Santa Barbara.

Pauline had come to Del Mar from Santa Barbara State College, later known as the University of California at Santa Barbara, where Pauline had earned a teaching credential. The best job offer his mother received after graduating, Ken said he was told, was one at the San Dieguito School District, so Pauline went to Del Mar and rented a room.

When Kenny first asked her on a date, other women in Del Mar told her to look elsewhere if she had any long-range intentions. After all, Kenny was by that time 44 years old, while Pauline was only 23; some thought Kenny would never get married.

On their first date, Ken said he was told, his father invited his mother to drive to San Diego to see the new movie, *Gone With the Wind*. They drove into the city in Kenny's Chrysler, with Brownie the dog at his accustomed spot on the running board of the car—it seems difficult to imagine that a dog could be trained to lie on a running board and not fall or jump off, but as Ken was later to point out, in the days of his father, cars didn't go quite so fast.

Kenneth Carroll Fitzhugh, Jr., was born on August 11, 1943, and was to grow up in the house his father had bought in the years before his marriage. It was a fine little cottage, just up from the beach; it was a quiet little house, in a quiet little neighborhood, not too much different than Escobita Avenue would be, some fifty-seven years later.

But by then, all of Ken's aunts and uncles, in their fifties or older at the time of his birth, would be dead, along with Ken's own parents—leaving Ken, as the only offspring of all the Fitzhughs, as the sole inheritor of all their estates.

The first to go was D. E. Thompson. He died the year before Ken Jr. was born. At his death, D.E. was 88 years old, while his widow, Ken's Aunt Helen, was 51. If the Great Depression had wiped out Marston Harding, it had left D.E. comparatively unscathed. According to his will, signed in 1938, filed a week after his death, and probated over the following year, D.E. left an estate worth $605,881 in cash, stocks, bonds and real estate, which was, for the most part, divided equally by Helen and D.E.'s only son, David Jr., then living on a farm in Sequim, Washington. As the last surviving spouse of D.E., that meant Helen received a little over $300,000 before taxes. By the time Aunt Helen died in 1984, this sum had grown into just over $2 million in cash, stocks, bonds and real estate, of which Ken's share would be one-third. It was principally this money that was to be the foundation for Ken and Kristine's own wealth so many years later.

Sometime the same year, 1942, Susie Miller's husband, the Navy psychiatrist Harvey Miller, also died, leaving Susie with some property, as well as a naval pension.

The next to go was Grandma Susie; she died in January of 1945, at the age of 87.

A little more than a year after that, Marston Harding died. He was only 54, but had suffered from a bad heart for years. Marston's death certificate listed his occupation as "retired financier," and his address as simply "The Castle, Del Mar, California." Marston left his widow Ruth a 1941 Mercury sedan; three $25 war bonds; 18 shares in a streetcar company located in New Bedford, Massachusetts, value unknown; six shares of preferred stock in another street car company in Worcester, Massachusetts, value unknown; $99.75 in cash; but most importantly, clear title to five lots on the Del Mar Crest, value unstated. It appears that Ruth subsequently sold this property, which marked the final passage of The Castle to other hands.

At some point in the 1950s, all three Fitzhugh sisters— Helen, Ruth and Susie—moved to San Diego, where they all had apartments in the same building. Thereafter, as each sister died—Ruth in 1976, Susie in 1982, and Helen in 1984—the assets of each estate were passed down to the survivors, principally Kenny, Pauline and Ken Jr. When Kenny died at 85 in 1982, his son was the beneficiary of his father's trust arrangement, as he was in 1997 when his mother Pauline died at the age of 80, leaving behind a similar trust. Both of these trusts represented the accumulated wealth of the Fitzhughs over the years since their arrival in Del Mar in the 1920s.

Thus, by the year 2000, Ken Jr. had inherited, from all his preceding family members over the previous twenty-three years, a total of about $1.5 million, as well as some of the furnishings from The Castle, including the carved chest with all the silver. To this was to be added another $450,000 inherited by Kristine Fitzhugh from her own family.

This, then, was the source of the reputed Fitzhugh family money in Palo Alto by the spring of the year 2000; it had come the old-fashioned way—they married it.

In his testimony, Ken had said that he had a "normal" childhood, and this seems to have been the case—if growing up in the shadow of The Castle, and as the nephew of two of his town's most storied residents could be considered normal. But then, Del Mar wasn't a "normal" community, not with so much wealth arrayed across its by-now densely forested hills. Of course, everyone in town knew that Ken's Aunt Ruth had once owned The Castle, and that tended to make Ken stand out from his peers.

Besides being small, Ken was very smart—at least according to a number of people who grew up with him in Del Mar. In some ways, he seems to have taken after his father: many saw him as a mild-mannered, almost meek little boy, somewhat shy and inhibited. Most of his closest friends were girls. He was rarely outspoken, and hardly ever lost his temper. He did have a precise, almost stuffy, way of speaking that inescapably communicated his intelligence, and as is often the case among children and teenagers, this mannerism made him seem fussy and pedantic to his contemporaries. Perhaps due to his small size, he wasn't given much to outdoor sports, instead playing indoor children's games like "Cootie," "Clue," and "Monopoly," although he did enjoy riding his bicycle around the town.

His father Kenny, as a former "confirmed bachelor," was busy during the day running the garage, and was seen by some of Ken's childhood friends as somewhat remote and distant; and it is likely that the age difference between Ken and his father may have limited their communications. It appears that Ken's closest confidante while growing up was his mother, Pauline.

Most people in Del Mar recall Pauline as a happy, cheerful woman. "She was June Cleaver," Ken's best friend, Alice McNally Stoll said. Both of Ken's parents strove to provide him "with all the amenities," Alice remembered. Ken was fascinated by electric trains, and a room was added to the house just for the trains, she recalled. The family paid cash for everything, Alice said.

With his mother as a teacher, Ken grew up prizing education, and in fact, was so well-prepared for school that he skipped the first grade. Other kids in Del Mar tended to resent Ken, "because he was so smart," Alice remembered; in turn, this tended to drive a wedge between Ken and his contemporaries, and doubtless contributed to his well-remarked introversion. Likewise, Ken's strong interest in music made him seem different from the other kids. "He was always showing off," one childhood acquaintance recalled.

If Ken did not make friends easily, those he did make tended to be extremely loyal to him. Years later, after Ken was arrested for the murder of Kristine, most of those who knew him refused to believe that he could have committed the crime. Even when provoked as a youngster, some recalled, Ken never lost his temper, but kept his own emotions in check. The idea that Ken could become homicidally aggressive seemed impossible.

There was, however, a less attractive side to young Ken's personality. Alice, for one, recalled that Ken had something of a calculating and sly nature. Once, while visiting Ken's house, Alice saw him disappear into a closet, where his father kept a supply of candy bars that were sold at the garage. Ken Jr. felt entitled to eat the candy, but apparently wasn't willing to share it with his playmates, Alice remembered. Years later, a psychological profile of Ken, prepared by the California Department of Justice, would suggest that deep within Ken lay an abiding "sense of entitlement"—that he believed he deserved everything because that's just the way things were.

Together, these observations of Ken seem to depict a shy, vulnerable boy who found his refuge in his intellectual superiority—as well as in an exterior rigidity of personality in which there were rules to follow; those who failed to adhere to the rules were to be condescended to, as a defensive measure, if nothing else. For the rest of his life, in fact, Ken would be a stickler for rules, a master of the "Gotcha" game, whose forgiveness of others' obvious transgressions of the rules would be a source of personal validation and empowerment. It was not for nothing that everyone—every single person who knew Ken—would say that he had an absolute horror of being late. Adhering to the clock was one primary way of always being right.

Ken himself recalled both of his parents as very supportive, and eager to see him do well in school. Both his mother and father were responsible for disciplining him, Ken recalled—rather than just one parent, as is sometimes the case with people accused of crimes. Years later, Ken would recall his father Kenny as being both firm and fair with him.

In addition to his music and his schoolwork, Ken was an active member of Del Mar's Boy Scout Troop 713. This interest in scouting would continue throughout Ken's life; eventually he would become the scoutmaster for his own sons' troop in Palo Alto.

By his high school years, Ken's interest in music had grown; asked if he could have anything to do over in his life, what it would be, Ken answered that he sometimes thought about what would have happened had he made music his career instead of business. But, he said, his mother, while encouraging him to enjoy his interest in music, had cautioned him to prepare for a non-musical profession.

In the fall of 1960, Ken enrolled at California Polytechnic College at San Luis Obispo, where he majored in electrical engineering. Ken continued to pursue his interest in music while an undergraduate; in fact, he was president of the student band. In 1964, he discovered an old pipe organ at St. Stephen's Episcopal Church in San Luis Obisbo. He acquired the organ, disassembled it, and hired a moving company to haul it to Del Mar. The only place in town large enough to house the reassembled organ was the Exhibit Hall at the fairgrounds–racetrack. Ken traded his services as an organist at the annual county fair in return for the rental fees for the space. It was while playing this organ in the summer of 1964, following his graduation from college, that Ken first met Kristine Pedersen.

That summer, Kristine was sixteen, the only child of Einer and Helga Pedersen. Both Pedersens were immigrants from Denmark who had come to the United States separately in the 1920s. Helga Jensen Pedersen had relatives living in the San Diego area, according to Ken, and it was through these relatives that she met Einer.

Einer was a master builder, a developer of custom-built houses in the exclusive San Diego community of La Jolla. Like many other craftsmen, Einer was a methodical perfectionist. These traits Einer attempted to pass on to his daughter, an inculcation made the more powerful by the fact that Einer was a middle-aged man, set in his ways, at the time of his daughter's birth. When Kristine—baptized Anna Kristine—was born on September 18, 1947, Einer Pedersen was 47 years old, and Helga was 42.

From a very young age, Kristine showed a prodigious talent in music. Einer and Helga, in fact, hoped that she would become a concert pianist. Both parents pushed Kristine hard, it seems.

As she grew older, however, Kristine appears to have become beset by a crisis in confidence, ostensibly over her musical ability, but in fact reflective of difficulties that were rather more deeply seated. Her diary—written for herself, of course—shows that in the months before her death Kristine was revisiting some of the old issues of childhood, particularly those that related to wanting to please her father with her musical performances:

> *I felt very childlike this morning,* Kristine wrote on the morning of December 13, five months before her death, *like a child who did not want to go to school—fearful— some anxiety and wanting to hide and retreat—but from what?*
>
> *I have to let go of my need to appear perfect and "in control" . . .*

While the diary ostensibly is a record of Kristine's anxieties about teaching, the context seems to demonstrate that the teaching worries are simply a stand-in for deeper anxieties: problems that were so difficult for Kristine to articulate that a class of elementary school students became the symbol for them. Later, in January of 2000, for example, Kristine wrote:

> *Today there is less fear and anxiety but it is still there. I am so tired of having these feelings . . . I am working hard to handle them but I don't like feeling the way I do when I go to bed and wake up. I am afraid of what's going to happen in my work. I am afraid that I will not measure up and will appear a failure to my friends, family and colleagues. People will think I am incompetent. Maybe I am . . .*

In February:

> *Shame and injury. These are what I fear. It is the five-year-old little girl inside me that felt ashamed because she was different from others. She felt injured by others, classmates, teachers, but most of all her father. I felt approval based on my actions rather than for who I was. When I didn't perform well enough the consequences were severe—especially when the expectations were high. I was expected to obey and be a perfect little girl. If I was, my father was so proud . . . I learned to set my standard for perfection to guard against injury. I tried so hard as a child to be good but I always felt that I fell short. Friends didn't accept me. I wasn't like them. I tried to fit in by changing on the surface but never quite made it . . .*
>
> *The problem is that I have the standard set so high that I am bound to fall short . . . I don't know what to tell the five-year-old inside of me. The child that fears making mistakes and not being accepted and approved of, I guess. I just need to tell her that she doesn't have to keep struggling and obsessing over being perfect. That people will still love and care about her, because*

what people really love and care about cannot be changed. It is who she is, not what she does. How she dresses, how thin she is or how much money she has. Whether or not her performance is flawless. Believe in it!

As one can see from these excerpts, written more than forty years after her childhood, the origins of Kristine's perfectionism—and its antidote, the jumping over the lines of accepted behavior, such as in the affair with Robert Brown—were rooted in her powerful desire to please her father. In time, Ken would become the father figure in the relationship—a role that Ken was well-suited for, particularly with his rigid, rule-following personality. In rebelling against Ken—through the affair with Brown—Kristine was establishing a justification for her feelings of "shameful" inadequacy, while at the same time providing Ken with the means to play "Gotcha," and thereby feel superior.

No one can read these diary entries of Kristine's, however, without also feeling her pain. Subsequent excerpts from the diary make it clear that she was going through some profound changes in the months before her death—changes that were inexorably leading her to taking responsibility for her life, and her actions. Indeed, as she moved ever closer to the Gordian knot at the center of her being, she was moving away from her dependency on Ken.

The relationship between Kristine and her parents, particularly her father, is thus a key to understanding the riddle of what transpired so many years later in the house on Escobita Avenue. In Ken, Kristine had a suitor who met Einer Pedersen's criteria for a suitable mate for his daughter: a man who was gaining a professional degree, who came from an apparently wealthy family (who was known in the community for his connection to The Castle), and someone who was in line to inherit a substantial sum of money from his elderly, childless aunts.

In the fall of 1964, Ken enrolled at Stanford for a two-year master's degree course in business administration. Kristine—who, like Ken, had skipped a grade—enrolled at California Lutheran University in Thousand Oaks, where she continued her music studies.

Then, after Ken had taken his MBA and had obtained an accounting job at the San Diego aerospace firm of Teledyne Ryan, Ken and Kristine were married on June 19, 1966, at the La Jolla Lutheran Church. Ken was almost 24, Kristine was only 18. But here is a puzzle: a check of the San Diego County marriage records turned up no marriage certificate for Ken Fitzhugh and Kristine Pedersen, or even Ken and Anna Kristine Pedersen, for that year or any other year. Ken later insisted that a marriage license *was* issued; the fact that it could not be located was, he said, probably the result of an oversight by the San Diego County authorities.

In marrying Ken, Kristine may have believed that she was escaping her father, and the expectations that he had placed on her. Einer's main concern about the marriage, according to Ken, was that Kristine's education not be ended. Ken assured Einer that Kristine would continue to attend college by enrolling at San Diego State College. But the goal of becoming a concert pianist was dropped, probably to Kristine's relief. Instead, Kristine would study to become a teacher. According to Ken, this pleased Einer and Helga almost as much, because teachers had high status in Denmark.

Thus, in the summer of 1966, Ken and Kristine moved into a small apartment in La Mesa, California, just east of San Diego. Kristine attended classes at San Diego State, while Ken went to work in the cost accounting department of Teledyne Ryan.

It was in that department, two years later, that Ken met and became friends with Robert Kenneth Brown, eventually to invite him home to a fateful dinner.

IN retrospect, there is little doubt that Robert Kenneth Brown—"Bob" to his friends—was a charismatic, even flamboyant personality. Ken himself readily admitted that, years later.

"Robert Brown," Ken would say at his trial, "before drugs got to him, was a brilliant fellow."

Born on January 21, 1945—just three weeks after the death of Susie Amanda Edson Fitzhugh in Del Mar—Brown grew up in Compton, in southern California. He attended Brigham Young University in Utah, where he majored in accounting, eventually becoming a certified public accountant. In 1966, Brown moved to San Diego to attend law school; it was there that he obtained a job in the cost accounting department at Teledyne Ryan in 1968.

This was at the height of the war in Viet Nam, and draft quotas were escalating on a monthly basis. According to Ken, however, both he and Brown qualified for draft exemptions because of their jobs at Ryan.

The work, as Ken was to remember it later, had to do with determining the cost of components for a pilotless target drone the company was manufacturing for the Air Force. At some point, however, the drone was modified for use as remote-controlled air surveillance over the Ho Chi Minh Trail. In any event, it was considered defense work that was both critical and secret, so both Ken and Brown maintained their exemptions.

Kristine was still attending San Diego State when Ken invited Brown to come home with him for dinner.

Both Brown and Ken subsequently remembered the evening vividly—because Kristine, having been advised by Ken that he was bringing his co-worker home, rushed out and acquired a potpourri of Chinese takeout food, and was busily transferring it from the containers to cooking dishes to make it look homemade when Ken and Brown came through the door.

After this initial embarrassment, Ken, Brown and Kristine became extremely good friends. Eventually, Brown was to say later, and Ken was to confirm, they began having dinner together perhaps three times a week, and spent many weekends together as well.

"We were best friends," Ken would later testify. "For the years when we were married without children, I would say that Bob Brown was probably the brother that I never had, and the brother that Kristine never had, and vice versa, because we were [all] only [single] children. We were always doing things together weekends and week nights."

If Ken and Kristine had been quiet, stay-at-home conservatives until they met Brown, Brown himself rather enjoyed walking on the wild side. It wasn't long before Brown got both Ken and Kristine involved in a large variety of social activities, including dancing at a San Diego nightclub, and most especially, in hanging around with a group of fellow professionals who took the partying to the desert in the form of dune buggy jaunts and camp-outs.

"[When] I first met them," Brown was to tell Denson later, "they were social recluses. After I was around and [they got] involved with my friends, they began to break loose. They had never gone out dancing or having drinks or anything, or gone camping at the beach, or drove a motorcycle or dune buggies or anything like that. They weren't party people."

Brown was—a party person, that is.

This seems to have been a liberation of sorts for Kristine—the notion that someone could have fun in life, that the rules didn't have to be oppressive, appears to have done a great deal to relieve her of her anxieties. Ken, by contrast, was still a hanger-on—apparently content to tag along with Brown, while taking quiet pride in his attractive young wife.

Asked at his trial why he was never suspicious that Brown had designs on Kristine, Ken was blunt: "The primary reason

that I never suspected an affair," he said, "is because Brown
led a gay lifestyle."

"He always had a live-in lover," Ken would continue, in his
trial. "Brown was not an effeminate, but his live-in lover was
always an effeminate, plus there were gay people around all
the time. He expressed to me on numerous occasions his dis-
dain for women, and on a couple of occasions we would see
a gal that he knew in high school or in college, and he would
lament to me that he was unable to have sex with the girl, and
then after we'd known each other for about three years, he
finally got up the nerve to make a pass at me. And if I didn't
think he was gay before, *that* cemented *that*, cemented my
thoughts. And the way we handled that, I told him that I
wasn't interested. Keep your hands off of me. I accept your
lifestyle, but I don't want to be a part of it."

In other words, according to Ken, it was simply incon-
ceivable to him that Brown would have a sexual interest in
Kristine.

But Brown, when called to testify at Ken's trial, said he
didn't think most people believed he was gay. "Not to outward
appearances," he said. Nolan, representing Ken, tried to pin
this down.

"In fact," Nolan asked Brown, "you were gay at the time
[of the affair with Kristine], correct?"

"In fact," said Brown, "I was bisexual." And that fact,
Brown said, was known to most people within his circle of
friends.

The implication was clear: Ken had known of Brown's
bisexuality, and either ignored the possibility that his good
friend Brown might be having an affair with Kristine, or—as
Brown eventually came to believe—had actually encouraged
it.

Brown later wasn't sure exactly when the affair with Kristine
began. He gave several different answers to this question, once
implying that it had started within a few months of meeting
Kristine, and on other occasions suggesting that some time
passed before the affair developed. Probably the most likely

beginning, however, would be sometime in the year 1975, perhaps five or six years after he had met the Fitzhughs.

"She was two years younger than me, so she was twenty-eight, I was thirty," Brown told Denson, when Denson asked how old Kristine was when the affair began. Since Kristine was born in 1947, that would put the start of the affair in 1975. Brown got the impression that Ken was sexually indifferent to Kristine, although Kristine was reluctant to talk about it; Brown had the impression that Ken just wasn't the romantic type. "She was starving for affection," Brown told Mike Denson. But there may have been something else going on, as we shall see.

Kristine established a separate postal address so she and Brown could communicate without Ken knowing about it. She seemed to have a horror of anyone finding out about their affair. Still, they talked three or four times a week on the telephone, and once a week or so each would slip away to meet, either at Brown's apartment or the house Kristine shared with Ken.

Even while this was going on—and Brown said it lasted for almost a decade, which would put it into the 1980s—he, Kristine and Ken continued to have dinner together several times a week, and often spent much of the weekend together, at least while they all lived in San Diego. So close did they become that they all had pet nicknames for each other.

Ken later professed that he never knew why Brown gave him the nickname of "Weasel," or Kristine, "Snake." But Brown was later to tell Denson that he called Ken "Weasel" because, "Look at him, he looks like a weasel." And also, Brown said, the nickname fit Ken's nature: "weaselly," meaning secretive and tricky—especially when it came to money. For all of their life together, Brown said, Ken had control of all the money; he'd made Kristine sign a power of attorney that gave him complete control of all their assets. Brown drafted it for Ken.

As for Brown's nickname, "Aardvark," that happened, Ken said later, when he, Brown and Kristine had gone to a popular restaurant for dinner and learned that there would be a lengthy wait for a table. A few minutes later, the hostess called "Dr. Barker, table for two." Brown quickly jumped to his feet and presented himself, with Kristine and Ken in tow.

"That's Dr. Aardvark," he corrected, "and it was a table for three."

"Oh, I'm so sorry, Dr. Aardvark," the hostess said, and led them immediately to a table.

Ken, rule follower that he was, and Kristine, who had such a horror of looking foolish in public, were astounded and embarrassed at Brown's effrontery. Trying to hide their faces from the other diners, they asked how Brown had come up with the name "Dr. Aardvark." Brown said it was the first word he could think of that began with two A's.

That was, however, quintessential Brown—big, brash, a born performer.

As the 1970s unfolded, Brown, Ken and Kristine became increasingly involved, not only as friends, but also in joint real estate projects, investments, two boats, a motor home, dune buggies—all manner of commingling of assets, it appears. The first boat, a sixteen-foot sailboat, was named "Aardvark," naturally. Brown taught both Kristine and Ken how to sail it, at least until it sank one day. After that, the trio bought a twenty-five-foot sloop; this was named "Aardvark II." The trio entered the larger sailboat in the Newport to Ensenada International Yacht Race in several years.

And on the weekends, Brown, Kristine and Ken frequently traveled to sand dunes, either in the desert near Brawley, California, or up the coast at Pismo Beach. There they gathered with a number of Brown's friends, including Tom Schaide—who picked up the nickname Dr. Dump, a wry comment on his impeccable neatness—to race dune buggies and motorcycles, camp out—and drink, according to Brown. Brown's own capacity for alcohol and drugs was legendary, and while Ken and Kristine drank, according to Ken they eschewed using drugs.

To outward appearances, Brown, Ken and Kristine were just good friends; but as the years passed, a number of people began to suspect that Brown and Kristine were conducting a secret affair. Schaide, among others became aware of this; and eventually Kristine confirmed it—at least according to both

Schaide and Brown. As for Ken, he would maintain to the bitter end that he knew nothing.

Still, there seems to have been an underlying resentment of Brown on Ken's part—manifested by sudden "accidents" in which Brown was the target. According to Brown, one year Ken accidentally drove his car over Brown's foot, breaking it. Then Ken, according to Brown, refused to drive him to the hospital for several days, and as a result, an infection set in that was only beaten back after months of treatment. On another occasion, when Ken was at the helm of a sailboat, he made a sharp turn, knocking Brown unconscious by the action of the boom.

And there may have been something else going on, as well: where Ken was to testify that Brown had propositioned him for a physical relationship, Brown himself—a year before Ken took the stand—said it was the other way around.

"On one occasion when we were camping," Brown told Denson and Wong, "he reached over and grabbed me."

"Did anything follow through after that?" Denson asked.

"No," Brown said. "I said, 'What are you doing?'"

"He didn't answer?"

"No," said Brown.

After graduating from San Diego State, and obtaining a teaching credential, Kristine began a job as an elementary school teacher in the San Diego area. At one point, she made the front page of *The San Diego Union*'s features section.

Coincidence Puts Piano Duo in Tune, the paper reported. The story went on to relate that the principal of the school where Kristine taught, MacDowell Elementary, discovered that Kristine and a fellow teacher, Grace Allen, had both studied piano with the same teacher. The principal "nagged" Kristine and Ms. Allen to begin playing piano duets for charity benefits. The *Union*'s story noted that Kristine's husband Ken "not only plays, but restores organs."

Ken meanwhile, left his job at Ryan and took a new position as assistant to the president of Avco Community Developers, thus embarking on his eventual career as a real estate developer. Eventually, according to Ken, he became the company's director of finance. Later, he would join another San Diego development firm as a division president, coordinating the company's various construction projects in the San Diego area.

Sometime in the mid-1970s, Ken and Kristine bought a house on Myrtle Way, just north of the famous Zoo. Soon after moving in, they hosted a housewarming party for their friends. One long-time friend of Ken's from Del Mar later recalled attending the party and being introduced to Brown, who seemed to be in a rather ebullient mood. At one point during the party, Kristine told Ken that she and Brown were going out to get more ice. But when they did not return for several hours, Ken's friend began to get suspicious. She mentioned the disappearance to her own husband, who simply shrugged; Ken himself did not seem at all concerned about Kristine's absence.

Not long after Ken and Kristine moved into the house on Myrtle Way, Ken's mother and father sold their house in Del Mar—and bought another just around the corner from Ken and Kristine. Ken's mother Pauline had always wanted to live in a "Spanish-style" house, he said later, and now that Ken Sr. was retired from the garage, they could live in one. Besides, Kristine was pregnant.

YEARS later there would be enormous confusion in the various accounts as to what, if anything, different people knew about this pregnancy—and this is a considerable understatement, to say the least.

Brown would eventually provide approximately four different versions of the events, a circumstance which later caused Santa Clara County Deputy District Attorney Michael Fletcher to grind his teeth; initially, in fact, Brown indicated that it was several years before Kristine had told him that he was Justin's father. Later, though, Brown said that Kristine had told him shortly after she became pregnant, not several years later. The different versions would give Ken's attorney, Tom Nolan, the opening to attack Brown's credibility.

It nevertheless appears that Kristine herself provided support for some of Brown's later recollections of the events in statements she made to Dr. Schaide, and to Brown's aunt, Janet Moore, among others.

Ken, for his part, having maintained that he never knew that Kristine was having an affair to begin with, was hardly in a position to offer much contradictory evidence.

But Brown's next-to-last account, delivered to Mike Denson on the eve of Ken's trial, asserted that he first learned of Kristine's pregnancy during the summer of 1977. He said Kristine told him that he was the father, and "told me exactly where it occurred." He said Kristine told him it had happened when he and she had gone ahead of the dune buggy crowd, in the motor home they jointly owned, to rent camping spaces near Santa Barbara earlier in the same summer. Kristine told him that she'd gotten pregnant when they had pulled off onto a frontage road near the freeway, and that this was where "it happened."

Brown said Kristine told him that she wanted to get pregnant, and had stopped using birth control, and that she hadn't had sex with anyone else but Brown for the four months before she became pregnant.

"So she intentionally got pregnant, you believe?" Denson asked.

"Oh yeah," Brown said. "She told me she did."

Kristine's intent with this pregnancy eventually became one of the mysteries at the core of the Fitzhugh tragedy. According to Brown—who was apparently recounting something Kristine had told him, even if it was slightly garbled—Kristine had gotten pregnant to qualify Ken for the inheritances from the Fitzhugh aunts. Brown's remarks were sketchy and mumbled, but nevertheless quite suggestive:

"While we all lived in San Diego," Brown was to tell Denson in May of 2001, "I believe there was a condition. You see, they both came from pretty substantial families. I mean by substantial, they both had some money. He had some great-aunts who were worth millions. And she told me, and I believe Ken did too, that the inheritance wouldn't happen, unless there was an heir. So they tried for a long time . . . He went to a sex doctor and [unintelligible] working. Then allegedly his sperm count, it was like way up. She told me that that was a lie, and that it was just for show. I don't know, you know, I'm not a doctor. I never saw the results. All I know is, they were [childless] after being married for almost ten years.

"And," Brown continued, "they were both only children. [They had to have kids] before the money got transferred. I know that. Only because they both told me individually [that the aunts' wills required them to have children]. I never saw any documentation. But I knew the great-aunt very well [presumably Helen Thompson]. And I knew Kristine's parents. You know, they considered me part of the family."

The day after this conversation with Brown, Denson interviewed Brown's own aunt, Janet Moore. Janet's take on the Fitzhugh family history was also somewhat garbled, and with some resemblance to the old children's game of "Telephone," but still with a germ of fact:

"There was a big chest," Janet told Denson, "from the Civil War. It was buried. It was at a big home that was owned by Weasel's two aunts."

Here was an obvious reference to the Spanish chest filled with the sterling silver service, and The Castle. It takes only a little imagination to see how this story might have evolved: "Civil War" being a garble of "silver"; as for "buried," it's entirely possible that the chest and the silver might have been hidden to conceal it from Marston Harding's creditors back in the 1930s.

"And lots of silverware and lots of other pieces," Janet added. "And the chest was very, very heavy, and beautiful. I don't know where it is."

Then, abruptly and without any prompting by Denson, Janet turned to the issue of the inheritances.

"I do know," she continued, "that Kristine told me Ken couldn't have kids. And that she said that . . . you know, it wasn't my business to figure out anything . . . except that the two aunts wanted to leave money to Ken, but he had to have kids."

"Who told you this?" Denson asked.

"Well, Kristine told me that," Janet said. "That he had to have kids to get the money."

Much later, when asked about these assertions, Ken did not at first directly contradict them, except to note that none of the wills had any such "condition" in them. "You've seen the documents," he said. "Is there anything like that in there?" And Ken was right: none of the aunts—Ruth, Helen or Susie—specified any such requirement, although two of the three wills were drafted after Justin was born. Still later, to make this matter even more clear, Ken said, "I completely reject the ridiculous idea" that Kristine had gotten pregnant to satisfy some supposed inheritance requirement.

It is, of course, possible that such a "condition" for being named as an heir was oral, or even that it was implied. Certainly the aunts were under no legal obligation to leave their fortunes to anyone, since all were childless. For all the law cared, the aunts could leave their money to the Society for the Perpetuation of Left-Handed Redheads, or any other endeavor they chose.

On the other hand, both Ken and Kristine were still young, and the aunts were quite elderly. Who was to say when, or if, a new Fitzhugh might be born? As Ken was to point out, the absence of any such "condition" in any of the wills suggests that this have-kids, will-inherit imperative was simply not so.

This therefore leaves open the question of whether Kristine, having despaired of becoming pregnant by Ken in the 1970s, had simply told this story to Brown and Janet Moore to justify her decision.

This inheritance-by-conception story, however, wasn't at all what Brown told Denson and Wong at the outset of their contact with him in June of 2000. In fact, Brown had initially indicated uncertainty as to which *child* was supposed to be his, Justin or John; and was quite fuzzy about the details. At one point, in fact, he told the detectives that he was Justin's "step-father," and then corrected himself—he was Justin's "godfather," he said.

But in fairness to Brown, at the time of his first interviews with Denson, he was under the influence of two things: first, a large assortment of pain-killing drugs, as a result of his recovery from his motorcycle wreck; and second—probably more important—a natural desire to spare the boys the pain of having to hear the truth from the police. So it is clear that Brown was engaging in some degree of self-censorship at the outset, at least when speaking of his relationship with Kristine. Kristine herself had told some people that Brown was Justin's "godfather"; this seems to have been the cover story they'd agreed to, and Brown was simply trying to keep faith with Kristine.

It is also clear that by the time he learned this information—about Justin's paternity—from Kristine, whether in 1977, 1978, 1979 or 1980, Brown was beginning a long, downhill slide—a descent that would eventually cost him most of his friends, his position, his reputation and his health. It

was understandable that some of the details might have fallen
through the cracks over the years.

In the fall of 1977, Brown accepted a job as an attorney for a
large fast-food franchise, a corporation; the new job required
him to live in Fresno. Brown gave Kristine a power-of-
attorney over his San Diego property, and moved north, where
he bought another house on Harrison Street in Fresno. He still
talked with Kristine frequently, and often flew to San Diego
to see both Fitzhughs, but it was becoming increasingly clear
to many of his friends that Brown was on a road to big trouble.

Justin was born in March of 1978. Brown flew down to
be with Ken and Kristine when the day arrived. Schaide picked
him up at the airport and drove him directly to the hospital.
Brown later said he arrived at the facility ten minutes before
Justin was born, but it actually appears that he got there afterward.

For the first three years of Justin's existence, Brown was
to say later, he frequently saw both Kristine and Justin. As the
boy began to grow, Brown realized that Justin looked much
more like him than like Ken. Kristine even took Justin to a
Brown family gathering in 1979 and told Brown's grandmother that Justin was her great-grandson—at least, according
to Brown himself and his aunt, Janet Moore. Kristine and Justin, he said, also came to visit him in Fresno, where he owned
a house on Harrison Street. Eventually, Brown would show
the detectives a photograph of himself, Kristine and Justin
taken at the Harrison Street house (the house was later torn
down to make way for an office building) when Justin was
still a toddler. At one point in 1981, Brown gave Kristine a
diamond ring, which she habitually wore with her wedding
band from Ken. It was this ring that had been smashed so hard
into Kristine's finger that it cut the flesh on the day of her
murder.

In 1981, Ken and Kristine relocated to Palo Alto, when Ken's
employer was purchased by another company. He and Kristine
bought the house on Escobita Avenue in May of that year for
around $200,000. Brown, who assisted the Fitzhughs in the

purchase of the house with legal advice, was later to recall that it was filled with an assortment of valuable antiques— oriental carpets, clocks, the silver chest, a whole assortment of gleanings from the Fitzhugh clan, but principally from Ruth Fitzhugh Harding and Helen Fitzhugh Thompson.

Aunt Ruth had passed on in late 1976. Marston Harding's widow was 90 when she died. Aunt Ruth had a modest amount of cash put by—about $41,000—and this was divided six ways by her survivors, including Ken Sr., the four surviving aunts (including Frank Hallett Fitzhugh's widow in the Los Angeles area), and Ken Jr. But Ken—who'd had to act as Ruth's conservator in the final year of her life, was granted all of Ruth's "furniture, furnishings, paintings and pictures," a bequest that apparently included at least some of the valuable oriental carpets seen by Brown, as well as the fabulous silver collection.

Ken's new employer in the Bay Area was engaged in building and managing public housing projects in San Francisco and Sacramento. The following year, the new company suffered a "retrenchment," as Ken called it, and the bank foreclosed on some of the housing projects. For the next six months or so, Ken worked as a consultant to the bank, helping to straighten out the mess that had been left by the company's default; then he went to work for another construction company, this one based in Palo Alto. Again Ken was involved in building apartments, but primarily in Palo Alto and San Jose.

For the Fitzhughs, however, money was about to become less and less of a problem. Although Ken's immediate family had grown—John was born in 1981—the older Fitzhughs were passing on. Interestingly, two of Ken's elderly aunts— Susie and Helen—both had new wills drawn up after Justin was born, and both named Kristine as an individual heir.

In May of 1982, Aunt Susie died, leaving a total of $288,494 to be split among Ken Sr., Pauline, Ken Jr. and, curiously enough, Kristine as a separate legatee. Then in November of the same year, Ken Sr. died; his estate was encompassed in a trust, so the details of his arrangements were never made public, but presumably Pauline and Ken Jr. were named as beneficiaries.

Two years later, Aunt Helen died. The widow of D. E. Thompson left an estate valued at $2,050,811, the vast bulk of which, after taxes, was divided between Ken Jr., his mother Pauline, and the widow of Frank Hallett Fitzhugh in the Los Angeles area. That put Ken's share at about $440,000, with a similar share going to Pauline, then 67 years old. Kristine was again named as a separate legatee, qualifying to receive a one-third share of Helen's furs and jewelry.

Two years after this, Kristine's mother Helga died; she'd lived a little over four years after her husband Einer's death in 1982. Einer and Helga's principal asset was their house—actually two houses on a large lot—in La Jolla. The property was sold by Kristine in the spring of the following year for $495,000, which brought Kristine a net of $452,582. This money, if Brown is to be believed, went into the Ken and Kristine pot, for Ken to invest.

Thus, by the spring of 1987, Ken and Kristine together had inherited—so far—just under $1 million from their respective families. It was about that time that Ken left his job with the Palo Alto developer, and went into business for himself.

While the Fitzhughs were coming into this money in the 1980s, Brown, Kristine and Ken continued to get together for vacations and three-day weekends with others in the dune buggy/sailing gang at various beach and desert resorts. These vacation jaunts would continue into the 1990s, according to both Brown and Ken. Both Justin and John, who came on the beach and desert trips as well, had long ago accepted "Aardvark" as a member of the family.

In addition, during these years, Brown and Kristine often went skiing with some of the same gang, sometimes in Colorado, sometimes at Lake Tahoe; Ken came on some of these trips, but often separately, according to Brown. Occasionally, Kristine traveled separately with Schaide and other friends, including at least one trip to ski in the Alps, with a stop at Monte Carlo.

On some of these occasions, according to Brown, he, Ken and Kristine gambled. In fact, Brown realized that he was as addicted to gambling as he was to drink and drugs. "I have a problem with it," he told Denson. "Don't let me loose at Harrah's [Casino]." At one point he'd become so addicted to gambling, Brown said, he'd had a "$50,000-a-day limit at seven different casinos. I lost a quarter of a million dollars."

Brown's predilection for drugs and alcohol was obviously starting to catch up with him, and was affecting his health as well as his mind. Even before leaving San Diego, he'd been laid low with a recurring case of hepatitis, which had made it difficult to maintain his law practice. Soon, his judgment began to suffer as well.

In 1980, Brown got involved with one of his law clients in a bit of tricky business; the client owned him a substantial amount in legal fees, and in order to pay some of the fees off, the client offered Brown two IBM electric typewriters. Brown took the typewriters and subsequently sold them to another man for $800. When this man then attempted to resell the typewriters, he learned that they were stolen. At that point, the man began working for the authorities as an informant, and he soon convinced Brown to sell him a copying machine, which also turned out to be stolen. At length, Brown was arrested and charged with a felony count of receiving stolen property. In May of 1981, Brown pleaded *nolo contendere* to receiving stolen property, and was placed on four years' probation.

At that point the California State Bar began proceedings to suspend Brown's law license. In August of that year Brown received a formal four-year suspension, but the suspension was stayed, provided that Brown serve one year of the suspension, and make regular reports to the bar swearing that he'd been adhering to all the rules.

Two years later, Brown was again in trouble with the bar for a letter he'd written while on suspension, threatening to refer a civil business dispute he'd had with yet another man to the Fresno County District Attorney's Office for prosecution, a no-no if the intent was to pressure the man into a settlement. For this Brown was "publicly reproved" by the state bar.

In the 1990s Brown again got into trouble with the state

bar, over allegations that he had taken legal fees for services not performed, diversion of clients' funds from his trust account, and willful disobedience of a court order. The complaints dragged on until 1997, when Brown was ordered disbarred.

As these ongoing peccadilloes indicate, Brown continued to have financial troubles throughout the 1980s and into the 1990s. Several times the Harrison Street house went into foreclosure, but each time Brown or one of his friends was able to drag it back from the brink. At one point in this period, Brown, Ken and Kristine invested in a corporation that ran a bar in Fresno; where it was, and whatever happened to it are now lost to history, however—any records were destroyed long ago, according to Fresno officials.

By 1994, Brown had lost his house in Fresno, and his alcohol addiction had become unmanageable. At that point Kristine and Ken "intervened," and had Brown admitted to an addiction treatment facility; the Fitzhughs paid $12,000 to dry "Aardvark" out. Justin came to the hospital. He made "Aardvark" promise him that he would give up his drugs and drinking. Brown promised that he would.

But then Brown went on one last trip to the beach with Ken, Kristine and the rest of the group, in 1995. There something untoward happened, the details of which seem to have been repressed by all concerned. The short version, however, was that Brown relapsed into drink and drugs again.

After this, Ken called Brown and told him that he wasn't welcome in their house anymore.

"What happened was," Brown said, "on that trip I fouled up again and drank too much, took drugs and made a fool of myself, and embarrassed people. And with that, [Ken] and Kristine both said—and the boys said—that they didn't want to see me anymore. They didn't want to watch me kill myself. That was the next morning. And they packed their things up and they went home, and I went home, and that was the end of it."

But it wasn't.

THE TRIAL OF KENNETH
CARROLL FITZHUGH, JR.

As they talked to Brown, lying drugged in his sickbed southeast of Placerville in June of 2000, Denson and Wong were beginning to get some idea of the sort of man Ken was. "You don't get the nickname Weasel for nothing," Denson observed later.

Brown depicted Ken as a man who was sly and calculating, as well as controlling. A man who kept his cards extremely close to his vest, who was for all practical purposes very nearly the complete opposite of Brown in personality. It wasn't at all surprising, they thought, that Ken hadn't been very personally forthcoming in their three interviews with him.

Denson and Wong had several objectives for their discussion with Brown, almost all of them concerned with the still-nagging issue of Ken's motive. There was evidence suggesting that the killing of Kristine had been premeditated, such as the missing blue Suburban and the possible change of clothing before the murder. In fact, Deputy District Attorney Fletcher had charged Ken with murder in the first degree, which required proving that the crime was premeditated. But Denson and Wong both knew, as did Fletcher, that it is much harder to convince a jury that someone has planned a murder if no one can show a possible reason for such planning.

That was why the detectives wanted to explore the ramifications of Brown's affair with Kristine: to see whether Ken was aware of it, and whether he would have had any reason to believe that Justin had been fathered by Brown. If Ken had known of none of this—and had just found out—that might account for a motive to murder.

The trouble was, however, such a motive wasn't entirely consistent with the idea of premeditation. Usually, a jealous husband doesn't *plot* to get even with a straying spouse—instead, if there's violence, it happens in the heat of the moment: without premeditation. That was the difference between murder and manslaughter, because it came directly to the question of the killer's intent. It seemed hard to believe, calculating as Ken might be, that he might wait twenty-three years to take his revenge for being cuckolded. At this point, neither the detectives nor Fletcher were aware of the version of events that Brown and Janet Moore would eventually put forward: that Kristine had intentionally used Brown to father a child to qualify Ken for the inheritances from his aunts, and that Ken may have been aware of this.

In their first face-to-face interview, with Brown still in his sickbed southeast of Placerville, Denson and Wong questioned Brown carefully as to Ken's knowledge of the affair, but Brown was unable to say whether Ken had been aware of it or not. Certainly he had never confronted Brown with any accusations, Brown said. Nor had Brown brought the matter up with Ken. Kristine herself was adamant about keeping the secret, Brown indicated, and insisted that Justin's true parentage be kept quiet as well.

"She was very proper," Brown said of Kristine.

So—was Brown really sure that Justin *was* his son? Denson wanted to nail this down. Kristine had told him this?

"Yeah," said Brown, "it was years before she mentioned it . . . you've seen the pictures. Justin looks just like me."

"When she told you, did you guys make any plans about how you were going to handle it?"

"No."

Brown found a photograph of Justin and showed it to the detectives. "You can see," he added, "he's not as slight of build as John. Justin has light hair, like me, her. Big-boned. He followed me everywhere when I was around."

"Okay," said Denson, "so it was Kristine's wish that no one else know that you were the father of Justin?"

"Right. So I maintained the silence. I didn't know. It looked like it to me."

Denson asked Brown about some of the particulars of the affair. Brown was reluctant to go into details; he didn't want to give Justin any more pain than he already had. But Kristine was careful to keep the affair separate from the rest of her life, Brown said.

"Did you think outward appearances, to everyone, was real important to her, how everyone perceived her?" Denson asked.

"My feeling is that she would have been embarrassed by it having been known by people," Brown said. "Eventually, it was, to all my friends, because she just announced it . . ."

"Do you think Ken ever knew about it?"

"Till this came out, I had no clue," Brown said.

Driving back to Palo Alto, Denson and Wong discussed their impressions of Brown. It was clear that he was in pretty bad shape, at least physically. Besides all the broken bones he'd suffered in the wreck, Brown's liver was shot. Brown himself would later say the doctors had given him no more than six months to live. Denson and Wong wondered whether they needed to get a video camera up to Placerville to record Brown's testimony before it was too late. It seemed entirely possible that Brown might be a key witness against Ken.

They'd asked Brown whether he knew if Ken himself had been having any affairs, and Brown said he didn't know. What about money? As Fletcher had already said, ". . . sex or money is usually the motive." The detectives had previously discovered the $48,000 life insurance policy on Kristine, with a double indemnity clause, which meant that if Kristine was killed, Ken stood to collect $96,000. They had also discovered that the week following the murder, Ken had gone to a bank and asked to borrow a substantial sum of money on the Escobita house—which, of course, he now had sole title to, now that Kristine was dead. Besides this, they'd discovered that the Fitzhughs had bounced some checks just before the murder, and that there had once been a tax lien filed against them by the government.

And while everyone, including Brown, had first assured them that Ken and Kristine were more than comfortable, financially speaking, now that they'd talked to Brown in person, Denson and Wong began to have second thoughts.

Was Ken in need of money? Was that why Kristine was dead? For insurance? It hardly seemed likely, with only a maximum of $96,000 at stake. But maybe something else was going on—something they had so far missed.

Like the antiques. Where were all the supposed antiques that Brown had told them about? When Denson and Wong told Brown they hadn't seen any antiques in the house that struck them as particularly valuable, Brown had said that something had to be wrong.

"I can only think that they lost a lot of money," Brown had told them. "I do know that five years ago they had probably a million-and-a-half dollars' worth of antiques . . ."

Denson had said he hadn't seen anything like that in the house.

"This would be everywhere," Brown had said. "There'd be clocks worth $50,000, rugs worth $150,000 . . . the house was literally jammed wall-to-wall with very expensive stuff, and if it isn't there now, then it got disposed of . . ."

Brown had told them about The Castle, or at least a garbled version of it. "I know this . . . he was a direct heir of his great aunt's. I don't know if you're familiar with [the story, but] one of them owned a castle in Del Mar . . . a five-eighths replica of a castle in Scotland. It was the family's . . . [and there were] Thirteenth-Century rugs and what-have-you, that were priceless. I don't know if they still have all that . . ."

Denson had asked Brown to estimate the value of the house's contents.

"Three million dollars," Brown had said. Denson had told Brown that Ken himself had put the value of the contents of the house at $125,000.

"Oh, no," Brown had told them. "There's something really wrong."

Had Ken sold all of these supposed antiques? Had he and Kristine run through the $2 million or so they'd inherited, and then begun disposing of the antiques to keep afloat? Had Kristine known any of this? Had she and Ken had arguments about money? Had, for example, Ken planned to borrow on the house, and Kristine had said no? Was that why she was dead?

Were the Fitzhughs starved for cash as well as love?

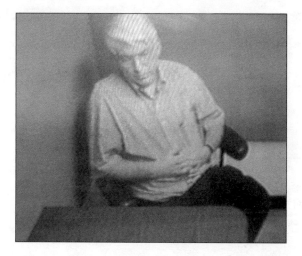

"Then I saw the black shoe . . . The God damn black shoes!" Family man Ken Fitzhugh on May 5, 2000, already under suspicion for the murder of his wife, Kristine, hours earlier. The police questioning Ken didn't buy his story about Kristine tripping over her shoes while descending the basement steps.

(Palo Alto Police)

Kristine Pedersen Fitzhugh, elementary school teacher, mother of two, for 33 years the wife of Ken Fitzhugh. And on May 5, 2000, his victim, a California jury decided.
(California Department of Motor Vehicles)

Prosecutors argued that Ken led two family friends to a staged scene at the bottom of the basement steps, where Kristine's body lay. From the beginning, he called their attention—and the attention of police and firefighters—to her discarded sandal, telling all who would listen that she must have tripped. (Palo Alto Police)

Palo Alto Police Sergeant Mike Denson, the primary investigator in the murder of Kristine Fitzhugh. He said he ran his investigation by the book, and quickly came to suspect there was something fishy about the crime scene. And Ken Fitzhugh's story about his wife's shoes.

(Carlton Smith)

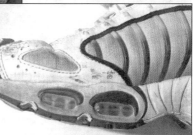

The case would hinge on another pair of shoes—Ken's. Police found blood on them. (Santa Clara County Crime Lab)

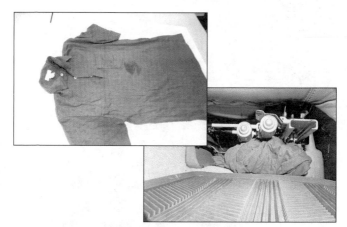

They would also find blood on Ken's green Polo shirt, which was bunched up under the passenger seat of the family's Suburban on the night of the murder. (Santa Clara County Crime Lab)

The beautiful Palo Alto home where Ken and Kristine Fitzhugh made their lives and raised their children. The luxurious foyer that greeted rescue workers offered no hint of the grisly scene that awaited them one flight down. (House and foyer: Palo Alto Police)

But the bloody mess at the bottom of the basement stairs did not distract them from other telltale clues: interrupted work, and an interrupted meal, at the kitchen table. An almost imperceptible blood residue spattered on the kitchen floor. Investigators soon surmised that Christine's attacker hit her with a blunt object while she sat at the table, then moved her body downstairs.

(Palo Alto Police)

Carol Gossett, manager of the Family Golf Center driving range in San Bruno. Ken Fitzhugh claimed he was on Family Golf Center property at the time of the murder, but Gossett testified she never saw him. (Carlton Smith)

Witness Tracy Wang, standing at the spot where she saw a vehicle that looked like Ken Fitzhugh's blue Suburban parked about noon on the day of the murder. Police believe that Fitzhugh moved his vehicle to the street behind his residence, then entered through a back gate. (Palo Alto Police)

Santa Clara Deputy District Attorney Michael Fletcher prosecuted Ken Fitzhugh's murder trial in July 2001. Large crowds turned out to witness the humiliating fall of the respected husband, father, and entrepreneur. (*Fletcher*: Carlton Smith. *Crowd*: Photo by Yuki Saito, courtesy *Palo Alto Daily News*)

Ken and Kristine's sons attending their father's trial. Justin Fitzhugh, whose paternity became a major issue in the case, holds the hand of his girlfriend, Angelina Whitesell. His younger brother, John, follows close behind. (Photo by Yuki Saito, courtesy *Palo Alto Daily News*)

That would be something—just three days earlier,
Fletcher had been arguing that Ken was too *rich* to be granted
bail. What if it turned out that Ken was, if not broke, at least
financially incapable of fleeing?

And there was something else: it was a supreme irony
that Kristine had tried so hard and for so long to keep her
secret. Now, because she was dead, the whole thing was certain to come out, and in the most public way she could have
ever imagined. It hardly seemed fair, literally adding insult to
injury. But then, there was nothing at all fair about murder.

FLETCHER had been caught by surprise by Nolan's talk about the lie detector test at the bail hearing. After Ken had offered to take such a test for the police, Nolan had arranged for a private examination first. That took place on May 12, and when the police heard about it, they decided no good purpose would be served by giving Ken one of theirs.

Now the fact of the private test had come out in court. Worse, a few days later, a reporter for the *Palo Alto Daily News* had been given the name of Ken's private examiner—from Idaho, no less—and had interviewed him.

"It's crazy that they're prosecuting this guy," polygraph examiner Ted Ponticelli told the newspaper. "He didn't do it."

The paper went on to point out that Ponticelli, a former examiner for the Defense Department, gave as many as three hundred such tests a year—virtually all of them at the request of defense attorneys.

The paper's reporter asked Fletcher what he made of the fact that this information had come out. "Draw your own conclusions," Fletcher said. It appeared to some that Nolan was trying to even the score somewhat in the pre-trial publicity department. "I don't talk to the media," Nolan had said in court. But someone had to have talked to the media to give them Ponticelli's name. It seemed like Nolan (or someone in his office) might talk when he thought it was in his client's interest to do so.

By the time Denson and Wong got back to town after their discussion with Brown, the Fitzhugh money situation was like one of those magnetic pointers that couldn't make up its mind about the direction of north: was Ken broke, and that's why he'd killed Kristine? Or was Ken rich, and if he got out, would he run away to Brazil? The signs were contradictory. An effort to sort out the Fitzhugh finances was begun that would last the better part of a year.

After almost a month in the Santa Clara County jail, Ken was sick of it. And who could blame him? After a lifetime of freedom, the clanging sound of the steel doors closing can be a shattering experience, made worse by the realization that to the jail guards, you are just another potential source of trouble. And as a high-profile prisoner, Ken was a natural target for other inmates intent on prying information out of him so they could try to make deals with the prosecutors. Ken had to watch his every step, and guard his every remark.

Fletcher, meanwhile, had begun to consider Brown's information more carefully, particularly as it shed light on Ken's possible motive. What if Ken had killed Kristine because of something to do with her affair with Brown? By now Fletcher had learned that the diamond ring that Kristine wore was from Brown. It didn't seem likely—to Fletcher it seemed highly *unlikely*—that Ken had been unaware of Kristine's affair.

"I mean, if my wife were wearing a diamond ring from some other man, that would—you know . . ." Fletcher said later. "Well, it would certainly raise a question, it would certainly say, hey, that's a very important person in her life. And the fact that the value of the ring exceeded the value of her own [wedding] ring, it might say something. And it would be a constant reminder to me of how close she is to this other person."

And if it was true that Brown was the true father of Justin—and Ken had just learned that fact—might that explain the murder? But what if Brown was wrong? What if Schaide was wrong? What if Ken was Justin's actual father? Fletcher wanted to make sure he didn't get too far out on a limb—he could easily envision Nolan sawing vigorously and sending him into the pit of judicial ignominy if it turned out that Brown was wrong. That's the problem with motive evidence—if it blows up in your face it can take your whole case down with it. Fletcher decided to see if he could get some DNA tests to make sure he knew what he was talking about before heading down that road. For the time being, he decided not to let Nolan in on what Brown was saying.

At this point, of course, Fletcher had no way of knowing that Brown and Janet Moore would eventually suggest that Ken had known about Justin's parentage all along—that wouldn't come out for almost another year. For the time being, Fletcher decided to try to develop the theory that Ken had murdered Kristine because he had just found out that Brown was Justin's true father. That at least fit with the savagery of the attack, even if it tended to undercut the notion of premeditation.

But first Fletcher had to get the case against Ken through the probable cause hearing. If he couldn't show that a reasonable person would have probable cause to believe that Ken and no one else had committed the crime, he would really be embarrassed.

Nolan was a formidable opponent, Fletcher knew: always ready to attack. Already there had been one foray, over the issue of the lie detector test. And Nolan had already tipped his hand to his likely line of assault in the bail proceedings, when he'd said that the Palo Alto police investigation was slipshod, that the detectives had misinterpreted the evidence in a rush to judgment to satisfy a clamorous community, and that the real killer was still out there.

In a probable cause hearing in a murder case, the burden of proof is quite low, which is why most prosecutors choose to limit the evidence they present. All they need to do is show evidence that someone had their life taken "unlawfully," and that there were facts sufficient to lead a reasonable person to believe that the person charged was responsible. The hearing is before a judge and, at the end, the judge has to decide whether the person charged should face trial. In such circumstances, a defense attorney will usually be content with a limited cross-examination, hoping to poke some holes in the state's case, to get some inconsistency that can later be exploited at trial. Rarely in California does a defense attorney mount a complete defense, Perry Mason–style, during the probable cause hearing, also known as a preliminary hearing or examination, because the burden of proof is so easily met for the prosecution; few defenders wish to tip their hand to the opposition that soon.

The hearing began on June 23, 2000, before a packed courtroom. The drama of Kristine's murder and the accusation against Ken had made the Fitzhugh matter big news throughout the Bay Area. Fletcher would stay completely away from the issue of motive.

After Fletcher called witnesses to show how the shirt and shoes had been found in the Suburban, he offered a stipulation—an agreement with the defense—that the DNA test on the shoes had shown that the red substance near the toe was Kristine's blood. Nolan accepted this, agreeing that the blood was from Kristine. Then Fletcher put on witnesses to show that the Suburban had been under Ken's control throughout the day until Kristine's body was found; that Ken was unable to explain how Kristine's blood got on the shoes, and the shoes into the Suburban; that bloodstains had been found in the kitchen, although the body had been found in the basement; that Ken's telephone records showed that he'd made no calls to the Fitzhugh telephone answering machine, despite his insistence that he'd called from the Redwood City area to check on Kristine. Fletcher finished with testimony from Denson— that he'd consulted with the medical examiner, Dr. Gregory Schmunk, and that it was Schmunk's opinion that Kristine had died unlawfully, that is, she was murdered by a series of blows to the head.

This took most of the day, and at the end Fletcher wanted Judge Hayden to find that probable cause existed to believe that Ken had committed the murder, and that he should be sent to Superior Court for trial.

That wasn't what happened, however; Nolan threw everyone a curve by asking that the hearing be continued for a month. He might, he told Hayden, want to call some witnesses of his own. Fletcher objected to this, but Hayden said he thought Nolan deserved enough time to decide whether he would call his own witnesses or not. Fletcher then agreed to a three-week continuance of the hearing. At that point, Hayden issued a gag order on all the parties, including the police.

"I want this case tried and heard and considered in the courtroom," Hayden said, "and I see no benefit to either the People or the defense for continued—I shouldn't say continued—but, for contact with the media."

And with that, Ken went back to jail.

When the hearing resumed on July 18, Nolan called one witness: Patrick Bowes, who had been on the Family Golf Center property on May 5. Bowes was a maintenance worker for the San Bruno Park School District, which actually owned the land, and which had a yard facility there.

The real estate that Ken had said he'd gone to view the day Kristine was killed was formerly occupied by a junior high school that had been torn down, leaving a large dirt area. The property was pretty large, Bowes said. The driving range was on the far side of the dirt from the maintenance facility.

Nolan asked Bowes if the police had come to see him after May 5, and Bowes said they had.

"What is it that they asked you?" Nolan asked.

"Asked me if I seen anybody walking around in that dirt area, or if I seen any unusual—any unusual events," Bowes said. "That's when I told them about the vehicle I seen, and why."

Nolan asked if police had told him what sort of vehicle they were interested in, and Bowes said no.

"They didn't ask me—they didn't give me a hint what they were looking for, but they asked me what I seen, et cetera, et cetera, and I explained, two vehicles I seen," Bowes said.

Bowes now said he'd told the police that one of the vehicles he'd seen looked like a Chevrolet Suburban.

"Did they ask you what color? What did you say?"

"Either a real dark blue or black," Bowes said.

It seemed as though someone from the police had found a witness to back up Ken's story—that he was at the Family Golf Center property on May 5. Now Nolan wanted to nail down the time of this possible sighting.

Bowes said he'd come to the maintenance shop at 11 A.M. for a meeting. Then, at 11:30, they'd all broken for lunch.

"I eat my lunch out front," Bowes said. "And then I step

outside the gate, 'cause I smoke, and you have to be off the school property to smoke. And that is outside the gate where the vehicles are, and that's why I was around my vehicle at that time."

"What time is your lunch over?"

"Twelve o'clock, sir."

"So it was approximately twelve o'clock, in your opinion, when you saw this vehicle?"

"Before then."

"A little before?"

" 'Cause when I left to go back to work, the vehicle was gone."

Bowes now said he was sure about the time, because he carried a pager with an alarm set to go off at 11:30—lunchtime. "They're very strict on it," Bowes said, "strict on rules when you can take breaks and stuff."

Well, this was interesting: here was a witness who had possibly seen Ken's Suburban, and at exactly the time that Ken had said he was there, in San Bruno, miles away from the Escobita house at the approximate time of the murder. Of course, Bowes was scrupulous to admit that he couldn't specifically identify Ken as the truck's driver; the suggestion was powerful nonetheless. But there was more to come.

Fletcher now cross-examined Bowes. He asked him what had drawn his attention to the Suburban-like vehicle.

Bowes said he'd seen a second vehicle enter the parking area—a little black four-door sedan. This car came into the parking area, passed the Suburban-like truck, made a U-turn, and then drove up to the driver's side of the Suburban to talk to the occupant.

But hadn't Ken said he hadn't talked to anybody while at the driving range? If this had been Ken, wouldn't he have mentioned this conversation with the person in the small four-door sedan?

Fletcher left the implication there for Hayden to ponder: this couldn't have been Ken, even if Bowes was right about seeing a Suburban-like vehicle around noon. It had to be somebody else.

After this, Nolan offered three stipulations: the first, that

Federal Express driver James Selby would testify that he hadn't seen Ken's Suburban parked in front of the Escobita house at 12:08 P.M. on May 5, which was possible evidence that Ken *had* been at the driving range; the second, that Scott Wong would testify, if called, that lawyer Thomas Moore had told him that the shirt Ken wore when working on the computer problem was *not* the bloody green polo shirt that had been found beneath the front seat of the Suburban; and the third: that Agent Sandra Brown would testify that Gaelyn Mason had told her that when Ken had picked them up at 1:30 P.M. to go for the gambling equipment, there was nothing unusual about Ken's demeanor—this at a time only minutes after he was supposed to have murdered Kristine.

With that, the testimony was concluded.

Nolan's proffered defense had no apparent impact on Judge Hayden. Reading from a prepared text, Hayden said, "it does appear to me from the testimony that I have heard on the preceding day or days in this preliminary examination and today, that the offense in violation of Section 187 of the Penal Code of the State of California, that is, murder, has been committed, and that there is sufficient cause to believe that the defendant, Kenneth Fitzhugh, is guilty thereof.

"I order that he be held to answer the same charges."

AT the end of the hearing, Nolan made a new attempt to get bail for Ken. Bail, he said, was essential to Ken's right to have a fair trial.

"The reason we presented much of the evidence we presented," Nolan said, "is to show you that by no means is this in any way a clear-cut case."

That didn't matter, Judge Hayden said.

Nolan persisted. By now, he said, the authorities had looked over Ken's finances, and they had to know that he simply didn't have the resources to flee; and if he wasn't a threat to the community, and he didn't have the resources to flee, he was entitled to a reasonable bail.

"As a practical matter, where's he going to go?" Nolan asked. "There's no place in the world that somebody can go and not be returned to this country."

"There are lots of places," Judge Hayden said.

"There really aren't."

"Well, I say there are some—Brazil for one," said Hayden.

"They'll bring you back," Nolan said. "They'll bring you back here for trial, for homicide. For homicide—first of all, he's not rich, and they'll bring them back for trial. He has no ties to Brazil. He has no means of getting to Brazil. He has no money. He has two kids here, he's not going to give up the kids. I mean, the idea that—I don't know what it is about, what this court is thinking about Mr. Fitzhugh, that makes it think that there's a possibility that he, among all other people, would somehow go to Brazil. I mean, it just astounds me."

"I'm not picking on Brazil per se," said Hayden. "I think my concern—I think the flight risk is quite large."

"How?"

"I don't know."

"How? How?" persisted Nolan.

"I don't know," Hayden said again. "I'm not going to get into a debate whether he could or couldn't, whether he has assets or not."

Nolan said there were people facing life in prison who had the privilege of bail. "They don't flee," he said. "When's the last time in the country that somebody who has been released on bail in a homicide case has fled, and cannot be brought back? It does not exist."

"Your Honor," said Fletcher, "can we talk about something that is relevant?"

"This is relevant," Nolan shot back. "This is reality, because we're talking about somebody who could not have done anything wrong. He did everything right. He's entitled to the opportunity to fight this case out of custody, without chains, without a red suit." Nolan meant the red jail jumpsuit worn by felony suspects.

"I mean, when I say he's entitled, he's earned it. He has earned it." The evidence against Ken was so skimpy, Nolan said, and when coupled with evidence that showed he wasn't even present when the murder had taken place, he had an absolute right to a reasonable bail. Besides, he said, his sons needed him.

Fletcher said any suggestion that Ken was innocent was contrary to what the judge had just held—that there was reason to believe that Ken had committed the murder. "If he cares so much about his children," said Fletcher, "he wouldn't have killed his wife."

Ken, Fletcher said, had planned the whole thing out. The fact that the Suburban wasn't seen at the time of the murder showed only that he'd hidden it, not that he was someplace else.

"This is a vicious, brutal crime," Fletcher said, "perpetrated by somebody who thought this matter out, and the flight risk is substantial, the risk of harm [to others] is substantial."

Nolan said the only reason the D.A.'s office wanted to keep Ken in jail was to help insure that a jury would see him as guilty. Fletcher said he was offended by this remark, castigating their motives—that kind of talk said more about Nolan, he said.

Hayden said he'd take the bail request under submission; he wanted to think it over until Ken's arraignment in Superior Court on July 31.

"See you back here," Hayden said.

Two weeks later, Ken was again brought before Hayden for his arraignment in Superior Court. Nolan's associate Dan Barton pinch-hit for him, and entered a plea of not guilty for Ken. Hayden set a preliminary trial date of September 11, although everyone understood there was almost no chance of it starting then. Hayden said the case would be moved from Palo Alto to San Jose for the trial, because the schedule at the Palo Alto facility was too jammed for a lengthy proceeding. Hayden said that if there were any settlement discussions—courtspeak for a possible plea—now was the time.

This had been a possibility almost from the outset, given the circumstances of the murder—the idea that Ken might forgo the pain and divisiveness of a trial, and especially its effects on Justin and John—by admitting that he had killed Kristine in a sudden outburst of rage. Certainly the wounds inflicted on Kristine were supportive of that notion; they suggested that the attack was spontaneous rather than planned. If that were the case—and if he told authorities the truth about what had happened—Ken might expect to receive a sentence for manslaughter, rather than murder. Manslaughter carried a maximum sentence of seven years, and a minimum of three. Murder, however, was punishable by a maximum of death, and a minimum of fifteen years in prison.

Ken's 57th birthday was approaching. If he went to trial and was convicted, he could conceivably spend the rest of his life in prison, maybe even get the death penalty. Denson and Fletcher, among others, thought that the physical evidence that Ken had committed the murder was so overwhelming that they expected to get a call any day from Nolan, offering to have Ken plead guilty to manslaughter. Of course, at that point, as Fletcher and Denson said later, Ken would have had to con-

vince them that the killing was on the spur of the moment,
and that he'd had no intent to take Kristine's life when he'd
hit her. That meant they would have to hear a truthful explanation for the apparent moving of the Suburban before the
crime, and the apparent change of clothes, which were the
principal circumstances indicating premeditation. And they
would have to hear of a motive that indicated sufficient prov-
ocation—such as Kristine telling Ken that Justin was not his
son—to warrant a finding of manslaughter.

But none of these obstacles to a manslaughter plea was
insurmountable. The absence of the Suburban could be explained by evidence to suggest that Selby was simply mistaken
about the day he hadn't seen the truck; after all, Selby had
made a number of deliveries in the neighborhood on other
days, so who was to say that he had the right day? The clothes
could also be explained: Ken might say that he was wearing
the green shirt and the tennis shoes when he'd erupted, and
that he'd changed afterward when he realized that they had
become splashed with Kristine's blood.

But as the days passed, there was no call from Nolan, at
least about a possible plea. Denson and Fletcher began to believe that even with so many years of his own life at risk, Ken
simply wasn't capable of admitting that he was responsible for
Kristine's death. It simply didn't fit with the image that Ken
wanted the world to see of him; and it certainly wasn't anything Ken wanted Justin and John to believe about their father.
It was as if Kristine had held her secret for years, and now
Ken was prepared to hold his own, as well.

As for Kristine's secret, Fletcher now decided to put his
plan into operation. He asked Alan Lagod, representing Justin
and John, to agree to make Justin available for a blood test.

Ever since the night of the murder—when Justin and John had
come into the police station to be interviewed—relations had
been ticklish between the authorities and Ken's two sons. The
boys, not unnaturally, thought that the police were being totally unfair to Ken. They refused to countenance any notion
that Ken might have been the killer, and at first, clung to the
idea that their mother's death was a probable accident. The

more the police rummaged around in the Fitzhughs' past, the more upset the boys got. Both of them blamed Denson. There were suggestions that Denson was trying to make a name for himself at their expense. Wong's suggestion that the boys get their own lawyer had helped to crystalize the "us against them" climate. Later, when Ken was arrested and the court proceedings began, Fletcher had made some initial attempts to sit down with Justin and John and explain why the D.A.'s office was doing what it was doing. After all, Justin and John were the surviving victims of the crime, and there was no one who didn't feel the pain they were going through, as Denson and Fletcher both said. But Alan Lagod, who had been retained to represent the two boys, demurred at a meeting; the boys just weren't ready to talk yet, he told Fletcher.

Now, as the month of August 2000 arrived, Fletcher was about to suggest something that he knew would further roil the waters: the blood test for Justin, to determine his parentage.

"I talked to him [Lagod]," Fletcher said later, "and tried to sort of finesse this without, basically, telling somebody that I think there's a chance that their father's not their father, until I really know what I'm talking about."

Lagod was taken aback by the request. He wanted to know whether Fletcher was suggesting that the crime could have been committed by Justin.

"So I say, 'Absolutely not,'" Fletcher recalled. After some additional discussion, Lagod agreed to ask Justin to provide the blood sample, and eventually Justin agreed to do this, without knowing exactly why it was wanted.

That state of affairs didn't last very long, of course, because Fletcher had to inform Nolan of what he was up to. Nolan's associate, Chris Pack, then went to visit Ken in jail, and told him that the authorities wanted to test Justin's DNA to see if Robert Brown was really Justin's biological father.

"My immediate reaction—I had two immediate reactions," Ken said later, during his trial. His first thought, he said, was: "What is Brown up to now?"

His next thought, he continued, was about Justin. "Justin is scared to death of needles. The poor guy, having to give blood."

Then, said Ken, "Justin visited me and wondered, What in the world is going on? And I told him I didn't know what in the world was going on, and he said he didn't know.

"He said, 'Is there any chance of this? What is it?' And I said, 'Not as far as I have ever known, or, it hasn't ever even occurred to me.' And I said, 'But who knows what this is all about, and where it's going to go? But if on the aught-one percent chance it is true, you are still my son. And I am still your dad.' And he said, 'Oh yeah.' "

Who can imagine what a poignant moment this must have been for both Ken and Justin? Since May both father and son had suffered a series of blows that would have staggered any-one; now there was the suggestion that they had both been kept ignorant of a tremendous secret that came directly to the heart of their relationship.

After Justin left, Ken thought about what he had just heard. "It didn't particularly affect me at the time," Ken said later, "because I knew it wasn't true."

On September 14, blood samples from Ken, Justin and Robert Brown were submitted to the Santa Clara Crime Lab for paternity testing. Swamped with the hundreds of other blood swabs that had previously been submitted in the Fitz-hugh and other cases, Cyndi Hall did not begin work on the paternity question until December 1, 2000. Four days later, the tests were completed. Cyndi called Fletcher the same day with the preliminary results: it was true—Robert Kenneth Brown was the biological father of Justin Fitzhugh.

LATE in August of 2000, the house on Escobita Avenue was sold for about $2 million. Half the money went into Kristine's estate, to be probated for the benefit of the boys. The other half presumably went into Nolan's client trust account, the remainder, after Nolan's fees and other legal costs, to be disbursed to Ken, if and when he ever got out of jail.

Before the house was sold, however, a ceremony of sorts was held:

Priest holds purification ceremony at Fitzhugh house, the *Palo Alto Daily News* reported.

A priest held a purification ceremony at the Palo Alto home where music teacher Kristine Fitzhugh's life came to a bloody and violent end in preparation for putting the house up for sale, an attorney said yesterday.

The house is expected to go on the market next month and has been valued at more than $2 million. Fitzhugh's husband Kenneth is awaiting trial for allegedly murdering his wife in the Escobita Avenue house.

Friends of the Fitzhughs, along with several real estate agents, suggested inviting the nondenominational priest to purify the house, said Palo Alto attorney David Spangenberg, who represents Fitzhugh's two sons.

"It seemed an appropriate step given the sad situation associated with the residence," Spangenberg told the Daily News. "And we also hoped it would bring some closure for the family."

While it's not uncommon in many faiths to ask a religious leader to bless a home when a new family takes up residence, it is unusual to try and purify a home, said

Father Pat Michaels of St. Raymond's Catholic Church in Menlo Park.

Michaels, who was not associated with the ritual at the Fitzhugh home, said the idea of a "purification" strays too close to the idea of exorcism, an area where the Roman Catholic Church tries to steer clear.

"The idea of bad spirits lingering after a tragic incident is more superstition than faith," Michaels said. "But if the goal is bringing some comfort to people either moving in or out of a place associate with a violent death, that's very reasonable. That's dealing with human emotions."

The hope with the purification ceremony and blessing is to ease the minds of people who might continue to associate the house with the murder, Spangenberg said. Purification rituals at the scene of a death are common in many cultures around the world, he said. . . .

Now the Fitzhugh case fell into the lull that so often occurs between the arrest and the trial. There were by now literally thousands of pages of reports that Fletcher and the police had to process, so they could be turned over to Nolan in some sort of coherent order. There were also hundreds of photographs, and well over that number of physical evidence items—including many blood swabs, which had to be carefully divided so the defense could subject them to their own testing.

Now that he was beginning to receive the documents supporting the state's case against Ken, Nolan had to envision the defense. It was one thing to stand in front of a judge and ask for bail while railing at the prosecution for rushing to judgment when one didn't have access to all the facts, but it was another thing entirely when those facts were finally available.

As would eventually become apparent at Ken's trial—now delayed until the year 2001 because of all the work that still had to be done to prepare for it—Nolan's strategy was to take on the state's case component by component, trying to kill off each portion, one by one. The idea was, if one part of the chain of logic fell apart, doubt would be cast on some or all of the others. After all, Nolan only needed one vote out of twelve for reasonable doubt.

That meant, for openers, trying to figure out how the shoes got under the Suburban's front seat, along with the bloody shirt. Nolan's associate Chris Pack visited Ken in jail, but try as he might, Ken couldn't tell her how the bloody clothing had gotten into the truck. He was still "dumbfounded."

Even if the clothes could be explained, there were other problems: the blood spatter in the kitchen, for example, along with the evidence of cleaning. This was a big one: if the jury believed that Kristine had been killed in the kitchen, rather than the basement, Ken was probably lost, because who else but him would have taken the time to wipe everything up? Nolan arranged to hire some experts in blood spatter and luminol, in the hope that these people could spatter some reasonable doubt on the state's tests.

Besides those two majors, there were other troubling aspects of the state's evidence: the phone calls that Ken said he'd made to the answering machine in search of Kristine. Why weren't there any records of them? What about the cellular telephone company's records that seemed to show that Ken was nowhere near Redwood City when he'd gotten the call from Phyllis Smith at 1:16 P.M.? Instead, the records, if they could be believed, seemed to show that Ken was in the area of the Escobita Avenue house at a quarter after one on the afternoon of May 5.

And what about the motive? Because Fletcher had subpoenaed all of Ken's banking and other financial records, Nolan suspected that the D.A.'s office was going to try to suggest that Ken had killed Kristine for some sort of financial reason. That meant Nolan had to hire some forensic accountants of his own, so he could counteract any testimony that Ken had murdered his wife for money.

Of course, there was Brown. At this point, he had only said half of what he would eventually say: so far, only that he'd had an affair with Kristine, years before, and that there was talk that perhaps Justin was his biological son, not Ken's. But even Brown said he had no way of knowing whether this was true, at least at the time Nolan was trying to figure out what to do about him; nor had Cyndi Hall done the paternity testing, so there was as yet no proof either way. Certainly, there was no indication from the D.A.'s office that it believed that Justin's parentage was in any way a motive for the murder. Nothing had been filed in court making that assertion, and Nolan, as well as Lagod, were relieved that the secret, if it was true, was still just that—a secret.

And even if Justin *was* the biological offspring of Robert Brown, what difference did it make, really? These things happened; it wasn't as if it was the sort of motive that might make a placid, even-tempered, judicious man like Ken mad enough to kill.

This gave Nolan an idea: why not have a psychologist give Ken a series of personality tests? Then, if the psychologist returned with an opinion that Ken was simply a docile, harmless personality, incapable of committing such violence, he could be called as a witness to show that the police had gone completely off on the wrong track. Nolan eventually hired a psychologist to interview Ken and give him the personality tests.

Early in February, Nolan got the word: the paternity test of Justin's DNA, double-checked for probabilities by a laboratory in Long Beach, showed that Brown was definitely the father of Justin. He and Chris Pack went to see Ken at the jail. It was, Ken was to recall later, the first time that both Nolan and Pack visited him at the same time.

"And Ms. Pack said," Ken recalled, during his testimony, which was still to come. " 'We have some bad news.' And Mr. Nolan proceeded to tell me that DNA tests had shown that Robert Brown was the biological father of Justin Fitzhugh.

"And I was in—I was in disbelief," Ken continued. "And I was devastated at the same time. Disbelief, because it didn't match anything that I had ever considered. And devastated because I knew that DNA is millions to one. And I—I really didn't know what to think. And I went back to my cell, and was very quiet for a long time, trying to—trying to think of— of anything that made sense. And I finally thought of what might make sense."

At this point, Ken was about to offer something to explain the DNA results, but Fletcher interrupted him with an objection. As a result, whatever Ken was about to say—whether, for example, it had something to do with the inheritances— was lost. Whatever the truth was, that part at least would remain Kristine's secret.

So much for the defense; now for the offense. Nolan had made his reputation attacking law enforcement for its inadequacies. In this case, he reasoned, he could easily show that the police had targeted the wrong man from the outset, and that there was hard evidence of the real killer that the police had simply, and tragically, ignored. He hired his own blood spatter and luminol experts; he intended to show that if Kristine had been murdered, the crime had happened in the basement, not the kitchen, and that there was no "clean-up" of the crime scene. If he could establish that, Nolan believed, the case against Ken would collapse.

He had been interested to note that the police evidence team had recovered a number of partial fingerprints from the house on Escobita Avenue. But these prints had apparently led nowhere; in fact, Nolan had the idea that the police hadn't even bothered to check them, so sure were they that Ken was the killer. Nolan wanted to widen the field of possible suspects so that it wasn't just Ken standing in the prosecution's cross-hairs.

In January of 2001, Nolan asked Justice Franklin Elia to order the Palo Alto police to submit a formal request to the Federal Bureau of Investigation to analyze the murder scene to see if it matched similar crimes in other jurisdictions. Elia was a member of the state's Sixth District Court of Appeal, but had been tapped by the Santa Clara County presiding judge to hear Ken's trial because of a shortage of judges; in California, appellate judges occasionally are pressed into trial duty under such circumstances. A former Palo Alto City Attorney before being appointed to the bench, Elia said he'd be happy to take over the case.

Besides asking the justice to compel the police to consult
the FBI's storied ViCAP (for Violent Criminal Apprehension
Program) computer data base, Nolan also wanted Elia to order
the Palo Alto department to turn over two years' worth of their
reports on residential burglaries in the neighborhood—a flash-
back to the anxieties expressed about the "rash of burglaries"
that had ended about six months before the murder. In this
way, Nolan hoped to generate enough ammunition to sustain
a defense that would suggest someone other than Ken was
responsible for the crime.

Fletcher opposed this—all of it. The only conceivable result of such an effort, he believed, would be to provide Ken
with an opportunity to muddy the water with irrelevant suggestions, and to divert a jury's attention from the facts that
showed he was the one who was guilty. In order to get this
information, Fletcher told Elia, Nolan had to demonstrate that
there was some definite basis to believe that the crime had
been committed by an intruder. But the facts, he said, showed
nothing like that—no sign of forced entry, nothing stolen, and
a crime scene that had been cleaned up by the perpetrator—
hardly the act of a random burglar. In February of 2001, Elia
denied Nolan's requests.

Now Nolan returned to another problem: the Goddamn *white*
shoes—the running shoes that had been found in the Suburban. Throughout the fall, as Chris Pack visited Ken, she kept
returning to the shoes. How had they somehow traveled from
Ken's closet to the truck? She pressed Ken to think of something to explain this, but Ken continued to be "dumbfounded."

Then, after the first of the year, Ken read a newspaper
article about the collision between a U.S. Navy submarine and
a Japanese fishing boat near Hawaii. Survivors of the accident,
Ken read, said they had significant gaps in their memory of
the traumatic events. Some things could be recalled, but not
others. When Pack visited Ken again, he brought up this possibility. Was it possible, Ken asked Pack, that he'd put the
shoes in the Suburban, but just didn't remember doing it—
because of the trauma? Was it possible that these memories,
if they existed, could be recovered? A week or so later, Pack

returned and asked Ken if he was willing to be hypnotized.

Hypnosis has long been a dirty word in the legal community; in the past, convictions in a number of cases were overturned because critical witnesses had been hypnotized in an effort to "enhance" their recollections. The trouble was, once a person had been hypnotized, it wasn't always possible to tell where true memory ended and imagination began. As a result, courts in most states have refused to accept post-hypnotic testimony, that is, the "enhanced" accounts.

But Nolan did not think this applied to the person who was *accused* of a crime, rather than the accuser; so far as he could tell, there had never been a court decision which would prevent a defendant from relating his own recollections after hypnosis. Nolan decided to consult one of the leading experts in the field, a Stanford psychiatrist, Dr. David Spiegel.

On February 28, 2001, Nolan telephoned Dr. Spiegel, who took notes on the conversation. One of the first things Spiegel did was tell Nolan that his consulting fee would be $500 an hour. This seems not to have deterred Nolan; he proceeded to brief Spiegel on the problem of the running shoes.

"Doesn't know how he got there," Spiegel noted, referring to Ken's memory blank. "?find how shoes got there . . . possible that in the period of time when he is getting dogs out of the car, may have picked shoes up and taken them to the car—doesn't have a clue as to how they got there . . . find a shirt under seat with blood . . . not worn by the perpetrator . . . may have taken at same time as shoes . . . figure where he went . . ."

A month later, in April of 2001, Spiegel went to the Santa Clara County jail, and with Nolan and Pack watching from a concealed position, attempted to put Ken into a hypnotic trance. At that point, Ken recalled what had happened: in the first minutes after he'd left the basement, after he'd gone into the bathroom to wash his hands and face of Kristine's blood, he'd remembered about the dogs: Boots and Reina had been left alone in the Suburban, and for all Ken knew, Gaelyn and Carol might have left the truck's doors wide open, and the dogs were now running loose. He decided to go outside to the truck to check to see if the dogs were all right. On the way out, he'd noticed that his white running shoes were by the front door; he'd left them there that morning, because he'd intended to wear them when he went to look over the Family Golf Center property, but had inadvertently forgotten them. Ken remembered picking up the white running shoes, going to the truck, and putting them under the seat. Presumably, some of the blood from his pants or the paper towel he was carrying had transferred to the shoes at that point.

What about the green shirt? Ken remembered about that, as well. As he'd left the basement, he'd noticed that his hands were bloody. He'd picked up the shirt from a pile of rags on the floor, and used it to wipe his hands. He'd taken the rag upstairs to the bathroom, where he'd washed, gone into the kitchen for the paper towel, then out to the truck, the green shirt stuck between his arm and his side as he'd picked up the running shoes, along with the crumpled, bloody paper towel.

True, this didn't account for the prosecution's most critical evidence—the alleged moving of the body from the kitchen to the stairs—but it might tend to show that the Palo Alto police had been less than precise when they claimed to have had Ken under observation at all times during the events of May 5. The trouble with the bloody shoes, shirt and paper towel, at least for Nolan, was that they didn't dispel the thrust of the state's case, no matter *when* they were put into the Suburban; but left unexplained, they went a long way to bolster it. Still, if the jury's attention could be focused on this apparent discrepancy, doubts might be raised about other claims by the prosecution—such as the moving of the body.

For the time being, Nolan decided to keep mum about this "recovered memory." There was no point in giving Fletcher a chance to figure out what to do about this part of Ken's defense until he had to. He would tell Fletcher he'd had a psychiatrist examine Ken, but that there was no written report on the session. And in fact, there would never be one, as long as Nolan was running the defense, because he'd told Spiegel not to write one.

In the same month, Nolan decided to attack another one of the linchpins of Fletcher's case: he wanted the luminol tests thrown out.

The problem with luminol, Nolan told Elia, was that it was only *presumptive* for blood. It didn't necessarily mean that blood was actually present, only that it could not be ruled out as the cause of the luminescence. Worse, from a defense point of view, the results could be "spectacular," as Nolan put it— witness the *Daily News* report about the supposed "blood bath," which cited a large basketball-sized "bloodstain" where none was actually found. The mere presence of a substantial amount of bluish-green glowing doesn't mean that a horrific amount of blood was shed, only that the luminol was reacting to one of any number of chemicals—including animal blood, household cleaners, fruit juices—indeed, an entire panoply of possible triggers. Luminol was extremely sensitive. As little as one part of blood in more than a million of other substances would be enough to cause the reaction, Nolan said.

"Therefore," said Nolan in his brief to Elia, "Luminol photographs can give the appearance of a bloodbath and clean up of major proportions when only an extremely small amount of blood is actually present." This could have the effect of prejudicing a jury, Nolan said. At the minimum, the state would have to prove that the substances that caused the luminescence were human blood, and even then, for it to be admissible, it had to be proven to be Kristine's blood. If that couldn't be done, the "spectacular" luminol pictures should be kept away from the jury.

In addition to throwing out the luminol photos, Nolan also wanted the trial moved. There was simply too much prejudicial publicity in the case in Santa Clara County, he said.

In asking that the trial be moved to another venue, Nolan fell back on the defense lawyer's old reliable, the Sam Sheppard case. In that infamous 1961 case, Ohio osteopath Sam Sheppard was convicted of his wife's murder after an enormous amount of negative publicity both before and during the trial, which took place two weeks before a local election in which both the judge and prosecutor were candidates. The judge in the Sheppard case gave the news media, including radio and television reporters, free rein in the courtroom by allowing them inside the bar that normally separates the litigants from the public. This had the inevitable effect of transforming Sheppard's trial into a sort of legal version of *This Is Your Life*. In more ways than one, the Sheppard case was the O. J. Simpson trial of its time.

Nor did the judge in the Sheppard case do anything to halt the spread of leaks and unsupported rumors, most of them highly inflammatory, by the police and prosecutors before and during the trial; he even allowed the jurors to receive messages from outsiders during their deliberations, including questions from the media. Five years later, the U.S. Supreme Court concluded the obvious, that Sheppard did not receive a fair trial, and found that the judge in the case had utterly failed in his duty to maintain order in the courtroom.

Outwardly, the Fitzhugh case had some similarities to the Sheppard matter. In both cases, the defendants claimed that the murder of a wife had actually been committed by an intruder—in Sheppard's case, the notorious "one-armed man" who later became the quarry of the fictional Dr. Richard Kimble on television and in the movies. And there could be no denying that both cases had received an abnormally high amount of publicity.

But the circumstances in Ken's case were a far cry from those that were at work in Sheppard's. For one thing, neither the judge nor prosecutor were running for reelection, with the election day just two weeks away; for another, the reporters were being kept at bay by the strict rules of court.

That didn't make any difference, according to Nolan. What really counted was the sheer amount of publicity. He cited several California appeals cases in which the courts had ruled that a "reasonable likelihood of unfairness may exist even though news coverage was neither inflammatory nor productive of overt hostility . . . when a spectacular crime has aroused community attention and a suspect has been arrested, the possibility of an unfair trial may originate in widespread publicity describing facts, statements and circumstances which tend to create a belief in his guilt."

That was exactly what was happening in the Fitzhugh case, Nolan said. He pointed to the basketball-sized "stain" as evidence of the excessive news coverage.

"The press coverage," Nolan said, "has not only been inflammatory, but has also been compounded by statements from the Palo Alto Police Department that 'We are confident that we have the right suspect in custody.' " Under the circumstances, Nolan concluded, it was impossible for Ken to receive a fair trial.

Elia took these motions under submission, and indicated he would rule on them, along with several other similar matters, on the eve of trial—set to begin on June 25, 2001, a little more than a month and a year after Kristine Fitzhugh was found dead at the bottom of the basement stairs.

Before that happened, though, the public at large would finally learn about the long-suppressed affair between Kristine Fitzhugh and Robert Kenneth Brown—along with some new revelations that would raise the prospect of yet another motive.

In May of 2001, as he was preparing his case for trial, Deputy District Attorney Michael Fletcher received a new police report from Denson. Denson had been in contact with Brown to make sure that Brown would be available to testify in the trial. The last time anyone had had any extended conversation with Brown was when Wong and Denson had interviewed him while he was still in his living room–based hospital bed.

The authorities had had limited contact with Brown since his interviews—enough to take a sample of his blood for DNA testing, and to inform him of the results of the test. But when he called Brown in the spring of 2001, Denson was shocked at the clarity of Brown's conversation. In contrast to the mumbles of the year before, Brown sounded like a different person. What was more, Brown's story had evolved. He told Denson he'd wanted to tell Justin that he was his father from the very beginning, and had only held back because Kristine asked him not to. In his report to Fletcher on Brown's availability for the trial, Denson mentioned Brown's new-found clarity, and suggested that Fletcher call Brown to see for himself.

Fletcher wasn't entirely sure what to make of Brown. He knew that Brown was something of a wild card in the trial. He could, for example, suddenly become reluctant to remember things.

"It would not surprise me, given Robert Brown's track record with being in trouble," Fletcher was to recall thinking, "that the last thing he really wants to do is be injected into the middle of a homicide case, particularly in a case with such notoriety."

If he intended to use the affair and pregnancy as a possible motive for Ken, Fletcher knew, Brown's credibility was certain to come under attack from Nolan. But he had the results of the DNA test, so it wasn't as if Brown was making things up. Still, Fletcher knew he'd feel a lot more comfortable if he talked to Brown himself, as he would with any important witness. So on May 9, Fletcher called Brown. Brown told him he'd remembered some important new details about his relationship with the Fitzhughs.

And now Brown told Fletcher that he'd talked to Kristine in January of 2000, five months before the murder. Kristine had told him that she intended to tell Justin who his biological father was when Justin graduated in May of that year, Brown said. The graduation, of course, had taken place two weeks after Kristine was killed.

This seemed pretty important to Fletcher. After all, if Kristine had told Ken that she intended to tell Justin the truth about his biological father after the graduation, was it therefore possible that Ken had decided to prevent this—by killing Kristine?

To Fletcher, it fit. An earlier psychological profile of the crime and crime scene, prepared by the state Department of Justice, had suggested that the murder was the result of "some perceived on-going conflict between the victim and himself."

Perhaps, faced with the prospect of being unmasked as a cuckold, of having his eldest son learn the truth about his parentage, Ken had felt trapped by Kristine's insistence that Justin be told—that, in fact, he felt his entire edifice of personality was under dire attack. Perhaps he had become so desperate to preserve his façade as a father, a scoutmaster, a pillar of the community (as Nolan had repeatedly referred to him), that he had decided the only way to be certain that Kristine kept the secret was to make sure she never told anyone—permanently.

Or so Fletcher speculated.

The next day, May 10, at Fletcher's request, Denson called Brown. Fletcher wanted to get this new information nailed down in a form he could use at trial. After all, he could hardly be his own witness, if something should happen to Brown.

Brown was just about to call his aunt, Janet Moore, when Denson rang through.

Brown told Denson he'd just left a message for him to call Janet Moore, because his aunt had remembered things about the Fitzhughs that might be important. Janet had reminded Brown of the time that Ken had broken his foot by driving over it with the car, and the other time, when Ken had knocked him out with the sailing boom.

Brown said he'd also remembered that Justin "called me 'Dad' up until he was six or seven years old" . . . and that he'd introduced Justin to his own family as his son when Justin was only two or so . . . and that he remembered Justin visiting him for Father's Day . . .

"Okay," Denson said. "Let me go ahead and record this."

Denson first wanted to make sure that Brown wasn't under the influence of any mind-altering pain medications. Brown said he wasn't.

"And how many times did he visit you out of the last twenty-two years, would you say?"

"Up until 1996, we probably spent every Father's Day together, except one."

Ken said Kristine came to visit on Father's Day "like clockwork—every time she had a chance." Sometimes Ken would come too, he added. Kristine and Justin also visited him on his birthday, Brown added, "same as Father's Day."

"And how about his birthday?" Denson asked. "Did you usually show up?"

"Always."

"Always?"

Except, Brown added, until he had become "persona non grata," after the 1996 beach fiasco.

Denson wasn't sure what to make of this sudden resurgence of memory on Brown's part. He asked whether Brown had been taking medications when he was first interviewed the year before, and Brown said that he had.

"And I believe you said that those medications could even affect your memory," Denson prompted.

"Yes, they could," Brown said.

"Because we're getting new information here that we haven't previously gotten."

Brown said his memory was clearer than it had been in some time, principally because he was no longer on the pain medication.

Denson now asked Brown to go over the relationship with the Fitzhughs again. Brown sketched in many of the same events that he'd already talked about, up until the Fitzhughs' move to Palo Alto.

"Now," Brown said, "Kristine told me one of the reasons [for the move] was, if you're interested, is because of me." He said Kristine wanted to be closer to Brown in Fresno.

"And then," said Denson, "how did you come to find out that Justin was your son?"

"Well, [when] she first got pregnant she told me it was mine."

Now Brown related the story about the trip to Santa Barbara and the motor home, and then, the story about the aunts and the inheritances, and Kristine's purported statement that she and Ken had to have children to qualify for the legacies.

About a year or so after Justin's birth, he realized that Kristine had been telling him the truth, Brown said—that Justin looked like him, not Ken.

Throughout the next twenty years, Brown said, he kept encouraging Kristine to tell Justin the truth about his biological father, but Kristine refused.

"She was pretty stubborn," he said. "She said no, she would never, until he was older."

"And when did she tell you that she intended to tell him?" Denson asked.

"Right toward the end of last year, she made that December or January phone call to me," Brown said.

"January?"

"Yeah. It was real brief. And she said she could only talk for a second. She missed me and that she couldn't talk. She had to go. And I said, 'When does he graduate?' And she said, 'June.' I said, 'Well, let me know where and when.' She said, 'I promise I will.' And we ended the conversation and I never heard from her again."

WITHIN a few days of this conversation, Fletcher had informed Nolan of Brown's new recollections. On May 21, 2001, he sent Nolan a copy of Denson's report, and a transcript of Denson's conversations with Brown and his aunt, Janet Moore.

At that point Nolan realized that the issue of Justin's paternity was likely to become part of the state's case against Ken—the motive—and worse, that the whole thing would soon become public. Until this point, the entire issue of Justin's paternity had been kept under wraps by both the prosecution and the defense, and the public at large had no idea that any such revelation was in the offing.

Up to this point, Nolan had believed that if the prosecution intended to assert a motive for the murder, it would probably be in the area of the Fitzhughs' finances. For that reason, Nolan had sent all of Ken's financial records to a former IRS expert, who provided him with an analysis showing that Ken had no need to kill his wife for money.

But now Fletcher had thrown Nolan a curve ball with the paternity issue. That meant Nolan had to get to work to find a way to discredit Brown's credibility. He got Brown's records from the State Bar, and obtained records of his criminal history. Then he decided to try to have Brown's possible testimony thrown out as unreliable, but without tipping off the press and public about the paternity issue. If he could get a favorable ruling on the reliability of Brown's proffered testimony, perhaps he could knock the whole thing out without it ever having to be revealed, thereby sparing Ken and Justin the notoriety that Brown's assertions were sure to bring.

On June 12, Nolan filed a motion asking that any motive

the state might assert for the murder be the subject of an evidentiary hearing; he wanted the court to rule that the prosecutors first had to establish the truth of the facts before offering them as a motive. That meant, in Nolan's view, that the D.A.'s office had to prove that Ken had known about the paternity issues before the matters could be considered relevant.

"It is the position of the defense," Nolan wrote in his brief to Elia, "that not only is there no motive in this case, but a lack of motive is going to be a significant part of the defendant's case. Assuming that the district attorney intends to present evidence of motive in this case, he must first affirmatively demonstrate, under evidence code section 402, before this evidence is introduced, that Mr. Fitzhugh knew of the facts which constitute this motive."

Nolan told Fletcher that his motion was intended to eliminate the paternity issue from the trial, since, he said, Ken had had no way of knowing about Justin until *after* the DNA test. If Ken hadn't known, he said, how could it be a motive?

In response, Fletcher filed his own motion, contending that Elia didn't need to have a full-blown evidence hearing on the motive—that the justice could decide on his own discretion, if an offer of proof was made. This Fletcher proceeded to do:

"The People," he wrote in a brief filed on Friday, June 15, 2001, "intend to establish that the victim informed the defendant of her intent to tell her oldest son that the defendant was not his father. This is evidence of his motive to murder the victim. The evidence that the People rely on to establish the defendant's knowledge of the victim's plan is not reasonably in dispute."

Well, that wasn't exactly the case—from his position, not only did Ken not know of this supposed plan by Kristine to tell Justin the secret, he didn't even know the secret itself, according to Nolan. Fletcher, however, was making a subtle distinction: the evidence—the fact that Brown had made the statements—wasn't in dispute; what was disputed was the *inference* Fletcher was drawing from the statements: that if Kristine had intended to tell Justin, she surely would have told Ken first.

With Fletcher's filing, the die was cast: the story of Brown's affair with Kristine, and Justin's paternity, would inevitably become public.

The matter was to be argued on June 18. Apparently none of the news media outlets bothered to check the court filings on Friday afternoon, because the whole issue of the paternity burst upon the assembled news media like a thunderclap when the argument began before Elia on the following Monday morning.

It was left to Elia to raise the issue in open court.

"I believe," he said, "the prosecution wants to introduce some evidence as to motive. And that involves the statement that—well, there's some information that the victim was supposed to advise her husband of the victim's son being fathered by another man . . ."

This assertion electrified the assembled news media; there had been just this sort of speculation for nearly a year—well, at least that there had been some sort of love triangle—and now it was finally coming out.

Nolan was apparently chagrined at the justice's decision to let the cat out of the bag so overtly. He said he'd tried to deal with the whole issue on a preliminary basis without delving into "the historical events."

"So I tried to limit it to that," Nolan said. "The district attorney responded by giving facts." In other words, it was Fletcher's fault that all this was now about to come out.

Nolan gave a brief summary of Brown's assertions, and suggested that Brown's admitted problems with drugs and alcohol made his story unreliable. Nolan slid over the DNA paternity test so quickly, it probably wasn't noticeable to the assembled reporters.

"I can tell you," he told Elia, "that at first I didn't believe I had to fully investigate Mr. Brown because his statement was, 'I haven't talked to her in five years.' If he did father the child, the child is still Mr. Fitzhugh's legally, it is Mr. Fitzhugh's child, et cetera. And it's completely irrelevant to the issue."

There still had to be some evidence connecting the information about Justin's parentage to Ken's supposed motive,

Nolan said. Even if it was true that Justin had been fathered by Brown, it didn't mean that Ken killed Kristine. The state had to show that Ken was aware of any of this before they could say that was why he'd killed her. And Nolan didn't believe they could do that.

Moreover, Nolan continued, Brown's own history showed that he simply wasn't a reliable witness—even apart from the question of whether Kristine had told Ken about this supposed plan to tell Justin, there was a real question of whether Kristine had even made the statement at all to Brown. They had checked the telephone records, Nolan said, and there was no evidence that Kristine had ever made a telephone call to Brown in December of 1999 or January of 2000.

Nolan sketched in the background: the Fitzhughs' friendship with Brown, his drug and alcohol difficulties, the Fitzhughs' attempt to detoxify him, the severing of the friendship in 1996.

Then, said Nolan, the police had unearthed Brown, in June of 2000. In that conversation, Nolan told Elia, Brown had admitted that he'd had the affair, and said that Kristine had told him he was the father, although he himself did not know for sure. Then Brown had told Denson that he hadn't talked with Kristine for more than four years.

Now, almost a year later, Nolan said—after he'd heard about the DNA blood test results—all of a sudden Brown recalled that Kristine had called in December of 1999 or January of 2000 to tell him that she planned to tell Justin the secret at his graduation. The change in Brown's story and the lack of any telephone records showing a call from Kristine to Brown made Brown's account inherently unreliable, Nolan said. That's why he wanted a hearing—so he could examine the evidence to see whether any of his story should be admitted as an underlying fact. If it wasn't reliable, it shouldn't be heard by the jury, Nolan said, and therefore, couldn't be used to support Ken's supposed motive. There wasn't even any evidence that Kristine herself knew for a fact that Brown was Justin's father, Nolan said.

When it was his turn, Fletcher said, "it is a reasonable inference that she would never tell her son without telling her husband. This was a secret, this wasn't something a lot of people knew. She knew it, as I'm sure somebody who has borne a child would be expected to know who the father was—particularly under the circumstances, where they had a long-term, intimate affair. It makes no sense whatsoever to go tell a son without telling her husband. There's no evidence that she expected this to terminate their relationship [with Ken]. This was telling the truth to a young man, her son, at a time, sort of a coming-out time, of life."

Brown naturally had no way of knowing whether Kristine had told Ken about her intention to tell Justin, but it didn't matter, Fletcher said. The fact remained, it was reasonable to infer that Kristine had told Ken what she was going to do.

Fletcher pointed out that when he was first interviewed, Ken had in fact referred to Justin as "her older son." He suggested to Elia that Ken had made a Freudian slip, in effect disavowing his biological parentage of Justin, but thereby demonstrating that he was aware of the secret.

In rebuttal, Nolan wanted to make another point: Brown's inconsistency, between the statements of June of 2000 and the statements of May of 2001, needed to be viewed in context of *Brown's* possible motives:

"Here we have somebody dying, not doing particularly well, who now has confirmed that this is his biological son, who's now, all of a sudden, trying very hard to make contact with his son, and is not being allowed to make contact, through the son's lawyer. And now all of a sudden he's talking about how this was common knowledge, and how he was introduced [as Justin's father] and every Father's Day he would come. There are a lot of new things coming out."

Nolan's implication was clear: Brown's sudden recollection was an indication that Brown desired to get close to Justin, and was so desperate to do this that he was now making things up.

Elia took the matter under submission, and said he'd let both sides know whether Brown's testimony would be allowed within a few days.

But the news media wasn't about to wait. The *Palo Alto Daily News* reported:

D.A.: Affair is key to murder

Jurors who will decide whether Kenneth Fitzhugh killed his wife must be told about her lengthy affair that produced a son, a prosecutor argued yesterday before a judge. The prosecutor also said jurors must hear from her lover.

The young man's paternity, kept a secret for 22 years, is at the heart of the murder case: It provides an explanation to bolster the state's case about why a man with no history of violence would kill his wife of 33 years.

Santa Clara County Deputy District Attorney Michael Fletcher claims Kristine Fitzhugh was beaten and strangled by her husband in their Palo Alto home on May 5, 2000, to prevent her from revealing to their older son, Justin Fitzhugh, the truth about his biological father. . . .

And the *San Francisco Chronicle:*

Murder trial takes a bizarre twist—Prosecutors say wife was slain because she planned to reveal her son's true paternity

The revelations were reported throughout the Bay Area, and led the evening news, doing more to focus public attention on the Fitzhugh tragedy than anything that had happened up to that point. Two days later, when Elia decided that Brown's testimony would be admissible, there was yet another flurry of publicity about the long-ago affair.

If Kristine had once gone to extraordinary lengths to keep her secret, she could never have dreamed how it all would finally come spilling out in the most public way imaginable.

KEN's trial began on Monday, July 2, 2001. Nearly three hundred potential jurors had been questioned the week before it opened, particularly about their knowledge and opinions about the crime in the wake of all the publicity. Nolan's attempt to get the trial moved had been turned down by Elia, who said that Santa Clara's 1.6 million residents provided a large enough pool of potential jurors to find at least twelve who were unbiased. In the end, after many were excused because of the expected six-week length of the trial, Elia found the requisite dozen—six men and six women—and three alternates qualified for service.

Elia—as noted, a former city attorney in Palo Alto—was well-regarded in the community for the acuity of his legal reasoning; he had a reputation for running a very formal courtroom, and wasn't averse to chiding the lawyers who practiced before him if he felt they wandered off the track in their zeal to represent their clients. As the trial unfolded, there would be several sharp exchanges between the thin, balding Elia and the two lawyers. Elia meant to let both sides know that he was in charge of the proceedings, not them.

The trial's beginning drew a large crowd of onlookers; Elia refused to allow anyone in who couldn't find a seat, and turned several late-comers away. The crowd included two television sketch artists—Elia had already ruled that there would be no cameras allowed—and a half-dozen reporters. To handle the large number of visual exhibits—the scores of photographs—Fletcher had produced a Microsoft PowerPoint presentation that displayed the photographs in full color on a large screen.

Fletcher began his opening statement by commenting on

the difference between outward appearances and reality.

"A perfect family, a beautiful home, thirty-three years of marriage," he said, ticking off the appearances first. Ken and Kristine had two sons in private colleges, a collection of nice cars, a beautiful Palo Alto home, a ski boat, and two dogs, Reina the Pomeranian and Boots the poodle.

But things were not as they seemed, Fletcher said, and the truth began to emerge when Ken, accompanied by two friends, came home on May 5 to find his wife dead at the bottom of the basement steps. Ken had tried to say that Kristine's death was an accident, but the evidence would show differently. It would show that Ken, in fact, had killed his wife—all because Kristine wanted to tell the truth about the paternity of their oldest son.

"No one saw it coming," Fletcher said. "Not Kristine, not her friends. No one. And the ruse worked for a while, but in time . . . the truth came out. Kristine Fitzhugh did not die in an accident. He killed her."

Fletcher sketched in the events of Kristine's affair, and said the jury would hear that Kristine had wanted to tell Justin the truth. "Maybe this is why the defendant killed his wife. We'll never know for sure," Fletcher said. "Only two people know why. One is dead, and one is on trial for murder."

But the evidence would show that Kristine's decision to tell Justin the truth about his biological father had sparked a killing anger in Ken, and "he proceeded to inflict his deadly anger on Kristine Fitzhugh."

Ken had attacked his wife with such force that there were seven separate wounds to the back of her head, he said. And the evidence would show that this attack had taken place in the kitchen, while Kristine had her back turned to Ken. The fact that there were so many bloodstains in the kitchen proved it, Fletcher said. The bloodstains showed that Ken had moved his wife's dead or dying body to the basement steps, trying to make the whole thing look like an accident. Then Ken had tried to clean everything up. But Kristine did not cooperate.

"Kristine left a trail that led right to the murderer, right to her husband," Fletcher said, pointing at Ken. "It's Kristine

Fitzhugh's blood, and it's been cleaned up, and her body was staged in the basement."

That fact alone, said Fletcher, should lead the jury to conclude that there could be only one man responsible for the murder: Kenneth Fitzhugh.

Nolan now rose to give his opening.

The police, he said, had gotten the wrong man. Worse, they had tailored the facts to fit their conclusion.

The evidence would show that, contrary to what they'd just heard, the attack did *not* take place in the kitchen, but in the basement. And the attack was the work of an intruder, which the police would have realized if they hadn't been in such a rush to blame Ken.

"There is an obsession with proving the crime took place in the kitchen," Nolan said, because they wanted to prove that Ken was the murderer. But if the attack had really occurred in the kitchen, he said, far more blood would have been found there later—even, he said, blood on the ceiling from the cast-off. There simply wasn't enough time for Ken to have cleaned up all that blood, Nolan said.

It was true, Nolan said, that Kristine had not died in an accident; but the evidence of what really happened in the basement was obscured by all of the attempts to resuscitate Kristine early on the afternoon of May 5. Whatever evidence of murder existed had been wiped out by all the foot traffic of the rescuers. The luminol results in the kitchen were inherently unreliable, he said. The triggering substance could be decades old; it could be from a steak or roast previously cut in the kitchen, so overly sensitive was the chemical.

And it was also true that Justin was Kristine's son by Brown, Nolan said. But it didn't mean anything. Because no one knew this for certain—not until the D.A.'s office had made Justin get a blood test to determine his paternity. Even Kristine herself might not have known for sure that Brown was Justin's biological father, Nolan said. Jurors would get a chance to read from her diary, to hear from her friends and her psychotherapist, and nowhere would they find any evidence that Kristine planned to tell anyone about the circumstances of Justin's conception.

"You will conclude from the facts that at this point in time she did not plan on telling Justin," Nolan said. "The evidence will show that she did take her secret to her grave."

The prosecution would make much of Ken's actions, Nolan said, but the facts would show that his actions were entirely consistent with a man in shock. "He loved his wife dearly," Nolan said. "They had a great relationship." The defense would put on expert psychiatric testimony to show that Ken's actions on the day of the discovery were as explainable as they were natural for a man in a state of terrible shock.

The police were so convinced that Ken was the killer, Nolan said, they'd never bothered to investigate any other possibility. Despite police statements to the contrary, there *were* a number of items missing from the Fitzhugh home, Nolan said—among them a small hatchet kept in the back yard in a pile of logs. That could have been the missing murder weapon, Nolan suggested, but no one from the police ever bothered to follow up on that lead. "They had already made their arrest," he said. "They had already made their decision."

Ken, he said, had cooperated with the police throughout the entire investigation. He had nothing to hide, and he was not guilty.

WITH the preliminaries out of the way, Fletcher began to put on his evidence. His plan was quite direct: first, show what had happened in the basement when Ken, Gaelyn and Carol had arrived, followed by the firemen and police officers; then show how the evidence was collected, followed by what it meant; then sum up his case with the motive evidence, consisting of the testimony from Brown, and his corroborative witness, his aunt, Janet Moore.

Fletcher began with Emily Nessi, the assistant manager at the Peet's Coffee shop, and established through her testimony that Kristine had been there for her latte and muffin that morning. Nessi remembered that Kristine had asked her to get more of a certain kind of scone she liked, and Nessi now produced a telephone record that showed she'd called the bakery at 11:27 A.M. on the morning of May 5. That seemed to demonstrate that Kristine had left the coffee shop shortly before 11:30 A.M.

Next, Fletcher called James Selby, the Federal Express driver. Selby told of making his delivery on May 5, and not seeing either the Suburban or Kristine's silver BMW. Fletcher was narrowing the time frame for the crime. After Selby, Fletcher called Brad Flores, and used his testimony to introduce the videotape of the crime scene, which showed Kristine's body sprawled at the foot of the basement stairs, a dark pool of blood clearly visible on the floor beneath her head.

After Flores, Fletcher called Gaelyn Mason, his first major witness.

In the immediate aftermath of Kristine's death—and as it became apparent that the police believed the death was more than an accident, that they even believed Ken was responsible—both Gaelyn and Carol Piraino had been loyal to Ken. While being cooperative with the police investigators who questioned them, it was clear to the detectives that neither Gaelyn nor Carol believed that Ken had murdered anyone, let alone Kristine. They were simply too close to the Fitzhughs to believe that.

This state of affairs continued to exist even after Ken was arrested, and as the investigation into his and Kristine's backgrounds unfolded in May and June. But as the evidence began to come in—the apparent absence of a true alibi for Ken, the luminol findings in the kitchen, the bloody shoes and shirt—Gaelyn and Carol began to believe that their friend had used them. By the time of the trial, both women, at least according to Denson and Fletcher, believed that Ken was responsible for Kristine's death. This put them in an awkward position, as both still felt quite close to Justin and John.

Gaelyn took the stand on the afternoon of July 2, and continued her testimony the following day. She described the arrangements that had been made for Ken to take them to San Jose to pick up the gaming equipment, Ken's remarks about Kristine's apparent disappearance, the trip over to the Escobita house, followed by the scene in the basement.

The critical thing in Gaelyn's account was the timing of the events. In order to make the point that the bloody shoes and shirt had to have been put into the Suburban by Ken after the murder, but before the discovery of the body, Fletcher needed to demonstrate that it was impossible for Ken to have put the articles in the car at any time after he, Gaelyn and Carol had arrived at the house. That meant tying everyone's movements down to within seconds, if possible.

In this Fletcher was assisted by the city of Palo Alto's computer-aided dispatch log, which showed the arrival times of the personnel who had come to the house—the firemen, the police and the paramedics. Fletcher believed the only possible opportunity that Ken had to go to the Suburban (if he hadn't put the articles in the truck after the murder but before the discovery of the body) was between the arrival of the firemen at just before 1:46 P.M. and the arrival of Officer Sascha Priess just after 1:47 P.M.—about ninety seconds, altogether.

After that, Ken had been under observation throughout the entire afternoon. Fletcher meant to show that there simply wasn't enough time or opportunity for Ken to have gone to the truck after the arrival of the firemen. The whole thing was like a fine watch, interdependent; or in another way, like one of those English murder mysteries, with everyone's movements carefully reconstructed to eliminate the alibi, as various people, witnesses, policemen, and firemen alike, popped out of doorways and tramped up and down stairs in constant view of one another. If he could show that Ken was lying about the shirt and shoes, Fletcher knew, he could give the jury grounds to disbelieve Ken's entire defense.

Under questioning from Fletcher, Gaelyn described everyone's actions, as best as she could recall them: the attempts she and Ken had made to revive Kristine; Ken's remarks about the "God damn black shoes"; the arrival of the firemen; Ken ascending the basement stairs, bloody hands raised like a surgeon; Gaelyn's own exit from the basement via the rear storm doors. The point Fletcher wanted to demonstrate was that during none of this time did Ken have the opportunity to go to the Suburban with the shirt and shoes, at least as far as Gaelyn had seen. Just to be sure, Fletcher asked Gaelyn whether Ken was carrying anything in his hands when he left the basement, and Gaelyn said no.

On his cross-examination, Nolan tried to induce Gaelyn to admit that her memory of the events of May 5 might have gaps in it, particularly when it came to where everybody was at any given point in time. He brought up Gaelyn's own exit from the basement.

"And so you decided to find a way out, is that right?" he asked.

"First I got trapped by the stuff they were moving [e.g., the ship's bell and the firemen's equipment]," Gaelyn said, "and then it got too much for me, so I asked them to help me get out, when I remembered that door that goes out of the basement."

"At first you didn't remember the door?"

"I didn't remember much of anything right then," Gaelyn said.

"And," Nolan prompted, "you have tried to re-create and figure out things, correct?"

"I have pictures that I see that don't go away," Gaelyn said. "I have sounds that I have, and as I start to look at those, yes, things begin to make sense."

"You're trying to make sense of this?"

"No," Gaelyn said, "I'm trying to look at what I saw and think about it. And when you see things like that, they are just slides, pictures of things."

"And between the time Ken went upstairs and after you finally went upstairs, you don't know what Ken did, or where he went, correct?"

"Personally, no," Gaelyn said.

After Gaelyn, Fletcher called Carol Piraino. She went over much of the same ground as Gaelyn, but from a different perspective. She hadn't actually gone all the way down the stairs in the basement, she said; she'd only watched after she'd called in the alarm.

Fletcher wanted to get Ken's movements covered, the same way he'd done with Gaelyn. After the firemen had arrived, he asked, what had Carol seen Ken do?

"I see him come out of the basement and go into the bathroom," Carol said.

"When you first observed him," Fletcher asked, "can you describe his hands—the position?"

"His hands were straight up in the air, like this," Carol said, and she raised her hands in the ninety-degree angle. There was blood on his hands, and blood on his face, Carol remembered.

Carol said she moved into the kitchen as Ken began to come up.

"Why did you do that?" Fletcher asked.

"When he came up the stairs, I was really overwhelmed," she said. "Because I didn't know what to say or do as he got up to the top of the stairs. And I needed a minute to kind of pull myself together. I was quite upset at the moment."

"Could you tell where he went when he came out of the basement?"

"He went into the bathroom," Carol said.

"Okay. And Mr. Fitzhugh goes into— When he came up the stairs and you saw him with his hands up, did he have anything in his hands?"

"No."

"Did he have a shirt?"

"No."

"When he's in the bathroom and you're in the kitchen, can you tell what he's doing in the bathroom?"

"I can hear the water running."

"Tell us what happens next," Fletcher prompted.

"A couple of minutes later, less than a couple of minutes later, probably thirty seconds later, I walked out of the kitchen to go back to the top of the stairs [to the basement]. I glanced into the bathroom and I noticed that he's no longer in the bathroom."

Here it was, the tiny chink in the state's case: Carol had said she looked into the bathroom at the end of the hall, and Ken was no longer there. Where had he gone? Was this gap "a couple of minutes"? "Less than a couple of minutes"? "Probably thirty seconds"? Was it enough time for Ken to get past Carol in the kitchen with the bloody paper towel, the bloody green shirt, and out the door with the bloody running shoes to the Suburban, without Carol observing him?

That was what Nolan was about to contend—that in his state of shock, Ken had unconsciously picked up the green shirt from a pile of rags while in the basement, that he'd gone into the bathroom, washed his hands and face, dried them on a paper towel, then had gone out to the Suburban to check to see that Gaelyn and Carol had shut the doors to the truck to prevent the dogs from getting loose, picking up the bloody shoes from near the front door on the way. *That* was when the shirt, shoes and towel had gotten into the truck, that was how the blood got on the incriminating articles, and that was where he was when Carol had looked into the bathroom and noticed that he wasn't there. That was what Nolan wanted the jury to believe. And if Ken could have gotten out to the Suburban with the bloody objects without the police noticing, what else had the police missed in their rush to judgment?

AFTER glancing at the apparently empty bathroom, Carol continued, she stepped onto the upper landing of the basement stairs and looked down to see Kristine on her back on the basement floor. She said she saw paramedics on the floor of the basement, "cutting her blouse and putting some patches on her chest." She saw Gaelyn edging toward the back of the basement, and realized that Gaelyn would leave the basement by the storm doors.

Then Carol said she left the landing area and returned to the kitchen, intending to meet Gaelyn as she entered the dining room from the patio area. Ken, she said, was then in the hallway, talking to police officers.

This seemed to be a case of Ken disappearing and reappearing within seconds. Where had he gone? Carol didn't know.

On cross-examination, Nolan tried to make this point more obvious to the jury.

"Now," he said, "he goes into the bathroom, right?"

"That's right."

"You go into the kitchen?"

"Right."

"And there's a period of time when basically you have a kind of memory loss, or there's just a lack of memory, correct, by you?"

"A lack of memory of what?"

"Of what happened and where people went."

"I know where I am and I know what's going— I leave the kitchen and go to the top of the stairs."

"But you don't see where he goes?"

"No."

"And you don't see where he went after he left the bathroom?"

"No, I did not see where he went after he left the bathroom."

Nolan asked Carol if she had ever told anyone that at that point she thought Ken had gone outside to the truck. Carol said that was true; she'd said that on May 5. But, she said, she didn't know that for a fact. She didn't know where Ken was, she insisted; at the time, she'd only been guessing.

Had she ever told Gaelyn that Ken went outside to the truck?

"I don't remember," Carol said.

"Didn't you tell Gaelyn that you saw him leave the residence after going into the bathroom?"

"I don't recall."

"There was a time when you didn't know where he was, when he could have gone out of the bathroom, into the kitchen, and outside, correct?" This was subtle; Nolan was trying to establish that the blood found in the kitchen—the myriad little spots of Kristine's blood highlighted by the luminol—could have come off of Ken's pants and loafers, if he'd gone into the kitchen before then going outside to the truck with the shoes, shirt and towel. This would also explain how the paper towel could have gotten into the Suburban.

"To go from the bathroom to the kitchen," Carol said, "he would have passed me, because I was in the kitchen."

"After you left the kitchen," Nolan persisted, "he could have gone into the kitchen, isn't that correct?"

"It's possible."

"Because there was a period of time when you don't know where he was?"

"That's right."

"And isn't it true that your memory back then was, that you saw him leave the house?"

"I don't recall."

When testimony resumed the next morning, Nolan tried to reinforce his gains. He induced Carol to admit that when she'd seen Ken in the hall talking to a policeman—or it might have been a fireman—Ken was standing near the front door; and that when police Agent Brown had talked to her in June of 2000, she had tried to cloud Carol's recollection of these events by asking for her "support," that they, the police, "were doing this for Kristine." The implication was that Carol's lack of recall was because of Agent Brown's influence.

Except for the problem of the lack of time, Nolan thus succeeded in laying the groundwork for his defense on the shirt and shoes: neither Gaelyn nor Carol could swear that Ken had not gone out to the truck after coming up from the basement. That left the firemen and the police officers.

Fletcher now called Palo Alto Fire Captain Patrick Morris, who had been one of the first rescuers to reach Kristine on May 5. Morris said he and his crew of two received the alarm on Kristine at 1:42 P.M., and got to the Escobita house just before 1:45. He and the others, Richard Sartor and Lee Caudill, were waved into the house by Carol, and descended to the basement, where they found Ken and Gaelyn performing CPR. Ken told them they'd been trying to resuscitate Kristine, Morris said.

"Can you describe his demeanor?" Fletcher asked.

"He was very quiet, very—almost appeared detached to what was going on around him. Not animated, moving around. Appeared very calm." Morris thought Ken's behavior was very unusual. "In my experience," he said, "most family members and bystanders are much more animated, much more emotional, and much less detached at the scene of an emergency than fire fighters and trained medical personnel." But in answer to a question from Nolan, Morris admitted that different people might act differently than usual, depending on their training and experience.

The paramedics arrived a minute or so later, Morris said, and helped them move some of the stuff in the basement out of the way, so they could attach electrodes to Kristine for an EKG. This apparently was when Carol witnessed them from the top of the stairs.

Fletcher called Sartor; Sartor said he, too, was struck by Ken's demeanor when they first arrived.

"How did he appear?" Fletcher asked.

"Unemotional," Sartor said.

"Did that cause you to ask him a question?"

"Yes, it did."

"What was that?"

"I asked him if he was a doctor," Sartor said.

After Ken and Gaelyn left the basement, the paramedics arrived, Sartor said. The lead paramedic, Toby McDonnell, asked Sartor what the situation was. Sartor told him as McDonnell applied the EKG patches.

"He then leans over to me and says to me: 'This could be a crime scene, couldn't it?' Yeah, could be," Sartor said he said.

"What was going through your head at that point?" Fletcher asked.

"Just how odd it was," Sartor said, "how odd she looked, for somebody who purportedly had fallen down the stairs. It just didn't jibe with the way she looked."

On his cross-examination, Nolan had Sartor admit that people showed emotion in different ways, and then turned to Ken's movements.

"I take it," he asked, "that after you took over [CPR from Ken], you didn't really pay any attention to where Mr. Fitzhugh went, correct?"

"Yeah, very little. I was busy working."

"You didn't notice how many times he went up and down the stairs?"

"A couple of times, to my recollection."

Suddenly, here was another possible chink in the state's case: Sartor was testifying that Ken had gone up and down the basement stairs "A couple of times, to my recollection." If this was true, it was possible that Ken had ascended the stairs, with empty, bloody hands raised the first time, and then returned to pick up the bloody green shirt, unseen by either Gaelyn or Carol—Gaelyn would have been exiting the basement through the storm doors, while Carol would have been in the kitchen, "to pull myself together" during the "couple of minutes" when she did not know where Ken was.

Nolan asked Sartor whether he'd seen a bloody tennis

shoe print in the basement. Sartor said he had. It was, he said, "probably about half a shoe."

Nolan asked whether Ken had been wearing tennis shoes when Sartor first saw him, and Sartor said he didn't know. Well, said Nolan, Kristine hadn't been wearing tennis shoes, had she? Sartor said, no, she hadn't.

Nolan asked if Sartor had mentioned the bloody shoe print to anyone, and Sartor said he hadn't, not until a couple of days later. It didn't seem important at the time, he said.

Nolan scored a double-hit on this supposed bloody shoe print. At the beginning, as Denson had told Ken, the police believed that there was a bloody tennis shoe print in the basement. Later, as the investigation progressed, Denson was forced to admit that the print did not exist—only that there had been a blood smear that looked like a print, but wasn't, really. Now Nolan was inducing Sartor to say that he'd seen the print, and that the print had not been preserved. No preservation—that meant the print might have come from the unknown intruder, or so Nolan's question implied.

The police, said Sartor, had never asked him to return to the house to point out where he'd seen the print.

Fletcher wanted to nip this in the bud. He asked Sartor to look through the photographic exhibits to see if he could find the shoe print.

"You've been asked to look through the photographs that were taken in the basement that day?"

"Uh-huh."

"Have you ever been able to find the print that you believe you saw?"

"No," said Sartor, "not at all."

THAT afternoon, Fletcher and Nolan agreed to a stipulation on some of the arrival times: based on the computerized log, the fire department had been called at 1:40:30 P.M. by Carol; Morris' fire engine had left at 1:42:28; it had arrived at the Escobita house at 1:45:42. That meant that if he hadn't put the shoes and shirt in the truck before the discovery of the body, the only other time he could have done it was between the arrival of the fire department at 1:45:42 and the simultaneous arrival of Officer Tom Pohl and the paramedics at 1:48:21. In between, of course, Sascha Priess had arrived at 1:46:51, and both Priess and Pohl said they'd had Ken under observation from the moment of their respective arrivals.

Now Fletcher called Santa Clara County Medical Examiner Gregory Schmunk. In calling Schmunk, Fletcher had two objectives. The first, of course, was to get Schmunk's expert testimony as to the nature of Kristine's wounds, and the unlikelihood that they had been caused by a fall down the stairs. But because Schmunk had been the first person to notice the possibility of bloodstains in the kitchen, Fletcher also wanted Schmunk to tell the jury how the police had first begun to consider that the kitchen was actually the scene of the murder.

Fletcher asked Schmunk to describe Kristine's injuries. "Basically," Schmunk said, "there was extensive bruising to the face, and there were bruises to the lips. There were burst blood vessels, what we call petechiae, present in the eyes and in the mouth, which indicated there had been a compression of the neck. And there was bruising in seven separate lacerations or tears to the back of the head."

Fletcher now began displaying photographs from the autopsy; the jurors had previously been warned that this would be upsetting, and it was.

One of the injuries to the rear of Kristine's head had caused a skull fracture, Schmunk said.

"Would you please describe the nature of those injuries?"

"One [is a] long laceration which appears to have been received from a dull-end . . . object," Schmunk said. "I'm not talking about anything with a sharp edge, like a knife or a hatchet, or anything like that. We're talking about something like the edge of a table, the edge of a chair, or possibly a two-by-four–type instrument, although this seems sharper than the edge of a standard two-by-four. The other injury is somewhat star-shaped, looks like it would be the end of an object, such as, again, a chair leg, table leg, corner of a desk."

"Doctor, did you notice any injuries to the victim's hands?"

"Around the left ring finger there was bruising," Schmunk said. "This is consistent with what we call a defensive-type injury. This is a wound which would be received when the decedent is either trying to attack her attacker, or fend off blows which are coming at her."

Schmunk said it was his opinion that the strangulation had likely taken less than a minute.

"Doctor, can you tell whether the strangulation occurred before the injuries to her head?"

"We know from the findings that Ms. Fitzhugh was alive, in the sense that her heart was beating and there was blood pressure in her body for both of the events," said Schmunk. "If she would have been strangled after her heart had stopped, and the blood pressure had gone to zero, we would not see the hemorrhages in the neck. Likewise, if she had been strangled to the point of death and her heart stopped beating before the blunt force injury occurred, we would not see the extensive hemorrhage or bleeding that we saw underneath the scalp . . . nor would we expect to see the degree of hemorrhage that we see in the brain."

Schmunk said that meant there were only two possibilities: that Kristine had been strangled into unconsciousness, then beaten about the head; or it was possible that she had been hit first and strangled after. There wasn't any way to know for sure, he said.

This wasn't completely accurate; it was also possible that the strangulation and the injuries to the back of the head could have occurred at the same time, as Schmunk's further testimony would suggest. It was a subtle but important point, because it came to bear on the issue of premeditation: if the injuries were sequential rather than simultaneous, it was stronger evidence of intent to kill. But if the injuries had been inflicted as part of one act of violence, it was possible evidence of an uncontrolled rage. That might mean the difference between murder and manslaughter. But it wasn't in Fletcher's interest to develop this distinction; that was Nolan's job, not his.

Schmunk now gave evidence that this simultaneous injury alternative might actually have been the case:

The injuries inside the brain, he said, suggested that "the head was actually used to strike a surface." The contrecoup damage to the brain indicated that the head was moving when it was struck, Schmunk said. The nature of the injuries, he said, also suggested to him that Kristine had been upright when first struck. It was the sheer number of injuries, both front and back, that made the idea that she had been injured in a fall a non-starter.

"This had become a very suspicious death scene," Schmunk said, after telling the jury how he had happened to come to the house, with Dr. Vertes, on the Sunday following Kristine's death. "When I went to the autopsy room and examined the wounds, I confirmed what I had already known, that these were not consistent with a fall down the stairs."

So by the following day, Schmunk indicated, he was prepared to look for another plausible location for the place where the injuries had occurred by actually going to the Escobita address. This was consistent with a policy he had instituted since becoming the Santa Clara County Medical Examiner, Schmunk said—having the pathologist visit the death location to better understand what had happened.

"I have done it throughout my career," Schmunk told the jury. "I enjoy it. It gives me a lot of insight into how a person has died.

"Once I got to the scene," Schmunk continued, "I accepted that she had been found at the bottom of the stairs, and that the fall scenario was still being considered, so I looked over the scene to determine if there was any blood evidence or any type of situation that made sense for that type of scenario, and I found no evidence at the scene to support a fall down the stairs, and extensive evidence to support the fact that in my opinion it was a staged scene."

This drew Nolan out of his chair with a vehement objection. "This witness has not been qualified to offer an opinion as to whether a scene was 'staged,' " Nolan said. "He's simply not qualified for that."

Elia said he'd decide whether Schmunk's opinion could be considered by the jury after hearing what it was. Nolan, inwardly fuming, sat down; he felt that Elia had missed the point of his objection, and in fact, it appeared that Elia had.

"Why did you say that?" Fletcher asked.

"I have seen hundreds of scenes with dead persons," Schmunk said. "I've also had the opportunity to examine many, many more scenes through photographs . . . and the simple fact that Kristine was at the bottom of the stairs and her head in a pool of blood—supposedly, when she fell down the stairs she was carrying some paper and some dry-cleaning in dry-cleaning bags, and that when she fell, she just sort of fell with her head right on top of this, all these papers and dry-cleaning bags. And that just does not happen. When a person falls down stairs with something in their hands, they don't hold it tightly against their head as they go down, and everything ends up right around their head.

"I also looked at ths scene for evidence of blood transfer or anything that might have occurred from her going down the stairs. I would expect to see blood in several locations as she went down. I didn't see that. I did not see any blood present at the bottom of the stairs other than this pool, and a trail of blood that went off to one side. So there was just nothing to support the fact that this woman actually received her injuries at that point. It just supported the fact that, yes, she was there when she had the injuries, and did bleed out from head wounds."

To Nolan, Schmunk had clearly strayed beyond his province; now he was assuming the role of a crime scene reconstructor. He renewed his objection, asking that this testimony be thrown out by Elia. Elia said he didn't think there was much dispute. "I thought both sides agree that this was somebody [who was] murdered this way," Elia said.

"He said, 'staged scene,' " Nolan said. "That's what I object to, the opinion that it's 'staged.' " Schmunk wasn't qualified to use such a loaded word, Nolan thought.

Elia decided to overrule the objection, but told Nolan he could cross-examine on Schmunk's qualifications as a self-appointed crime scene expert later.

Fletcher continued. He asked Schmunk what sort of blood evidence might be expected if Kristine had been killed in the basement.

Schmunk, over Nolan's continued objections, said he would have expected to see blood spatter from the impacts from Kristine's head wounds. He said he hadn't seen any "cast-off" as he had been expecting.

Having seen no blood spatter in the basement, Fletcher now asked Schmunk, had he then gone into the kitchen area of the house?

Schmunk said he had.

"And did you see anything in the kitchen area that seemed relevant?"

Again Nolan objected. "I think we're getting beyond his expertise as a pathologist," he told Elia once more. Schmunk was not qualified to offer evidence about "blood splatter," he said.

"It's 'blood *spatter*,' not 'splatter,' " Fletcher said. And besides—"Your Honor, he's not blind," meaning Schmunk.

Elia overruled Nolan's objection once more. Schmunk said he'd found "blood spatter" in the kitchen. "Once we had seen blood spatter in that area, we were—both Dr. Vertes and I were highly suspicious that—"

Nolan headed this off with another objection, and this time was sustained by Elia.

"Now, how much blood did she lose before she was placed downstairs?" Nolan asked, when it was his turn.

"I don't believe there's any accurate way of estimating that."

"How much blood did she lose if she was assaulted at the bottom of the stairs?"

"Again, there's no accurate way of estimating that."

"How big were— What would the blood splatters be if she was assaulted upstairs? How much? Would it be on the ceiling, on the walls? How much would it be?"

"It would depend on the nature of the assault."

"So it could be a large amount or a small amount?"

"Correct."

"How much blood would there be downstairs, of a blood splatter, if she was assaulted downstairs?"

"Same would apply," Schmunk said. "It would depend on the nature of the assault."

"Could be a small amount, could be a large amount?"

Now Nolan was zeroing in on his objective—showing the jury that it *was* possible that the attack had occurred in the basement, that, depending on "the nature of the assault," a small amount of blood might be "splattered."

"Correct," said Schmunk.

Nolan wanted to know whether the ship's bell could have caused the injuries, and Schmunk said it wasn't likely—the surface of the brass bell simply wasn't flat enough.

Nolan asked Schmunk to give him some examples of blunt instruments that might have caused the injuries, and Schmunk said he'd already done that—a table, a chair leg, some sort of edged furniture. When pressed, Schmunk said he thought Kristine might have been hit with a lighter object moving at a high rate of speed. That was because only one of the wounds caused a skull fracture, and that injury was more consistent with the head being shoved into an immobile object "rather than the object striking the head."

If it was Nolan's plan to get Schmunk to admit that the missing woodpile hatchet could have caused the wounds, he wasn't succeeding. Schmunk's answer made it sound like the attacker had thrust the back of Kristine's head into a hard object, at least once and probably several times. If a weapon *had* been used, it was used in a very controlled manner, Schmunk said.

This exchange opened a brief window on one of the still-unsolved riddles of the Fitzhugh case—the failure to find a murder weapon. In part because the police believed that Ken had premeditated Kristine's killing, it almost required them to believe that he had used some sort of blunt object as a weapon, such as a two-by-four. But Schmunk's evidence indicated that this might not have been the case—since the most severe injury was the skull fracture to the rear of the head, and the brain showed evidence of being whipped around inside the skull, it seemed more likely that Kristine had been killed when someone smashed her head into a stationary object, such as a table leg or even the floor—probably while the attacker had his hands around her throat.

Taken in summary, in fact, the injuries rather strongly suggested that the attack was actually spontaneous: begun with an attack by fists, which knocked Kristine to the floor, and followed by the attacker putting his hands around her throat and thrusting her head into some hard object. This was potentially quite contrary to the idea of planning: after all, what sort of murderer *plans* to use his bare hands, when a vast array of more suitable objects can be found? That is, if there is planning. But the concept of murder by bare-handed assault didn't fit into either side's theory of the case, so it was not worth exploring further, despite its utility, at least to the defense, as possible evidence in support of the charge of manslaughter.

Nolan spent most of the rest of the afternoon trying to denigrate Schmunk's expertise as an expert on blood spatter, with little to show for it. In the end, he asked Elia to order Schmunk to return with any reports he'd been given that had helped him form his opinion, and with that, the testimony wrapped up for the day.

WHEN testimony resumed, Nolan caught Schmunk short by asking him about his testimony in response to one of Fletcher's questions on the day before. Schmunk, reading from his office's report, had said that Kristine was five feet three inches tall. Nolan knew that was a mistake. Kristine was actually five seven. Schmunk admitted that the measurement taken in the morgue hadn't been accurate, but it was because of changes in the body's posture after death. Still, Nolan's point was made: Schmunk's opinion wasn't necessarily always accurate.

After another morning of wrangling with Schmunk over the nature of Kristine's wounds, Nolan apparently realized that he wasn't getting anywhere; Schmunk was unswerving in his opinion that the missing hatchet, even blunt side up, could not have caused the wounds. Nor could anyone tell the velocity of the major blow to the head, or even much about the direction.

"It would be most consistent with directly into the photograph," Schmunk said, as he inspected one of the autopsy photographs of the wounds.

"In other words, directly down?" Nolan asked.

"Correct."

"It's a direct contact?"

"Not a glancing blow," Schmunk agreed.

"Not a glancing blow," said Nolan. "So it doesn't come across the wound in any direction, it's down on?" Nolan was trying to establish whether the skull fracture blow had been caused by a left- or right-handed person.

"Right," said Schmunk, meaning "correct."

"Can I demonstrate on Mr. Nolan?" Fletcher asked, a jest that indicated his frustration with the pace of questioning.

"That is a soft object," Elia cracked.

"It might be, it might do the trick," Fletcher said.

"No, it's not going to do the trick," Nolan said. "Good luck."

Schmunk finally left the witness stand early that afternoon, to be replaced by the school district's Phyllis Smith. She testified that she'd been alerted to Kristine's absence by the clerk at Addison School, where Kristine was to have taught the 12:50 P.M. music class. The discovery was something of a fluke, Phyllis indicated. The clerk had been delivering invitations to an upcoming school social event when she'd passed the classroom where Kristine was supposed to be teaching, and saw that she wasn't there. The clerk asked the regular teacher where Kristine was, and the teacher, who had taken over the class, told her that Kristine had never arrived. The clerk went back to the school office and telephoned Phyllis.

Phyllis had then called the Fitzhugh house, trying to find Kristine. The answering machine picked up, she said, so she left a message asking Kristine to call her. Then Phyllis called Ken's office number, which also went to the Escobita house. Ken answered. She told him that Kristine had missed the class, and asked if he knew where she was.

Ken told her that he didn't know where Kristine was. He told Phyllis he was on his way home, and would check the house when he arrived. Phyllis said Ken told her he was driving through San Mateo at that moment, so Phyllis assumed that Ken had forwarded his office telephone to his cellular phone, as he had done in the past.

Then she'd called Kristine's cellular number, and was connected with her voicemail—Ken had actually recorded the greeting for Kristine, so she got Ken's recorded voice. She'd left no message because she'd already left one on the home telephone.

Nothing like this had ever happened with Kristine before, Phyllis told Nolan when it was his turn.

"When you talked to Ken on the phone, he did not say to you that he was going to call Kristine at home, did he?" Nolan asked. Nolan was trying to whittle away some of the evidence that Ken had told people—Gaelyn and Carol, for example—that he'd tried to call Kristine himself on his cellular phone while he was returning to Palo Alto. He knew the defense would have to explain why there were no messages from Ken on the answering machine, as Ken himself had initially seemed to suggest there would be.

"I don't recall him saying that," said Phyllis. "I told him I would . . . get back to him. I mean, I am thinking in terms of—"

"Right," said Nolan, cutting her off. He'd gotten what he wanted from Phyllis. Ken had made no statement to her that he intended to call himself to see what was wrong. "We appreciate your testimony very much. Thank you."

Fletcher next called Craig Frost, a telecommunications engineer for the cellular telephone company. Frost gave a primer on how cellular telephone technology worked. As the cellular phone user moved around, the signal from the telephone was picked up by various antennas. Each antenna had three "faces," that is, 120 degrees of arc apiece. Depending on the location of the phone in relation to the antenna, one of the three faces would pick up the signal and pipe it into the telephone system for relay to the call's recipient. As the caller moved around, the signal would be "handed off" from one antenna to the next. The antenna usage left an approximate record of the time and location of each caller as the call unfolded.

When Ken had received the call from Phyllis Smith on his cellular telephone at 1:16 P.M., said Frost, in his opinion, the call had been routed to Ken's portable from the south face of the antenna located near Stanford University, which was about a half-mile north of the Escobita house. That evidence suggested that Ken was actually near the Escobita house when the call was put through—perhaps even inside.

"Is it possible for this call to have been received by the phone assigned to Mr. Fitzhugh while he was in San Mateo?" Fletcher asked.

"My opinion, no," Frost said.

"Okay. You wouldn't go through the south face of the Stanford cell site?"

"If you were in San Mateo?"

"Yes."

"No."

"Is it possible, in your opinion, for the phone assigned to Mr. Fitzhugh to have received this call and generated these records and to be on [Highway] 101 in Redwood City?"

"In my opinion, no."

"On [Highway] 101 at Woodside Road?"

"No."

"Anywhere on 101 in Santa Clara County?"

"Not through the south facing sector, no," said Frost.

Now Fletcher asked if a record would be created by the telephone company if someone had used a cellular telephone to place a call that was picked up by an answering machine, and Frost said yes.

Fletcher had already demonstrated that the answering machine was on, with Phyllis' testimony. Now he had evidence that if Ken had really called the machine, there should have been a record of the call.

Nolan was prepared for this testimony; he'd hired his own expert to see if there was some explanation for why Phyllis' 1:16 P.M. call had gone through the Stanford cell site. He was convinced that the technology sometimes caused calls to be routed through other antennas, particularly if the first-choice antenna was overcrowded.

Under Nolan's questioning, Frost had to admit that the cellular company had never done a study to show how often a call was bumped to another antenna for reasons of overcrowding. Wasn't it true, he asked Frost, that sometimes a call was bumped even when the telephone wasn't moving? Frost said that was known to happen.

In other words, asked Nolan, establishing a person's location by tracing his cellular telephone calls wasn't foolproof? Frost said it wasn't. But he insisted that Ken could not have been returning to Palo Alto from San Bruno when Phyllis' call came through.

"Are you saying that it is impossible, *impossible* for a phone to be at Highway 101 and Woodside Road or Marsh Road and receive a signal from the Stanford site? Is that what you're saying, sir?"

"Yes," said Frost.

"Impossible?"

"I'm saying it's impossible," Frost reiterated.

With that, the testimony from the first week of the trial was concluded.

WHEN the trial resumed the following Monday, Fletcher called Officer Sascha Priess as his next witness. Nolan was looking forward to Priess' testimony; he had an idea that he could exploit it in a way that might buttress Ken's version of the events at the Escobita house.

Priess told of getting the initial call from the dispatcher to go to 1545 Escobita about 1:42 P.M. on May 5. He'd driven to the house, and entered right after the firemen, he said. He had seen Carol Piraino still holding the cordless telephone near the front door. He'd asked Carol where the victim was, and Carol had pointed toward the basement doorway. Priess had gone down the hall and turned onto the landing, and walked partway down the steps.

Fletcher asked Priess who he'd seen in the basement when he first went down the stairs.

"The only people that I recall were the victim and possibly two fire personnel," Priess said. Thus, almost from the start Priess was providing Nolan with his anticipated opening, because Priess made no mention of seeing either Ken or Gaelyn in the basement—which suggested that he hadn't gone down the stairs until some time, perhaps a few minutes, had already passed after his arrival. Nolan intended to show that Ken could have gone to the truck during this short period of time when he was not under Priess' observation.

"You come back up the stairs and you speak to Ms. Piraino, and what happens?" Fletcher asked.

"I ask her what happened, and she says that the victim's husband came home, found his wife at the bottom of the stairs, and that when he came home the front door was open."

"Then what's the next observation that you recall?"

"At that point I'm facing toward the basement and I see a subject come up out of the basement," Priess said.

"Do you see that person in court today?"

"Yes, I do."

"What's that person's name?"

"Mr. Fitzhugh."

"You see Mr. Fitzhugh come up out of the basement, and do you notice anything about his appearance?" Fletcher asked.

"I notice that when he comes up, he comes up like this," Priess said, and he held his hands upright at a ninety degree angle—like a surgeon waiting to be gloved, as Gaelyn had described it.

"And [with] what appears to be blood on his hands," Priess added. "He doesn't say anything as he comes up, and then he turns to his right and walks away from me further down the hallway."

He watched as Ken went into the first-floor bathroom, Priess said.

"So what do you do, at this point?" Fletcher asked.

"At this point, as I step in that direction, I hear a noise behind me and Officer Pohl enters the residence."

So now Fletcher had testimony supporting Gaelyn's observation that Ken had left the basement before she did, and that he had ascended the stairs with his hands up like a surgeon waiting to be gloved, as well as support for Carol Piraino's observations that she saw Ken come up out of the basement with his bloody hands raised, and go into the bathroom. That meant, if the jury believed Priess, there was no time for Ken to go out to the car to deposit the white running shoes, the green shirt and the bloody paper towel, because Pohl had just come in.

But Fletcher had a looming problem: Priess' testimony seemed to contradict that of Carol Piraino on an important point: while Carol had also said she'd seen Ken come up the stairs with his hands raised and go into the bathroom to wash, she'd never mentioned talking to Priess at that point in time, and in fact had said she had gone on to the basement landing to check on Gaelyn. And even Priess had just said that when he first looked in the basement, he saw neither Ken nor Gaelyn. Yet Priess was now saying he too had seen Ken go into the bathroom, hands raised, and that he had been talking to Carol while this was happening.

Fletcher decided to keep going, thinking that he'd straighten the matter out when he was able to put more of the computerized arrival times into evidence. He was still confident that there simply wasn't enough time for Ken to do everything he was saying he'd done between the arrival of the firemen and Pohl's arrival a little over two minutes later, even if Priess' recollection wasn't entirely accurate.

"And so," continued Fletcher, "you hear Officer Pohl. And he is coming in through the front door area?"

"Yes, he is," Priess said.

"So then what happens?"

"Officer Pohl comes in, I tell him that the victim is downstairs in the basement, he passes me and goes down in the basement."

"And what do you do?"

"At that point I'm still speaking with Ms. Piraino," Priess said. "And shortly thereafter Mr. Fitzhugh comes out of the first-level bathroom and walks up the hallway."

"And then what happens? Does he have to actually walk by you at this point, or is he walking toward you?"

"He's walking toward me, not past me. He's walking toward the bathroom. He's coming up to the threshold to the downstairs basement at the same time Officer Pohl comes up."

Boy, this was a mess: It sounded as though Priess had Ken walking simultaneously toward the bathroom and toward the basement landing, which of course were in opposite directions. It was beginning to seem like there had been a platoon of Ken doppelgangers deployed around the house: he was down the stairs to the basement twice, according to one of the firemen; he was going up the basement stairs, according to Gaelyn; he was in the bathroom twice to wash, according to his own story; he was in the kitchen, possibly dripping blood on the floor; he was near the front door talking to the police or firemen, according to Carol; he was out at the Suburban, depositing his bloody shirt, shoes and paper towel, while checking on the dogs, again according to his own story; he had disappeared completely for some short period of time, also according to Carol Piraino.

"And what happens?" Fletcher asked. He had to keep on going.

"Officer Pohl confronts Mr. Fitzhugh and they began to talk, and they keep on walking toward me in the hallway. At that point I ask Ms. Piraino for the cordless telephone, and I walk down the hallway."

At that point, Priess said, he'd entered the family room and called the station, informing Agent Buck that the scene looked suspicious because there was too much blood.

When he finished the call, said Priess, he left the family room and returned to the hallway. As he walked back down the hallway, the paramedics were arriving with their collapsible gurney. A few minutes later, the firemen came up the stairs and told Priess that Kristine was dead.

"What happens next?"

"At that point the paramedics take the gurney and begin to go back out of the residence. Mr. Fitzhugh comes from the dining room area of the hallway and rushes toward the basement threshold. And he mentions something of the fact that 'I knew she was dead,' or something similar to that."

"And then what happens?"

"Mr. Fitzhugh goes back into the landing and gets onto the first step of the basement stairs, and Officer Pohl gets hold of him and escorts him back to the foyer area."

Curiouser and curiouser: now Priess had Pohl twice accosting Ken on the basement landing, the second time after Ken had been in the dining room, and this, a few minutes *after* the paramedics had arrived.

If anything, Priess' testimony threatened to widen the window for Ken to get out to the truck, or so it appeared.

When it was his turn, Nolan tried to zero in on what he thought were the discrepancies in Priess' testimony.

"Do you recall," he asked, "at the beginning of your testimony, the district attorney asked you some questions about the circumstances surrounding your entry into the residence on May fifth, 2000?"

"That's correct."

"Your testimony in that regard was not complete, was it, sir?" Nolan asked.

Fletcher objected, saying that Priess could only respond to questions he was asked.

But Nolan was trying to make a point: he did not believe that Priess' testimony while under Fletcher's questioning completely accounted for everyone's movements in the confusing minutes after Ken had first walked up the stairs with his bloody hands raised. By artful questioning, Nolan implied, Priess had been permitted to leave some things out.

Priess now testified that he'd entered the house, walked down the hallway, asked Carol where the victim was, followed her pointing hand to the basement door, and then—

"She pointed toward the basement, and then what did you see?" Nolan asked.

"I walked down the hallway—" Priess began.

"Excuse me," Nolan interrupted. "I asked you, 'what did you see?' *Who* did you see?"

"In the hallway?"

"Right," Nolan said. "Then *who* did you see in the hallway?"

"Actually, I—"

"Who did you see in the hallway, sir?"

"I actually made an error in my report," Priess said.

"Who did you see in the hallway?" Nolan persisted.

"Let him answer the question," Fletcher called out.

Justice Elia intervened. "He's just asking you, who did you see?" he said. "If you didn't see anybody, that's fine. If you did, tell us who it is."

"Actually, there's an error," Priess repeated.

"Excuse me, sir," Nolan said once again. "I think the judge just said: who did you see?"

"I did not see anybody," Priess admitted.

"No one at all, is that correct?"

"That's correct," Priess said.

"You know that for a fact, do you not?"

"I recall it happening."

"Do you know it for a fact?"

"Yes, I do."

"You prepared a report of the events that took place in this case on May twelfth, year 2000, isn't that correct?"

"That's correct."

"And at that time you had no notes, did you?"

"I had some notes."

"Where are those notes, sir?"

"Long gone. I shredded them."

"When did you shred them, sir?"

"Shortly after I finished the report."

Nolan asked Priess if he had been trained to prepare accurate reports, and Priess admitted that he had.

"And since the time of preparing your report," Nolan continued, "you in fact heard that Mr. Fitzhugh said he went out to the car and he put things in the car, checking on the dogs, that he walked out there, he had a paper towel, that he had shoes, he went out to the car. You've heard that, have you not?"

"I have heard that," Priess said.

Nolan asked if, when he'd prepared his report on May 12, Priess hadn't yet had a chance to read any newspaper accounts about Ken's claim that he'd gone out to the car twice, that he hadn't had a chance to talk to either Denson or Fletcher about any problems with his report, and Priess admitted that he had not.

"And at that time," Nolan pressed on, "May twelfth, one week after this event, you said: 'I asked Piraino where the female victim was, she pointed toward the basement doorway. I then saw another female subject later identified as Gaelyn Mason standing in the hallway.' Isn't that correct?"

"That's what I wrote in my report," Priess admitted.

"You wrote that in your report, correct?"

"That's in error," Priess said.

Now Nolan had succeeded in introducing another element of reasonable doubt into the equation: if Priess' original report, written a week after the event, said he'd seen Gaelyn Mason in the hallway with Carol Piraino, that had to have happened after Ken and Gaelyn had separately left the basement. If Gaelyn was present, therefore, Priess could not have seen Ken come up the steps, bloody hands raised, and go into the bathroom to wash, because Gaelyn had seen the same thing from the basement floor, and Gaelyn could not be in two places at the same time.

Had Ken, in fact, already been in the bathroom and was he actually out at the Suburban, depositing bloody shirt and shoes and paper towel, while Priess continued on his way past Carol Piraino and Gaelyn Mason to the basement? And was Priess' report, indicating that when he first saw Carol, she was with Gaelyn, evidence that Priess' entry into the house had come *after* Gaelyn had left the basement by the storm doors and entered the dining room? If that was the case, wouldn't there have been enough time for Ken to go out to the Suburban, come back into the house, re-enter the bathroom, wash up a second time, and then emerge to encounter Pohl? If Priess had seen Gaelyn with Carol, how could he also have seen Ken come up the stairs, bloody hands raised? Was the vaunted computerized arrival log in error? Or was Priess simply collapsing the order of the events as part of the "rush to judgment"?

Priess indicated that when he'd written that he'd seen Gaelyn Mason with Carol Piraino in the hallway, he'd made a mistake; actually, he'd first seen Carol, and Gaelyn only later.

Nolan now asked when Priess had discovered that he had made a mistake in his report. Priess said he'd only discovered the mistake in recent weeks.

"When you read your report," Nolan asked, "this is the first time, now, you discovered you've made an error in your report. Is that correct?"

"That's correct," Priess said.

"Who did you tell?"

"Actually, at first I didn't tell anyone."

"Who did you first tell?"

"Later on I told the district attorney."

Nolan asked where this conversation had occurred, and Fletcher objected, saying it was irrelevant. But Elia instructed Priess to answer.

Priess said he'd told Fletcher about his error while they were at the police station about a week before the trial, while

Fletcher was going over the questions he intended to ask Priess.

Now Nolan tried to get Priess to admit that it might have been four or five minutes before Pohl arrived at the front door in time to see Ken emerge from the bathroom. Priess insisted that Pohl had come into the house only a minute or two behind him.

Nolan continued pressing Priess. He asked if it was true that it was only after seeing Gaelyn and Carol in the hallway that he'd then gone into the basement for the first time. Priess said that was what he'd had in his report, all right.

"You didn't see Mr. Fitzhugh down there, did you?" Nolan asked.

"No, I did not," Priess said.

Nolan asked if Priess had gone partway down the stairs before coming up once again, and Priess said that was true, too.

"Now, at this point you walked back up the stairs into the hallway, and you asked Ms. Piraino what happened?"

Priess said that was so; he and Carol had been standing near the stairway to the upper floor. Priess said he had his back to the front door and was facing down the hallway. That was when he'd seen Ken come up out of the basement with his bloody hands raised, Priess said.

But Nolan pressed Priess again: wasn't it true that he did not know for sure that Ken had come out of the basement at that time? Priess admitted that he hadn't actually seen Ken come up the stairs.

Now Nolan sprang his trap.

"And now," he said, "show me in your report, if you would, please, where you describe his hands, as you described them on direct examination."

"I don't," Priess admitted.

"You don't?"

"It's not noted in my report."

PRIESS' imprecision in writing his report on May 12 had given Nolan an opening. Not only did the discrepancy leave wiggle room for Ken to claim he had gone to the truck either before Priess' arrival, or while Priess was briefly in the basement, it also underscored the theme he wanted to drive home: that the police investigation had been sloppy. Reasonable doubt, reasonable doubt, that was what the game was all about: or so ran the defense lawyers' refrain.

Fletcher still believed he could put a patch on this potential puncture well before the air ran out of his case. So what if Priess had smashed together some of the events? Despite this, there was simply overwhelming evidence, in his opinion, that Ken could not have gone to the Suburban with the shirt, shoes and towel at any time after the arrival of the firemen. Even in the best of all possible worlds, Ken would have had to ascend the stairs, wash off the blood, go into the kitchen for a paper towel, go down the hallway; find the bloody shoes (wherever they had been, if not in the upstairs closet) open the front door, go out to the truck, put the towel and shoes and shirt inside, and return to the house, go back into the kitchen to get a second paper towel, then back to the bathroom to wash up one more time, emerge into the hallway once more, and head toward the basement landing, all from 1:45:42 P.M., when the firemen first arrived at the scene, to 1:48:21 P.M. when Pohl came through the front door—a span of 2 minutes, 39 seconds. And he would have had to do all this without Priess, Carol or Gaelyn seeing him carrying anything other than his own bloody hands. It was simply impossible. Not only that, it did absolutely nothing to alter the principal piece of evidence: that someone had moved Kristine's body after the murder, and had tried to clean up after himself.

Over the next several days, Fletcher concentrated on getting the rest of the physical evidence in—mostly the blood. Priess testified as to how the evidence-recording process worked, Agent Gary Brooks talked about his discovery of the telltale running shoes under the seat, Agent Sandra Brown about her "rediscovery" of the shoes and the bloody paper towel; Con Maloney was called to tell how he'd swabbed the kitchen floor, recovering the 144 different swabs, sample and control. Fletcher called the Fitzhugh house cleaner, who testified that she cleaned the kitchen floors with a wet mop on a regular basis—once a week, in fact, on Mondays. Fletcher also called another telephone expert, who said that if a person using a cellular telephone called a number hooked up to an answering machine, the telephone system would have a record of the call if the machine picked up; and another Palo Alto police officer, Robert Bonilla, who said that a bloodstained portion of the Escobita house kitchen flooring had been taken up and submitted for DNA testing to the crime lab. All of this was tedious, but necessary to show where the evidence against Ken had come from.

Fletcher concluded this portion of his case with testimony from a San Jose Police Department crime scene expert. Todd Lonac was a blood spatter expert. He and a second officer had come to the Escobita house on Saturday, May 6, at the request of the Palo Alto department. At this point, of course, Schmunk hadn't looked at the kitchen, and the Palo Alto police were still puzzled at the apparent lack of blood spatter in the basement. They wanted Lonac—who had experience with more than seventy suspicious death investigations, including a number that involved battering and consequent blood spatter—to look over the basement to see if he could help explain what happened.

Lonac now testified that he spent less than an hour in the basement, inspecting "boxes, and cabinets and walls and floors and the like, looking for blood spatter."

"Why were you looking for blood spatter?" Fletcher asked.

"Because, an assault of that nature, I would expect to find blood spatter consistent with a bludgeoning," Lonac said.

He and the second officer had looked all around the basement, Lonac said.

"Did you find any evidence of blood spatter?" Fletcher asked.

"No," Lonac said. Nowhere in the basement or the stairwell did he find any blood that looked as though it had landed with the sort of velocity he would expect from spatter, he added. At that point, he said, he'd recommended that the Palo Alto police call in Schmunk.

The following Tuesday, May 9, he'd returned to the house with another San Jose officer, and they had helped Maloney and his men locate the blood spatter there.

On his cross-examination, Nolan tried to induce Lonac to say that the absence of blood spatter in the basement didn't necessarily mean that Kristine wasn't killed there; Lonac admitted that it would depend on the manner of the attack, but reiterated that, given the wounds Kristine had sustained, he would still expect to see some blood spatter if she'd actually been attacked in the basement.

Nolan turned to the supposed bloody tennis shoe print that Fireman Sartor thought he'd seen, and hit a clunker: Lonac said the supposed shoe print didn't look anything like a shoe print to him.

Nolan tried another tack: would Kristine's attacker have sustained injuries to his hands, especially with all the bruising to her face? It was possible, Lonac said, but it depended on "variables." One such variable was whether the attacker was wearing gloves, but Nolan didn't ask and Lonac didn't volunteer this. Fletcher knew that Ken had complained to the police that a pair of gardening gloves was missing from the house; he'd find a way later to suggest that Ken had been wearing the missing gloves when he'd attacked Kristine; this itself, Fletcher felt, was possible evidence of premeditation.

Nolan continued with his cross-examination. What about the other evidence found in the basement, such as the broken

eyeglasses and earring? Wouldn't that indicate that the attack
had occurred in the basement? Lonac said it was possible, but
that the information had to be combined with the entire scene
for a proper interpretation.

After this fairly extended run of technical testimony, Fletcher
wanted to move back to the human element of his case; he
knew that there was nothing more tedious to a jury than long,
complicated, dull, scientific testimony. What the jury wanted
to know was what happened, and why.

Fletcher now called Tracy Wang, the Fitzhugh neighbor
who had told police that she'd seen a blue Suburban parked
on the street behind the Fitzhugh house on May 5. She said
that she'd seen the large vehicle parked in front of the property
behind the Escobita house around noon on the day of the murder. The implication was that Ken had hidden the truck so he
could conceal himself in the Escobita house, and still have an
alibi after the killing.

When it was his turn, Nolan tried to show that originally
Tracy had said that she'd seen the truck around ten in the
morning, and that when she'd come back to her house, after
2 P.M., the truck was gone. Widening the window of time
made it less likely that the truck Tracy had seen was that of
Ken Fitzhugh. Nolan tried to get Tracy to say that she'd re-
fined her story *after* Ken was arrested, when she knew that
the noon hour was the critical time for the truck to have been
at the scene—more than two weeks after the event. Tracy admitted that she'd read some of the newspaper articles, including the police theory as to when the crime had occurred. But
she said her recollection wasn't influenced by what she'd read.

Fletcher next called Carol Gossett, the manager of the
Family Golf Center driving range in San Bruno. Carol said
she knew Ken quite well, from his previous work on the property. Because she'd been instructed to keep people out of the
dirt area of the site, she made a practice of watching it closely.
But on May 5, she said, she never saw Ken.

"Did you ever speak to Ken Fitzhugh that day?" Fletcher
asked.

"No."

"Did he ever come by the office, to your knowledge, and speak to anybody on that day?"

"No."

There wasn't much Nolan could do with this testimony; about all he could manage was to ask Carol whether Ken would have talked to her anyway, if he knew that Family Golf Centers didn't actually own the property—thereby suggesting that Ken might have been there, regardless, but just hadn't talked to Carol Gossett. It was weak, but it was the best that could be done.

Following Carol Gossett, Fletcher called yet another Carol who knew Ken: Carol Gibson, who had a Palo Alto dog grooming business. This Carol had the account, if that's the right word, for Boots and Reina. On March 7, 2000, Carol said, Ken had brought Boots in for grooming.

"And did Mr. Fitzhugh say anything, or did you hear him say anything, relative to the next time he would be back in the shop?" Fletcher asked.

"He said his wife was not going to be here the next time the dog was due in," Carol said.

"Did he make any mention [of] where she would be?"

"He mentioned Placerville," Carol said.

This was potentially damaging testimony for Ken. After all, this sounded as if he and Kristine had been intending to split up, and that Kristine had intended to go to Placerville—and Brown.

Nolan tried to blunt this by inducing Carol to admit that, first, she had only relayed the statement to police in September 2000—seven months after Ken had supposedly said this, and five months after Kristine had been killed—and further, that Ken had made the statement to another person, and that she had only overheard it.

Nolan asked Carol if she knew where Kristine was on April 14, 2000, which was one of the Fitzhughs' days to bring the dogs in for grooming, according to Carol's records. Carol said she didn't know.

In fact, Nolan had evidence of where Kristine was "the next time" Ken brought Boots in for grooming: according to the Fitzhugh family calendar, Kristine had noted that she and

Ken were to be in Stockton for the University of the Pacific's family weekend. When the time was right, he intended to introduce that calendar to show that, far from rushing off to Placerville to be with Brown (or anyone else, for that matter), Kristine had planned to be in Stockton with Justin and Ken. In that way, he hoped to blunt the implication that Kristine had intended to leave Ken.

As Carol left the stand, Fletcher called as his next witness Robert Brown's aunt, Janet Moore; he had decided to bring Janet on before her nephew to help set up Brown's testimony.

In Fletcher's eyes, Janet Moore was a sweet, mature woman who appeared to be utterly guileless; no one, he would say later, would ever doubt her sincerity; this would help bolster credibility of her somewhat ne'er-do-well nephew, he believed.

Janet said she'd known the Fitzhughs, both Ken and Kristine, since the early 1970s. She had met them through her nephew, Robert Brown. Once, in fact, she'd spent a week at Ken and Kristine's house in San Diego. When she'd first met them, Janet said, the Fitzhughs had no children. Over the years, she had seen Kristine with Ken, with Robert, and occasionally, by herself.

She had come to know Justin, as well, after he was born; in fact, when she had married in 1982, Ken, Kristine and Justin had all stayed at her home.

"Was there ever an occasion when Kristine told you who the father of Justin was?" Fletcher asked.

Nolan objected, but Elia overruled.

"She didn't tell me directly," Janet said, "she told my mother . . . she said that she wanted my mother to meet her grandson."

Obviously this wasn't right; Janet meant great-grandson, since Robert Brown was Janet's mother's grandson, that is, the child of Janet's sibling. Well, it was confusing, all right. But Fletcher didn't think any real harm was done—the jury knew what Janet meant.

Now Fletcher produced three photographs, and asked Janet if she'd seen them before.

Yes, she had, Janet said. "They came from a party at my

mother's house," she said. "Kristine, Bob and Justin came to the party." It was, Janet said, her mother's 76th birthday.

"There's a small boy in the picture . . . with blond hair," Fletcher said. "Who's that?"

"Justin," said Janet.

"And he's in somebody's arms. Who is that?"

"Robert Brown, my nephew."

"And seated next to your nephew is a woman with a nice smile. Who is that?"

"Kristine Fitzhugh," Janet said.

Now came the moment that the news media had been waiting for: the star witness. Robert Kenneth Brown, Kristine Fitzhugh's one-time lover and the father of her child, took the witness stand.

In his lifetime, Brown had suffered a vast assortment of broken bones—from a motor vehicle accident that had once broken his legs and back, from the time at the beach when Ken had run over his foot with the car, to his most recent crash on the motorcycle, from which he was still recovering. As he approached the stand, stooped, his painful limp was obvious, as was the wooden cane that bore his weight. Once a burly bear of a man, Brown now appeared battered by time, almost fragile. It was difficult to believe that this man had once been so vibrant, so full of life, that he and Kristine had for years been lovers.

Answering softly, almost mumbling, Brown responded to Fletcher's questions. Had he known the Fitzhughs? When and how had they met? Were they good friends? Did Ken and Kristine have any children before he met them? Had they all invested in things together? As he replied, Brown bit by bit sketched in a portrait of the lives that had been led by Aardvark, Snake and Weasel.

"Can you think of anybody in your life," asked Fletcher, "who's been a closer friend to you than Kristine Fitzhugh?"

"No," Brown said.

"Did you and Kristine—did your friendship develop into more than just a friendship—did it become intimate?"

"Yes."

"You were aware that she was married?"

"Yes, sir."

"To your knowledge, was Mr. Fitzhugh aware that you were being intimate with Kristine at that time?"

"Not to my knowledge."

"Did Kristine become pregnant during the period of time consistent with you having sexual intimacy with her?" Fletcher's question, while hardly artful, at least got the point across.

"Yes," Brown said.

Fletcher now showed Brown a photograph of Brown, Kristine, Schaide and two other people taken at a friend's chalet in Aspen, Colorado. The photograph was taken while Kristine was pregnant with Justin, Brown said.

"And after Justin was born, did Kristine ever make a comment to you to indicate that you were the father of Justin?"

"Yes."

"Can you tell us what your recollection is about that?"

Now Nolan lodged his first objection. The sought-after testimony was hearsay, Nolan said, and shouldn't be allowed. Elia said he'd already ruled on this issue before the trial. The record protected, Nolan sat down once more.

"She told me," Brown said, "that she was positive I was the father, because she had quit taking the birth control pills, and that she hadn't had sex with anyone but me for a period of four months or so before she was diagnosed as pregnant."

"Were you convinced at that time that you were actually the father?"

"I didn't know for sure."

Over the next hour or so, Fletcher took Brown through his relationship with the Fitzhughs after Justin's birth.

"Had a lot of fun together?" he asked.

"Great time," Brown said, mumbling again.

Fletcher now wanted to be sure that he was the one who first asked the hardest questions of Brown.

"Mr. Brown," he asked, "how did it feel to you to be involved with another man's wife?"

Nolan objected on the grounds of relevance—Brown's feelings were beside the point. Besides, *he* wanted to use this aspect of the relationship to make Brown look bad, if he could.

Letting Fletcher do it for him would take the sting out of it.

Fletcher said he wanted to show the bias of his own witness—a rather unusual maneuver, but allowable. Elia said he could go ahead.

"You were having sex with somebody else's wife?" he asked.

"Yes, sir," Brown said.

"You know she is married?"

"Yes."

"And the husband is a very good friend of yours?"

"Yes."

"Did it ever trouble you that you were doing that?"

"Yes," Brown said. "I have felt guilt about it, yes."

This out of the way, Fletcher now asked Brown if Kristine had ever come to see him—without Ken—when he lived in Fresno. Brown said that she had, with Justin. Fletcher showed Brown the snapshot taken of Brown, Kristine and Justin, and Brown identified everyone in the picture.

Now Fletcher showed Brown the diamond ring that had been taken from Kristine's left hand after her death.

"It appears to be the ring I gave her," Brown said, his voice breaking and trailing off. "One of them."

"Who told your grandmother she had a great-grandson?"

"Kristine," Brown said.

"Mr. Brown, while you lived in Fresno, did you begin consuming drugs and alcohol to an extent that it became a significant problem in your life?"

"In Fresno?"

"Yes."

"Yes."

"And did it impact your professional life?"

"Yes."

"You were a lawyer at the time?"

"Yes, sir."

"How did it impact your professional life?"

"I flatly made a lot of mistakes," said Brown, "and made some large errors, and it caused me to lose my business, eventually lose my home, and I lost my health, and eventually I lost my best friends."

"And was anybody forcing you to take drugs or alcohol?"

"No, sir. I have no one to blame but myself for that."

"You were ultimately disbarred from being a lawyer, because of various acts of misconduct?"

"Yes, sir."

"Do you have anybody to blame for those?"

"Myself," Brown said. "Nobody forced me to do any of this. I made mistakes on my own, and I am responsible for them."

Fletcher took Brown through the litany of his past mistakes, leading up to his recent plea of guilty on the illegal use of someone else's car in Placerville in 1999.

Fletcher turned to the question of how Brown had found out about Kristine's death. Brown said he'd gone into a state of shock at the news, and that at first he couldn't believe it. He'd just gotten out of the hospital after his motorcycle wreck, and was taking pain medications, which made the whole thing seem even more surreal, when he first heard of Kristine's death from his aunt Janet Moore.

Fletcher now asked whether Brown had ever had contact with Kristine after he'd moved to Placerville in 1997. He said he'd sent two postcards, each time indicating his new address and telephone number, including one in December of 1999.

"In December of 1999, January of 2000, after sending a card indicating your new address, did you receive a phone call from Kristine Fitzhugh?"

"I had sent a card," Brown said, "indicating that I was doing better, that I had quit everything, and that I had moved ... and so when I got the phone call from her, she said, 'I got the letter. I am not home. Justin is graduating in June. You and your aunt are invited up. How are you doing?' I said fine. She said, 'Will you be coming to his graduation?' and then I said yes. And she said at some point after graduation she intended to tell Justin."

"Tell Justin what?"

"About who his biological father was—me."

FLETCHER now took Brown through his conversations with Denson in June of the year 2000. Brown admitted that he had first told Denson that he hadn't talked to Kristine in four years. Brown hadn't told Denson that he'd heard from Kristine only five months earlier, had he?

"No, I didn't," Brown said.

"Why is that?"

"The only reason I can think of," Brown said, "is [that] I didn't think it was important, and I was—wasn't asked the question directly, and I was under the influence of these strong medications. I barely remembered the interviews at all. I remember them, but if it weren't for the transcript, I would have very great difficulty with it."

"Is it true Kristine made this phone call?"

"Yes."

"Any question in your mind about it?"

"No," Brown said.

Now it was Nolan's turn. There was really only one thing he could do with Brown, but it was one of the most important tasks he faced during the whole trial: he had to show that Brown was an unreliable witness, and that he was either wrong or lying about the December/January telephone call from Kristine.

Nolan began by asking why, if he'd sent a card to Kristine with his telephone number on it, the number wasn't written down in the family telephone list kept by Kristine. Brown said he had no way of knowing where Kristine would have kept his number.

Brown had said he received this telephone call around the

time of his birthday, January 21. Wasn't that so? Brown said the call had come before his birthday. He thought it had come before Christmas, but after he'd moved. He'd moved around December 7, 1999, and then had sent the card, he said.

Nolan wanted to know if Brown had ever told anyone that the call might have been in December of 1999, not January of 2000. Brown said that was what he'd told Fletcher and Denson. Nolan was trying to suggest to the jury that Brown's "recollection" of the date of the crucial phone call was sufficiently slippery as to be untrustworthy.

Didn't Brown know that there had been an agreement between the prosecution and the defense that the Fitzhugh telephone records showed there was no call to Brown's number in January, February or March of 2000? Nolan asked.

"Was I told there was an agreement between counsel?" Brown asked. He was befuddled by Nolan's abrupt switch of topic to the lawyers' agreement, which had had nothing to do with him.

"Right," Nolan said. He wanted the jury to get the idea that when he found out there weren't any telephone records for January, February and March, Brown had conveniently moved the telephone call to a month in which there were no records. This was a bit of slipperiness on Nolan's own part, because the transcript of the May 10, 2001, conversation between Denson and Brown clearly showed that Brown had said the call could have been made in December, and since Nolan had the transcript himself, he had reason to know that. Or perhaps Nolan had failed to adequately prepare for this critical witness, which seems unlikely.

"That there was [an agreement]," Nolan continued, "or you were told, that the records didn't reflect the phone call in January by—"

"I knew that," Brown broke in. "She told me she wasn't at home when she called me."

"I see," Nolan said, making his disbelief obvious with his tone. "She told you—"

"She said, 'I am not at home. I only have a minute.' And the phone call proceeded."

"And she wasn't on her cellphone?"

"I don't know what phone she was on."

"I am asking you whether or not Mr. Fletcher or Mr. Denson told you that there were no records of her phone call in January," Nolan said.

"I believe they did tell me," Brown said. "That doesn't surprise me. She told me she wasn't on her home phone, and she wasn't on a cellphone. She was at friends'."

"I see," Nolan said again. "*Now* she told you she wasn't on a cellphone either?"

"She didn't tell me that," Brown said. Brown may once have been an attorney, but he was in no shape to bandy words with Nolan. All Nolan had to do was bait Brown, and Brown rushed into the gap with information he had no way of backing up. This, indeed, was how to discredit a witness—make it seem like he was making things up as he went along. But Brown was literally correct: he hadn't said that Kristine said she wasn't using a cellular phone. He'd only said that Kristine had said she was at some friends' house, nothing more. Brown had simply inferred that she wasn't on a cellular phone.

As his cross examination continued, Nolan tried to make Brown look as if he was retaliating against Ken for his banishment from the Fitzhugh home in the mid-1990s.

"You were very upset, were you not, that he didn't let you know, so you could come to [Kristine's memorial] services, correct?"

"I don't recall saying that," Brown said. "I was upset that I wasn't invited to come, yes."

"Then a phone call was made by you to the police in response to a card they left?" This made it sound like the only reason Brown had called the police was because he hadn't been invited to the memorial service.

"It was not, 'and *then*,' " Brown said, getting upset. "I did make a phone call to the police in response to a card left on my window. The chronological order is out, and you're out of—out of line on that. That is not the way it went. I didn't call the police after Ken Fitzhugh called me."

After this, Nolan began a game of verbal three-card monte with Brown, with the cards being the dates of his various conversations with Denson and Kristine. By switching his questions around between the dates and the years, it appeared that Nolan's purpose was to confuse Brown into making a mistake, so he could then hammer him with new questions. Brown tried valiantly to keep up with the moving times and dates, and for the most part, managed to stay with Nolan. At one point Nolan suggested that Brown was saying he'd received a telephone call from Kristine in January of 2001, when, of course, Kristine had been dead for seven months.

Fletcher finally interposed an objection, and said that Nolan was misstating the evidence.

Nolan asked Brown about his May 9 conversation with Fletcher, the one he'd had after Denson suggested that Fletcher call him. Brown said he'd had a number of conversations with Fletcher. Nolan asked how long the conversation had lasted. Brown said he had no idea, that he didn't keep a diary of all his telephone conversations.

"You can't say it lasted an hour?" asked Nolan. "You can't say it lasted three minutes? Is that correct?" Nolan was hoping to get an answer that would allow him to suggest that Fletcher had prepped him on what to say about Kristine's supposed phone call.

"I don't recall," Brown said. Nolan had at last succeeded in forcing Brown into that most unsatisfactory refrain.

"So you can't give us any idea?"

"I can't recall. I have had many conversations, and I can't recall how long each one took."

"Have you ever read a transcript of the conversation you had with Mr. Fletcher?"

Fletcher objected. Nolan's question assumed there was a transcript; there wasn't.

"Assumes facts not in evidence," he said.

"No, it doesn't," Nolan said.

Nolan and Fletcher now started to argue with each other, which made Elia mad. "Do you gentlemen mind [not] dealing with the objections yourselves?"

At length, Fletcher made it clear that he had talked to Brown on May 9.

"I didn't know that," Nolan said.

Nolan went on. Wasn't it true that Brown himself believed

that Kristine would never have told anybody that he was Justin's biological father? Brown said he didn't believe that.

Well, said Nolan, wasn't it true that he'd told a defense investigator in January of 2001 that Kristine would never have told Justin the truth?

"I don't believe so," Brown said. "I don't recall."

Nolan found a document prepared by his private investigator, who had attempted to interview Brown in January. The investigator had reported that Brown had told him Kristine would never tell Justin the truth about his paternity.

Nolan now asked whether Kristine had insisted that he keep their affair secret, and Brown said that was so. Nolan asked if Brown was perceived to be gay, and Brown said not to "outward appearances." He wasn't gay, he was bisexual, he said.

Now Nolan peppered Brown with the inconsistencies between his first statements to Denson, and the new statements made nearly a year later. Brown said he was under the influence of the pain drugs, so some of the first statements were wrong.

Nolan asked Brown for a single instance in which Kristine had ever told anyone other than Brown that Justin was his son. Brown, getting tired, apparently misunderstood the question. He said Kristine had told Schaide, among others, while on the Newport–Ensenada yacht race in 1975. That couldn't be right, because it was three years before Justin was born. Apparently Brown was thinking of when Kristine had told others that she and Brown were having an affair.

But hadn't Brown told Denson that he'd "maintained the silence" about the affair, and kept quiet about Justin's paternity, to comply with Kristine's wishes? Even when Denson asked him point-blank in June of 2000?

"Yes," Brown said. "I was trying to— At that time I believe I was worried about—It's a touchy subject. I didn't want her reputation tramped into the ground. I loved the whole family. I didn't want any—any more bad publicity. I didn't know. I didn't say anything more than I had to."

THAT ended the testimony for Wednesday, July 11, 2001. It was no surprise that the news media played Brown's testimony big. The *Palo Alto Daily News* headlined:

'The other man' takes the stand,
Leaning heavily on a wooden cane, Robert Brown limped to the witness stand yesterday to tell jurors a secret he'd kept for decades, a confidence the prosecution says is the key to Kristine Fitzhugh's slaying. . . .
Brown testified yesterday that Kristine Fitzhugh, his long-time lover, told him several months before her death that she planned to tell Justin the truth around the time he graduated from the University of the Pacific in Stockton. The Palo Alto music teacher was found dead in her Escobita Avenue home on May 5, 2000, two weeks before the graduation . . .

Ex-lover testifies at trial, the *San Francisco Chronicle* reported. **DNA proves witness fathered woman's son**
Could it get much worse than this? Not only was Kristine's secret out, it was being spread all over the public prints and airwaves; if Ken really hoped to keep this all quiet by killing Kristine, it hadn't worked, that was for sure. And beyond what people now knew or were saying lay the real tragedy, not the apparent one: Kristine was dead, the boys had no mother, Ken was on trial for his life and the most favorable outcome would be going broke to stay out of prison. No, it couldn't get much worse than that. Not a bit worse.

When Brown was finished—not before Nolan had raked him over all his past peccadilloes to remind the jury that Brown

had on occasion in the past told less than the whole truth—
Fletcher was ready for his next witnesses. From here on in,
almost everything would depend on proof found in the blood:
swabs, paternity, luminol and all their permutations—after
that, the ball would be in Nolan's side of the court, to see if
he could refute the state's case.

Fletcher called Cynthia Hall, the DNA expert from the
Santa Clara Crime Lab. It had been Cyndi who had tested most
of the swabs taken by Maloney and his merry men on the
week after the murder; it was also Cyndi who'd subjected
many of the same swabs to the DNA testing that proved it had
been Kristine's blood in the kitchen.

It appeared that Fletcher had prepared for a long siege of
qualifying DNA as acceptable science, and Ms. Hall as an
expert, because he was thrown for a loop when Elia summoned
him and Nolan to the bench for a sidebar conference. Perhaps
Elia wanted to cut through all the scientific mumbo-jumbo
about DNA, because when he was finished, the two lawyers
agreed to stipulate that bodily fluids had been taken from Ken,
Kristine, Bob Brown and Justin, that all the samples had been
tested by Cyndi Hall in the Santa Clara Crime Lab.

"That should save us a few hours," said Elia. "And of
course this witness' expertise is also stipulated by both sides—
that she's an expert in DNA analysis, is that correct?"

Nolan agreed to this, and so did Fletcher. "Yes, Your
Honor," he said. "Let me try to collect myself. My plan's been
blown, now." Now that Elia had truncated his presentation,
Fletcher had to think on his feet to figure out how to get started
again.

He began by asking Cyndi to identify the tests she had
done on various swabs, starting with those found on the first
floor, with the intention of working his way through the entire
group of sixty stains that had tested positive for Kristine's
blood. At one point Fletcher pulled out his diagram, the one
Maloney had prepared from the blueprints Denson had obtained—the diagram with all the red circles showing where
Kristine's blood had been found. But Elia, still anxious to cut
to the chase, interrupted. The chart, with the enlarged red cir-

cles, made it look as if Kristine had shed copious amounts of blood in the kitchen, even though it represented only microscopic traces.

"Counsel," he said, "I want to make sure I understand this. This diagram has circles, red circles. Wherever it's circled in red, that means the test showed that that's Kristine Fitzhugh's blood?"

"That's correct," said Fletcher.

"What are we doing here?" asked Elia. "Why go through every one of them? Can she just testify that every one of them is presumptively positive for blood?"

Fletcher said they could do that, but he didn't want to be attacked because they hadn't done DNA tests on *all* of the swabs, just a representative sample. To avoid that, he said, he wanted to demonstrate the tests that had been done.

"All right, go ahead," Elia sighed.

Eventually, Fletcher finished all the swabs from the various parts of the house, and turned to the running shoes. "Did you do an examination of the shoes that were submitted to you?"

When Hall said yes, she'd examined the white running shoes, Fletcher asked her what she had discovered. The blood on the running shoes, she said, had come from Kristine Fitzhugh. What about the green polo shirt found wadded up under the seat? There too, said Cyndi, the blood had come from Kristine.

Fletcher now asked whether Cyndi had tested the DNA of Ken Fitzhugh, Justin Fitzhugh and Robert Brown. When Cyndi said she'd performed those tests as well, Fletcher asked what she had concluded.

"Mr. Fitzhugh is excluded as being the father of Justin Fitzhugh," she said. The tests showed that Robert Brown's DNA exactly matched half of Justin's DNA, and showed that there was no doubt that Brown was Justin's biological father.

When it was his turn, Nolan asked whether there was enough blood on the bottoms of the running shoes to indicate that one of them might have left a print someplace; he was still trying to validate the supposed tennis shoe print that Fireman Sartor had seen in the basement as evidence of an intruder.

Cyndi said the bottom of the shoe did not contain enough blood to have left a print. Nolan's implication was, if Ken's shoe hadn't left the "print," whose was it? But the implication assumed that what Sartor had seen really was a shoe print.

Now Nolan asked whether there was any "foreign" DNA found in any of the blood samples, including those taken from the floor and walls of the kitchen. Cyndi said there was, in fact, some DNA in a few of the blood swabs from the walls and floor that did not match either Kristine or Ken. These could have been left innocently before the murder, or could have become mixed with the samples during the collection process; there was no way to say for sure, she said. But as Nolan's question implied, they could also have come from the unknown intruder.

Now Nolan was able to get an admission from Cyndi that the crime lab hadn't tested *all* the samples submitted by Maloney for DNA, in part because of the expense. Cyndi said the lab was still involved in doing some tests that had been requested by Nolan himself, but that hadn't been completed yet.

"Wouldn't it be fair," Nolan said, "[to say] that the history of this case has been our desire to get a split of every single sample, and you're delaying and making that extremely difficult and extremely costly, because you wanted to have it done at your own laboratory? And if there wasn't enough, then you wanted to observe it [a private test], and you wouldn't give us a sample unless you could keep one, and you didn't have time and it was costing too much money, and all of those issues? Isn't that the history for about the last year on these swabs?"

Nolan's question should have sparked an objection from Fletcher, because it was really three questions, and compound, as well as argumentative. But Cyndi fielded the question(s) cleanly:

"Actually," she said, "I wouldn't say that's quite accurate."

Fletcher next called criminalist David Chun, who testified about the luminol tests, which gave Fletcher the opportunity to introduce the luminol photos, with the apparent wiping marks in the midst of the greenish-blue fluorescence. Nolan asked Chun where he'd sprayed the luminol, and induced Chun to admit that sometimes when too much luminol was sprayed, the accumulation itself can cause a reaction, as in the case of the "basketball-sized" stain. Nolan asked Chun who had directed him as to the places to spray. Chun said it was Denson. Nolan's implication was that Denson, having already decided that Ken was guilty, had overlooked places where additional luminol spraying might reveal blood evidence that didn't fit with his theory. But Nolan decided to reserve most of his criticisms of the luminol process for the testimony of the state's expert, still to be called.

That took place the next day, when Fletcher called John Thorton, a private forensic scientist who had taught at the University of California for twenty-four years. He'd had significant experience with luminol, Thorton told Fletcher, and had taught its use in crime scene processing for many years.

It wasn't always true that luminol could trigger a reaction from substances other than blood, he said; in most cases—such as fruit juice, or bleach—once it was dry, it no longer caused a reaction. Metals were different, he said. Because blood contains iron, its capacity for reaction lasts quite a bit longer. But even then, the luminol can't be used as positive proof for the presence of blood; for that, other tests, such as DNA tests, are required.

Thorton said he'd reviewed the luminol testing done at the Escobita Avenue house, including the photographs that had been taken there during the tests. The photographs, he said, indicated that an effort had been made by someone to wipe up the substance that caused the luminescence. Shown one of the photographs of the swipe marks on the floor near the kitchen entrance—one of those with the animal paw prints—Thorton said he was struck by the edging of the marks.

"It would be my opinion that this material had been fairly recently deposited, prior to the testing," he said. "I don't believe that the stain as we see it there . . . would survive any serious subsequent attempt to clean it up." In other words, it looked as if the blood had been wiped up by someone in a hurry. The paw prints alone showed that the clean-up had been a rush job, he said: the longer the time after a crime—or

rather, the more time that goes by after a clean-up of blood—
the harder it would be to see the distinctive wiping edges,
Thorton said.

Nolan now asked Thorton how much blood would be required to cause a luminescent reaction; he was trying to lay
the groundwork for the proposition that the blood that had
been found in the kitchen had come off Ken when he entered
that room to obtain the paper towel after his resuscitation efforts. Thorton agreed that only a very small amount of blood
was necessary.

"If there were a thimble-full of blood in a gallon of water,
for example," he said, "that could certainly account for the
type of reactivity that we're seeing in that stain."

This was a very small amount of blood indeed.

"If you took a thimble-full of blood in a gallon of water
and mixed it up, then took a thimble-full of that substance and
poured it on the ground, then you took water and a sponge
and moved it around?" Nolan asked.

"I think so," Thorton responded.

In fact, Thorton said under more questioning from Nolan,
even a tiny amount of blood in urine could cause a similar
reaction.

"For example," Nolan asked, "an animal with a recent
operation?"

This was interesting: the Fitzhughs had a small dog, Reina,
that wasn't yet completely housebroken. Nolan seemed to be
heading for the notion that some of the blood that had caused
the reaction seen in the swipe might have come from the dog.
That didn't account for why it had Kristine's DNA, though.

After some more questioning, Thorton said some of the
spots that had reacted to the luminol appeared to have been
dropped on the floor *after* the wiping down. This, of course
was consistent with the idea that Ken had dripped Kristine's
blood on the kitchen floor after the resuscitation efforts. In this
way, Nolan was able to suggest that at least some of the blood
in the kitchen had an innocent explanation.

That afternoon, Fletcher called Denson to the stand. Denson's
testimony gave Fletcher the opportunity to tie all the events

of the investigation together—the discovery of Kristine's body, the reactions of Ken, Gaelyn Mason and Carol Piraino, and the subsequent discovery of the blood evidence. Denson also provided a way to get more of the arrival times into evidence; Denson had prepared a timeline that reflected when each of the responders had punched a button on their patrol car's computer to show when they had reached the scene.

After the fire department had come at 1:45:42, Denson said, Sascha Priess had arrived at 1:46:51. At 1:48:21, both the paramedics and Officer Pohl had punched their buttons. That meant that from the time the firemen reached the basement, probably shortly after 1:46 P.M., to Pohl's arrival, less than two full minutes had elapsed. That was, Fletcher felt, an extremely short amount of time for Ken to do all the moving around he was now claiming that he had done.

Denson's testimony also gave Fletcher an opportunity to introduce the two video/audio tapes of Ken's interviews on May 5 and 6. Someone had made a written transcript of the tapes, and copies were passed out to the jurors to follow the often–hard-to-hear videos. Listening to the tapes, the jury got its first chance to see Ken actually say something—until that moment he had been sitting quietly at the defense table, almost as if he were an uninvolved bystander, rather than the main character, in the drama that had been unfolding.

The tapes took the entire afternoon to play, and most of the following morning. There was little doubt that the videos did not make Ken look good. At first he seemed detached, too detached, for the circumstances; then supercilious, his penchant for precision in his speech no help. Then came the explosion—the pounding of the fists on the table top, the shouting about "the Goddamn black shoes!"—followed by his obvious nervousness.

If anything, the second tape was even worse—particularly with all of Ken's denials at the end of the midnight grilling. Where was Ken's anger when he needed it? If he were truly innocent, why didn't he yell at the police, go into a rant, tell them quite emphatically that they were wrong, wrong-wrong-wrong? It just wasn't there.

The rest of Denson's testimony was taken up with his

description of how he had proceeded with his investigation. There was in fact, little that Nolan could do with any of this testimony, because it was so darned factual. In the end he contented himself with having Denson admit that in his first conversations with Brown, the Placerville man had never said that he'd had a telephone call from Kristine only five months before the murder.

Now Fletcher was finally nearing the end of his case, almost two-and-a-half weeks after he had begun. He called another San Jose police officer, Robert Froese. Froese was an expert on blood spatter—that is, the interpretation of blood-stains for the purpose of determining the direction and velocity of such stains. Careful analysis of this sort of evidence can be crucial in determining where and how a person was assaulted.

Froese said he'd looked over both the kitchen and the basement of the Escobita house, and had come to the conclusion that based on their shapes, the stains in the kitchen—particularly those on the chair at the kitchen table—showed that the blood drops had landed on the rungs of the chair with "medium velocity." In other words, they hadn't gotten there by mere casual dripping, they had to have been flung through the air at some speed. That supported the notion that Kristine had been struck by a blunt object, or possibly, that her head had been moving while the blood was cast off, as would have been the case if someone was thrusting her head repeatedly into the floor.

Other blood evidence—such as a stain on Kristine's pants, and the large stain on the green polo shirt—indicated that Kristine had been dragged across the floor to the basement landing by someone wearing the shirt, Froese said. That was "transfer," not "cast-off." Moreover, blood stains on the school papers found with Kristine in the basement indicated that they had been on the kitchen table when they were hit with flying blood.

Nolan tried to get Froese to admit that the attack could have occurred in the basement, but Froese was resolute: there was no blood in the basement that had come from any attack; it had all come from Kristine's already dead body.

AFTER Froese, Fletcher rested his case. Now it would be up to Nolan to try to present a completely different spin on all the events—to show that there was another explanation for the death of Kristine Fitzhugh, one in which Ken wasn't the person who had killed her.

The truth was, Nolan did not have much to work with: despite all his efforts over the previous two weeks, the evidence that the attack had occurred in the kitchen was essentially unshaken. That was the big one: who else would make an effort to clean up after themselves but a person who didn't want the police to suspect him? And who else would that be but Ken?

All the talk about the running shoes and the green shirt, and how they might have gotten into the Suburban, was just so much misdirection on Nolan's part, a sideshow to the main event. Even if he could show that Ken had put the shirt and shoes in the truck *after* the resuscitation effort, what did it prove, really? It didn't say a thing about the location of the attack, or the testimony about the clean-up. *That* was the 10,000-pound gorilla sitting on Ken's back, and all of Nolan's efforts to demonstrate that somehow an intruder had caught Kristine carrying dry-cleaning down into the basement and had attacked her on the stairs had come to no avail. The Suburban evidence was no real help to Nolan, even in the best case scenario; whereas, at worst, if Fletcher's view of it was right, it showed that Ken had been lying. So the best that Nolan could get from it was a determination by the jury that the police had been somewhat sloppy, and that Ken was telling the truth—about that limited part of the case only.

Nolan still had three arrows left in his quiver, however:

two blood experts, both members of the San Francisco Police Department, and Ken himself. Nolan had to hope that the blood experts would cast enough doubt on the state's inter-pretation of the bloodstains to convince the jury that reason-able doubt existed as to the location of the attack; and further, that Ken would show himself to the jury as the sort of man who could never have committed any violence, let alone the murder of his wife.

To set up the last, in fact, Nolan wanted to undercut the state's motive evidence. He needed to show that Kristine was perfectly content in her relationship with Ken, and that there had not been a single shred of evidence to indicate otherwise. He began by calling Kristine's psychologist, who presumably would know if Kristine had been thinking of leaving Ken, or even if she had been wrestling with the dilemma of whether to tell Justin about Brown.

Dr. Nicholas Ney had a psychotherapy practice in Palo Alto; he'd been seeing Kristine on a weekly basis for a little over three years prior to her death, for "personal growth, and also issues around sleeping difficulties, and work-related mat-ters." Ney said he had been granted permission to speak of Kristine's therapy by the executor of her estate, Dr. Schaide.

"In regard to her therapy," Nolan asked, "prior to May [of 2000] did you see any significant change in her mental state or behavior?"

"I saw her making progress," Ney said.

"Did there ever come up any issue of a deep, dark secret of any kind?" Nolan asked.

"That's a broad question," Ney said.

Nolan said he meant, had Kristine ever discussed the issue of Justin's paternity?

"Not to me personally," Ney said.

"And in the course of your treatment, did you see any change in her anxiety, about having to make an important decision, or something significant?"

"That's hard to speak to," Ney said.

Well, this was maddening: Ney seemed to indicate that there *might* be something, but Nolan wasn't exactly asking the right question.

Nolan asked if Kristine had ever told Ney that she had once had an affair that had resulted in a son.

"No," Ney said, "she did not to me."

This seemed to suggest that perhaps Brown had been dreaming about Kristine's decision to tell Justin the secret; or at least, she'd never told Ney that this was what she was thinking of doing.

Nolan now called a Fitzhugh neighbor, a dermatologist, who testified that he'd examined Ken's hands in the week after Kristine's death, and had found no wounds that would be consistent with injuries that might have come from attacking someone with his fists; on cross-examination, Fletcher asked if any such marks might be visible if Ken had used a weapon, but Nolan headed this off by objecting that the doctor wasn't an expert in forensic medicine.

After the doctor, Nolan called a man who said he had phoned Ken the day before to ask about the prospect of building a church school on the San Bruno property; this reinforced Ken's story about his alibi, because it proved that there indeed had been a real estate inquiry on the day before the murder. That was a plus for Ken, because it showed that his story to the police had some basis in fact. Nolan next called Patrick Bowes, the school district maintenance man who had said he'd seen a dark Suburban-like truck in the driving range parking lot just before noon on May 5. Bowes repeated his story, and then Fletcher did the same thing he'd done at the preliminary hearing, and demonstrated that the driver of the vehicle had stopped to talk to someone, which seemed to eliminate Ken.

The rest of the day went forward in similar fashion, with Nolan calling witnesses who he hoped would put a dent in the state's chain of evidence; one, for example, was a man who had been working at a construction site in the neighborhood, who testified that he hadn't seen any Suburban-like vehicle parked on the street where Fletcher's witness Tracy Wang had said she'd seen one. He called Officer Pohl, who said that he, too—just like Priess—had made a mistake in writing his report; when he'd written that he'd seen both Carol Piraino and Gaelyn Mason together in the hallway when he'd entered the house, he was inexact about the timing of this observation.

The next morning, Nolan called Dr. Rogers, his own pathologist, who testified that, just as Schmunk had already said, Kristine had died of a combination of blunt trauma and strangulation. Rogers said there was no way to know for sure what had caused the head injuries. Nolan asked if it could have been the ship's bell. Rogers said it was "within the realm of possibility" that the bell could have caused the seven wounds to the back of the head.

"Is there anything inconsistent in the autopsy . . . with a person running up the stairs, with their being grabbed from behind and strangled, with their being forced down the stairs, hitting their head on the bell, knocking them unconscious while at the bottom of the stairs, based upon your examination of the body as a forensic pathologist?" This would be Nolan's pitch to the jury: that Kristine had been attacked in the basement by an intruder, was running up the stairs to get away, had been grabbed, choked, and had fallen backward into the awkwardly placed ship's bell. This at least accounted for the right black shoe being on the left side of the stair.

"I could not exclude that," Rogers said.

After Rogers, Nolan called a string of witnesses in an attempt to contradict some of the elements of Fletcher's case, including a neighbor to the rear who said she hadn't seen Ken traveling through the rear yard, or any sign of the blue Suburban in the rear of the property around noon, and several co-workers of Kristine's who said they hadn't noticed anything unusual about Kristine's demeanor on the morning of her death. He also called a fingerprint expert from the San Jose Police Department, Henry Tempelman, to ask whether he had examined any fingerprints taken by the Palo Alto police at the house.

Tempelman said he'd been given twenty different prints to check in the county's computerized fingerprint data base of 400,000 known prints. Of those, approximately four could not be checked, because they had insufficient detail, and most of the others did not turn up in the database. One of the twenty turned out to be a police officer, so that left nineteen unidentified prints found in the house. Nolan wanted to make the point that the unidentified prints could be those of the supposed intruder, but this wasn't getting anywhere—not if no one knew whose prints they were. As Fletcher told Elia, they could be anyone's prints—and likely were the prints of Fitzhugh family friends, deposited over the years, who weren't in the county's database. Elia agreed, and ruled that the whole issue was irrelevant. Nolan wanted the nineteen unknown prints preserved for later re-checking; it was always possible, he suggested, that a match might someday turn up.

To Fletcher, this was like conjuring an intruder out of whole cloth, and Elia agreed. Nolan said he wasn't trying to pin the blame on the unknown culprit so much as to demonstrate to the jury that the police had been so focused on Ken that they'd failed to keep any accurate records of which prints had been checked, and why. If they ever actually caught the perpetrator, Nolan said, they'd have no way to tie him to the Escobita house.

It was all rank speculation, said Fletcher, and Elia agreed. In the end, however, he agreed to permit Nolan to argue to the jury that the police still had nineteen unknown fingerprints taken from the house on the day of the murder, and that the police had failed to identify any of them.

ON the following Monday, July 23, Nolan arrived at the heart of his defense, or at least what he hoped would be the heart: his own blood experts.

In calling Jim Norris, Nolan hoped to get an interpretation of the evidence that would cast doubt on the expertise of the Palo Alto police in collecting the blood swabs, and suggest that there was more evidence to be had, if they had only looked properly, in the basement.

Norris was the director of the Forensic Services Division of the San Francisco Police Department, which processed all the crime scenes in San Francisco. He was appearing as a witness for Ken because the San Francisco department allowed him to work on private cases on the side; in other words, Norris was moonlighting from his regular, government-paid job, a circumstance which caused more than a few raised eyebrows among his law enforcement counterparts in Santa Clara County.

Norris said he'd been hired by Nolan shortly after Ken's arrest, and was being paid by Nolan (who presumably was in turn billing Ken). He'd reviewed all the crime scene reports, he said, along with all the photographs that had been taken—over 1,000 of them, including those taken both by the police and the defense. He read all the reports of the Santa Clara County Crime Lab; he'd also been given daily transcripts of the testimony of all the experts who had testified so far, including the blood spatter expert, Officer Froese. Like Fletcher, he'd prepared a PowerPoint slide show to illustrate his testimony.

Nolan asked that Norris' disk be marked for identification, the ordinary procedure before it could be used in questioning.

"I've given a copy to counsel," he told Elia. Then turning to Fletcher, he asked: "Do you have a copy?"

"No, I don't," said Fletcher. "But I'm sure you'll give me one. Just in the nick of time."

Fletcher's sarcasm wasn't lost on anyone. Throughout the trial, he and Nolan had feuded about the discovery process, where, in California, each side is supposed to provide copies to the opposition of the materials they intend to use at trial. In Fletcher's view, Nolan had consistently evaded those requirements by contending that nothing had been written, so he didn't have to turn anything over. Now he was giving Fletcher the supporting documents for Norris' proposed testimony at the same time Norris was testifying, which gave Fletcher no time to consult with his own experts. It wasn't fair, but that was how the trial game was played by some, including, apparently, Nolan.

Nolan now asked Norris if he had any experience with luminol, and Norris said he did indeed. The advantage of luminol was that it was extremely sensitive to small amounts of blood. The disadvantage was that it was chemically unstable and sensitive to other substances. In fact, if it wasn't used within an hour or so after being mixed, it began to glow by itself. Once that happened, Norris said, the luminol user had to make up a new batch.

Norris' PowerPoint demonstration involved his putting some of Chun's luminol photographs directly over the same photograph taken in ordinary lights. The effect was to create a shadow on the ordinary light photograph. The double-layer, he said, showed where in some cases, the luminol appeared to be reacting where there was no blood at all. In one such case, he said, it was actually the wallpaper of the kitchen that was reacting to the luminol, not blood. This made him question whether the luminescence photographed by Chun hadn't actually come from some other source, he said.

He also doubted some of the wiping mark evidence, he said; he wondered whether what was actually being photographed was the luminol reacting with itself. That included the large patch in the hall between the kitchen and basement landing, the one with the animal prints, he said. It didn't look to

him like there were any wiping marks there, only that somebody had stepped in some wet, clear liquid, and the luminol's
"auto-luminescence" had only made it appear that there were
wipe marks.

"So basically," Nolan said, "between these two areas
there's no evidence whatsoever of any drops of blood that
have occurred?"

"Right," said Norris.

"What conclusions do you come to as a result of your
examination regarding the luminol found upstairs, in terms of
what it most likely means, what it least likely means, et cetera?" asked Nolan.

"Well, after I prepared these pictures and looked at them,"
Norris said, "I sort of had sort of serious reservations about
all—just all of the luminol found upstairs . . . I just felt very
uncomfortable using the luminol at all in reaching any conclusions, because there seemed to be some problems, frankly,
with what was reacting up in that house."

"If the theory of the prosecution was that there was a
serious assault up in the kitchen area, and that the individual
was then moved and relocated at the bottom of the stairs in
the basement, does that give you any more concern about the
interpretation upstairs, of the luminol?"

"Well, yes," said Norris. "The pictures of the hallway, if
the victim were bleeding in the kitchen and lying on the floor
or whatever, and then has—and is continuing to bleed, and
then has to be transported out of the kitchen, across the hallway and downstairs, I don't see any really good way for that
to happen and not have blood deposited in that hallway. And
[if] blood's deposited in that hallway, then you should either
still see the blood there, or you should have seen evidence that
the blood was cleaned up. But all I saw were the footsteps of
mainly, a little dog or cat, or whatever."

Now Nolan threw a knuckleball at Fletcher's case, one
the prosecutor hadn't anticipated.

He asked if Norris had seen the photographs of the ship's
bell in the basement, and when Norris said he had, Nolan
asked if the bell's composition would have any effect on the
luminol. It most certainly would, said Norris, particularly if

the brass bell were washed with water, and some of the copper and zinc from its brass composition were to be sloshed onto the floor. "Copper is the classic cross-reactant to luminol," Norris said.

Well, so what—the bell was downstairs, not in the kitchen, wasn't it? But Nolan would come back to this later.

There was more, as Norris continued to question the procedures employed by both the Palo Alto police and the Santa Clara crime lab. Elia began pressing Nolan to finish up.

"Based on everything that you reviewed in regard to this case," Nolan asked, "do you have an opinion as to whether or not there was a clean up upstairs of the scene?"

Norris began to hedge, but Elia told him he had to commit himself. "I'm sorry, sir," Elia said. "You have to answer the question. It was very specific."

Norris apologized to Elia. He turned to Nolan.

"A clean-up of blood?" he asked.

"Yes," Nolan said.

"I would have to say that I think other explanations are better than that."

"Do you have an opinion as to whether or not the assault took place in the basement?"

"The fact that the glasses were found and the earrings were found, and the glasses were found in the condition in which they were found [broken], seems consistent with somebody being attacked in the basement."

"And what about the amount of blood? Does that come into play at all, the amount of blood in the basement versus the upstairs?"

"Well, yes," said Norris. "There's a lot of blood in the basement and certainly when the crime scene was investigated, there was very little blood upstairs."

In fact, Norris now said, the blood upstairs—on the landing, in the hallway, on the kitchen floor—"some of it is clearly [from] a contaminated crime scene."

"What does that mean," Nolan asked, "a contaminated crime scene?"

"Well, in the situation, of course, emergency workers had arrived to try to assist the victim. And it's been my experience

. . . they can often, if there's wet blood at a crime scene, they will track it around."

So here it was, the main thrust of the defense: the blood in the kitchen, if it hadn't come from Ken when he stopped there to get the paper towel, after the firemen had arrived, had instead been tracked in by the police or firemen themselves before anyone realized that this was even a crime.

But a careful listener would have noticed that, Elia's abjuration notwithstanding, Norris had begun to hedge again. He didn't really have an opinion, yes or no, he only thought there were better possible explanations; two pieces of evidence found in the basement "seems consistent" with an attack there, but didn't show that conclusively; there was more blood downstairs than up, but so what, if it had been cleaned up; and true, rescue workers sometimes tracked blood around, but it didn't mean *all* the blood came from that, particularly since the firemen had never gone into the kitchen . . .

It was a dodgy, artful performance: truthful within the limits of the possibilities, which was exactly what Nolan wanted from his expert witness.

Late the same morning, Fletcher had his chance at Norris. He began attacking his testimony from the start. He pressed Norris to say which documents he had read of the 4,500 or so that the case had generated, and Norris admitted that he hadn't read nearly that many. In fact, Norris said, he had primarily concentrated on the Santa Clara lab reports.

Fletcher asked if Norris had read the state Department of Justice's crime scene profile, which had concluded that the crime scene was staged. Norris said he'd read it all right, but couldn't remember exactly what it said. It wasn't science, Norris said.

Fletcher pressed Norris to say whether he'd ever written a report for Nolan on his findings; if he had, Nolan should have turned it over before Norris testified. Norris said he had given Nolan no written reports of his analysis. He made Norris admit that this was poor "scientific" procedure. Norris said he had done the PowerPoint presentation. "That's a form of a report, certainly," he said.

Well, had Norris ever spoken with the medical examiner, Dr. Schmunk? No. Had he spoken with Dr. Vertes, who did the autopsy? No. Officer Froese, the blood spatter expert? No. And Dr. Thorton, "preeminent expert in the field"?

"Absolutely," Norris agreed, Dr. Thorton was the top expert in luminol.

"And you read his testimony and you agree with it?"

"Basically I agree with it, yes."

Fletcher asked if Norris thought Thorton had said anything that was wrong. "His testimony—" Norris said, "basically I would say the same thing."

Fletcher was annihilating Norris's previous testimony, wiping it out as if it had never taken place.

He asked if Norris had spoken with Denson before the trial. Norris said that he had, but that he'd told him he couldn't speak with him without Nolan's say-so.

"Just out of curiosity, Mr. Norris," Fletcher asked, "how much are you paid as a consultant in this case?"

"How much have I been paid to date?"

"Are you charging by the hour or flat rate?" Fletcher asked.

"By the hour," Norris said. "Actually, I haven't billed anything yet. I will, but it's been many hours, and I charge $175 an hour."

"That's about twice what you make as the head of the crime lab in San Francisco?"

"More or less, about."

Fletcher now took Norris through the luminol exhibits, and caused him to admit that in each case, there was evidence of swiping consistent with a clean up. As for the spot in the hallway with no blood, wasn't it possible that something— "like dry-cleaning, maybe?"—had prevented drops from hitting the floor as the body was moved? Norris said that was possible.

What about the chair in the kitchen, the one that Froese had identified as having the blood spatter? Norris said he wasn't the blood spatter expert for the defense, somebody else had handled that.

As the afternoon wore on, Fletcher continued pressing

Norris, until his usefulness as a defense witness was virtually destroyed. Then came the coup de grace:

"Mr. Norris, how many hours did you work on this case?"

"You kind of asked me that before," Norris said. "It is in the low hundreds."

"Does that mean a couple of hundred, or does that mean hundreds—?"

Norris said it had "easily" been more than two hundred hours.

"You know," said Norris, "I really haven't added it up. I'm going to do that."

"I'm sure you are," said Fletcher, drily.

Nolan tried to rehabilitate Norris' testimony by asking him if the blood that had been found in the kitchen, while having originally been Kristine's blood, could have been deposited in that room by Ken or someone else who had come in contact with the large pool downstairs, and Norris said that was "reasonable." He still thought it was more likely that the murder had taken place in the basement, he said, and because of the possible problems with the luminol, still felt that there was insufficient evidence of a clean-up.

Norris' testimony had taken most of the day. Nolan still had another San Francisco Crime Lab expert, blood spatter expert Michael Block, but he decided to put on two new witnesses to get evidence of Brown's character before the jury.

His associate Chris Pack called Susan Cielo, a Fresno-area teacher, who was a long-time acquaintance of Robert Brown. Susan had known Brown for more than twenty-five years, and had worked for him in addition to being his friend. She had also known Kristine Fitzhugh.

"Over that time," Pack asked, "have you formed an opinion of Mr. Brown's character for truthfulness?"

"Professionally," Susan said, "Bob does not have a very good, or did not have a very good reputation in the legal profession, for being truthful. Among his friends, they discounted his word greatly. And as my friend, I knew that he did not always tell the truth."

"Given that opinion, would you believe Mr. Brown under oath?"

"No, I would not," Susan said.

On his cross-examination, Fletcher asked if Kristine Fitzhugh had ever told her that Justin was the natural son of Robert Brown. Nolan and Pack objected simultaneously; this was beyond the scope of their questions, and shouldn't be allowed. Elia agreed. Fletcher said he'd just recall Susan as his own witness; he was simply trying to save her another long trip from Fresno to Palo Alto. Elia said Fletcher could reopen his case to call Susan as his own witness when Nolan and Pack were finished for the day with their witnesses. Both sides had already agreed that Fletcher could reopen his case to call as witnesses Justin Fitzhugh and Angelina Whitesell, who hadn't been available to testify earlier when Fletcher had rested. Now Cielo would also be called by the prosecution. But first Nolan called another witness, Terry Bradley, also from Fresno; like Susan, Bradley said he'd known both Brown and Kristine. He said he didn't trust Brown, at least when it came to telling the truth.

Elia now permitted Fletcher his reopening. The prosecutor recalled Susan Cielo, who said that yes, Kristine had once told her that Justin was Robert Brown's son, that she had indicated this even before Justin was born, when Kristine had come to visit Brown at his job in Fresno.

Now Fletcher called Justin himself to the stand.

JUSTIN'S appearance as a witness was no surprise—not after weeks of testimony about his very origin. Fletcher knew he had to produce Justin and give him a chance to tell what he knew, or be accused of trying to hide something. Indeed, Fletcher had asked that Justin be excluded from the courtroom during most of the trial, because he'd intended to call him as a witness from the beginning.

The only reason that Justin and Angelina hadn't already appeared was that by the time Fletcher had been ready to call them, they were about to leave on a short vacation to Lake Tahoe, and Fletcher didn't have the heart to tell them they couldn't go. Nolan had agreed to interrupt his case when they returned so Fletcher could put them on.

In the weeks leading up to the trial, Fletcher had finally had a chance to sit down with both Justin and John. He felt bad for both sons; how could he not? First their mother had been murdered, then the police had arrested their father, then their mother's long-past, secret affair with Robert Brown had been plastered all over the newspapers and airwaves. The sons had done nothing to deserve any of this, and it seemed grossly unfair that they were paying the price.

Fletcher had taken pains to tell both the boys why he believed that Ken had committed the crime, and why the authorities felt obligated to bring Ken to trial. As he discussed the evidence, Fletcher felt he was helping both sons understand a bit better why this had to be done. It didn't make it any easier, however.

Fletcher was enormously impressed with both boys—actually, they were men, now. Justin particularly, he thought, had a good head on his shoulders. As Fletcher put it later, he didn't know if *he* would have been able to cope with everything that had happened as well as Justin had. And as he thought about it, Fletcher realized that whatever else Ken might have been, whatever else he might have done in his life, Ken had been an excellent father. In another way, too, that might have explained what had happened: the upbringing of the boys was by far the best thing that Ken had ever done in his life, his crowning achievement. Perhaps Kristine's decision to tell Justin about Brown had, in Ken's own mind, been a repudiation of his importance that he simply could not abide. If that was the case, the death of Kristine was doubly tragic: the very real accomplishments of Justin and John were undeniable, no matter *whose* sperm had been employed to give Justin his life, and this was to Ken Fitzhugh's credit, not Robert Brown's.

Justin took the stand on the afternoon of July 23, 2001. In truth, there was little new information that he could add to what the jury had already heard. Justice Elia tried to put him at ease. "There is no reason to be nervous," he said. "We're all very friendly here."

After some preliminary questions to establish Justin's situation in May of 2000, Fletcher asked him about the brass ship's bell. How would he have gotten it from the back yard into the basement, if he had wanted to move it there? Justin said he would have taken it through the storm doors. Or, he added, if not that way, then through the dining room doors, into the hall, then down in the basement. In neither case, it did not have to be added, would the bell have gone into the kitchen.

This was significant, because Nolan had just tried to establish, with Norris, that if Ken had washed the bell in the kitchen, the water runoff, with its traces of copper and zinc, might have accounted for the positive luminol readings.

"Justin," Fletcher asked, "to your knowledge, are you aware of an event [in which] your mom shed blood in the kitchen?"

"No," Justin said.

Fletcher asked if Justin, in the two weeks before Kristine

died, had seen whether she had an injury to her hand. Justin said he hadn't seen any.

Fletcher asked Justin about Ken's clothing habits. He said Ken often wore black jeans, usually with tennis shoes.

"Would you find it unusual if he was wearing black loafers and white socks with those pants?"

"It would be unusual," Justin said.

Nolan objected, but Elia overruled him.

"Justin," said Fletcher, "in the course of this case, you've come to find out that Robert Brown is your biological father, is that correct?"

"Yes."

Fletcher asked if Justin recalled whether Brown had treated him differently than John, and Justin thought this was true, "at times."

"Did your mother wear a ring, a diamond ring, on her wedding finger?"

"Yes."

"And did she tell you that it had been given to her by Mr. Brown?"

"I don't know if she told me directly," Justin said. "But I knew. I had known. She may have told me directly. Actually, yeah. The information comes from her. I don't remember the exact time, but . . ."

"Would it be very unusual for her not to be wearing that ring?"

"Yes."

Now Nolan began his cross-examination.

"During your entire life," he asked, "did you ever suspect that you were being treated differently than your brother?"

"By who?" Justin asked.

"By your parents."

"No."

"By either of your parents?"

"Differently," Justin said, "but not unfairly. I was the older one, so . . ."

"Was there ever any sense from your mother or your father that your father was not your biological father?"

"No."

"Specifically in 2000, we're talking like January through May, were there any changes in, for example, the attention that was paid to you by your father or your mother?"

"No."

"Any heart-to-heart conversations where it appeared as if someone wanted to tell you something, but didn't quite do it?"

"No."

Nothing in his entire life had ever given him reason to think, even in retrospect, that Ken was not his father, Justin said.

"Since your father's arrest, you continue to see him in the jail, is that right?"

"Yes."

"And talk to him on the phone?"

"Yes."

There it was: Nolan had established that even after all that had come out, Justin still loved Ken, and continued to be supportive of him.

The next morning Fletcher called Angelina Whitesell, Justin's fiancée. Angelina had graduated from the University of the Pacific the year before Justin. She, like Kristine, had studied to be a music teacher, and had a job in Concord, on the east side of San Francisco Bay. Like Justin, Angelina had been excluded from the courtroom for all the previous testimony.

Fletcher took Angelina over some of the housekeeping arrangements she had observed while living part-time at the Escobita house; Angelina confirmed most of the earlier testimony of Justin and others.

Fletcher now asked if Ken had ever told her that he'd called to check on Kristine on May 5. Angelina said he had. "He said that he called the house and received no answer, and then called Kristine's cellphone and it was off, which was not unusual," Angelina said.

"When you were outside the house initially, after coming back from Stockton with Justin, did the defendant make any comments about the shoes?"

"Yes."

"Tell us what you recall about that."

"We were standing near my car talking and Ken said those—yelled, actually: 'Those Goddamn black shoes.' "

Angelina said she knew which shoes Ken was talking about, because Kristine had tripped in them "several times."

"Did Kristine wear a ring, a diamond ring?"

"Yes."

"And on what finger did she wear the ring?"

"On her wedding ring finger," Angelina said.

"Did she tell you where she got the ring?"

"Yes, from Bob Brown."

"Did she use a different name to describe him?"

"Aardvark."

"Did you and Kristine ever have a discussion about paternity?" Fletcher asked.

"Yes."

"How did the discussion come up?"

"We were taking a walk around the neighborhood," Angelina said, "and we were talking about my cousin, who was about to turn sixteen. And the person she thought was her father, who had raised her as her father, wasn't really her dad ... and they hadn't told her. And I was talking to Kristine, and I was saying that I thought they should tell her, and this, and that. And she replied, 'Yeah, they should have told her.' "

When did this conversation take place? In the summer of 1998, Angelina said.

Fletcher asked Angelina to describe how strongly Kristine had felt about this.

"It was close to adamant," Angelina said. "She felt very strongly."

AFTER Angelina, Nolan resumed his defense case. He called Michael Block, a blood spatter expert employed by the San Francisco Police Department. Like Norris, Block was legally moonlighting from his regular job when he'd agreed to be Ken's expert witness.

Like Lonac and Froese, Block had received specialized training in recognizing blood spatter patterns, and what they might suggest about the nature of an assault. Like Norris, he had reviewed the crime lab reports and photographs, as well as the testimony of the state's witnesses.

In contrast to Norris, Block was considerably more circumspect in providing his opinions. Under Nolan's questions, Block said that if the attack had occurred in the kitchen, he would have expected to see more blood spatter there. The amount of blood found by Maloney was far less than what he would have expected, given the nature of Kristine's wounds, Block said. He hadn't seen any pattern of bloodstains in the kitchen that made him think the crime took place there.

It was possible, he added, that the blood that had been found in the kitchen had come from Ken or the firemen, after the CPR.

But Block said he wasn't an expert in luminol, so he couldn't offer an opinion on whether more blood had been cleaned up after the murder.

At length, Nolan asked Block where he believed the attack had taken place: in the kitchen or the basement? Block said he couldn't say for sure. "I wouldn't want to specify one place or the other," he said. "I think there's an argument for both the upstairs and for the basement . . . I don't think I can confidently say it happened in one or the other."

• • •

Late that afternoon, Nolan called his own expert on cellular telephone technology, Stephen D. Stearns. Stearns was an electrical engineer, and had helped design systems similar to the one used for cellular telephones.

Stearns said he thought it was, in fact, quite possible for Ken to have received Phyllis Smith's 1:16 P.M. telephone call on his cellular while driving on Highway 101 on May 5. And, he said, it was entirely possible—technically speaking—that Ken could have made his own calls, as he had said, without there being any record of them.

As for this, Stearns said, one explanation might be that Ken had inadvertently hit the wrong button on his cellphone. That would mean he'd tried to make the call, but then had no connection. Or, said Stearns, the phone could have malfunctioned. Or the switching equipment could have dropped the call before it was completed.

The cell system's coverage, Stearns explained, wasn't uniform. "It is full of little holes and little islands," he said. "Holes like Swiss cheese, places where there is no coverage, because the signal is blocked by shadows." "Shadows" meant hills and tall buildings, he said.

Moreover, the coverage system had little spots where other antennas' signals jumped in from time to time, depending on the traffic capacity.

But how did Stearns explain the fact that the records showed that Ken had received Phyllis' call from the south face of the Palo Alto antenna? Simple, Stearns said. The signal could have gone to an antenna within reach of Ken's truck on Highway 101, then been reflected off a tall building to the north of the Escobita house, and then bounced into the antenna nearby.

On his cross-examination, Fletcher established that when he'd interviewed Stearns, Stearns had admitted that the most likely explanation for the use of the antenna nearest the Escobita house was that Ken was at or near the house.

Stearns admitted that, but said it wasn't the only possibility. Fletcher asked if Stearns had been able, in testing, to replicate the "bounce." Stearns said he had not.

With that, Nolan was ready for his most important witness: Kenneth Carroll Fitzhugh, Jr.

KEN finally took the witness stand in his own defense late on Tuesday, July 24, 2001—more than three weeks after the trial had begun. He'd had to sit silently by, unable to protest, while the other witnesses had dissected his life with Kristine, and the crime he was supposed to have committed. It was frustrating, Ken later admitted. But now it was his turn, and all eyes were on him.

Nolan began by asking Ken about his background. Ken responded with a series of long, wordy answers that soon sparked an objection from Fletcher. Fletcher told Elia that Ken wasn't answering questions from Nolan, he was giving a speech. Elia said that under the circumstances—with Ken's life in the balance—he would allow him a little leeway.

After a lengthy introduction establishing Ken's life and work history, Nolan turned to Ken's alibi: his drive to San Bruno to see the Family Golf Center property. Again Ken gave long-winded answers, so Fletcher objected again.

"Calling for a narrative," he said. "Ask a question."

"I believe there is a question," Nolan said. "Why did he go out there?"

"It is getting a bit lengthy," Elia said. "I think you can ask a very specific question."

"I think he is still answering that, because it is important why he went there, Your Honor," Nolan said.

"Yes," Elia said. "I understand that. And as I said, I will give him a great deal of leeway. Ordinarily I wouldn't, [with] another witness. But I think you need to be more succinct in your answers, please."

Ken said he'd try.

"Can we have a question?" Fletcher persisted.

"Counsel," Elia said, "may I please conduct court myself, or do you—"

"Sorry," Fletcher said.

"I will get another chair up here for you," Elia said. To Nolan: "Ask a question."

Thus chastened, Fletcher sat back down and let Ken continue.

Eventually, Nolan got to the question of Justin's paternity. Ken told the jury how he'd found out the truth from Nolan and Chris Pack while he was in jail.

He'd gone back to his cell, Ken said, and tried to think the whole thing through, trying to see "anything that made sense—"

At this point Fletcher interrupted once again, calling for another question, thus cutting off whatever Ken might have been about to say.

"What did you do as a result of this information?" Nolan asked.

"As a result of this information," Ken said, "I did two things. First, Justin came to visit me. And he said, 'Dad, did you know about this?' And I told him, 'No, I did not.' And I said, 'Just as we talked about before, you're still my son, and I'm still your dad,' and he said, 'Yes, that's right. It doesn't really make any difference, does it?'

"And I said, 'It doesn't make any difference, except perhaps with regard to health.' And as far as I knew, Brown's— Brown's parents were healthy. 'And you have predisposition to drug abuse, which so far you have escaped.' "

The second thing he'd done, Ken said, was to ask for a new DNA test. Nolan's office had arranged one, he said, and the results confirmed the first test. "I was not Justin's biological father," Ken told the jury.

"How have you and Justin been coping with this?" Nolan asked.

Fletcher interrupted with another objection, which Elia sustained. Fletcher didn't want Ken launching into a long, sad tale in which the jury would have no choice but to feel sorry for Ken and Justin.

Well, said Nolan, had the news caused him to understand anything that he hadn't understood before?

Yes, said Ken. He now understood why Justin was so much smarter than either he or Kristine. Because, Ken said, "Robert Brown, before drugs got him, was a brilliant fellow."

Nolan now took Ken through the preliminary events of May 5, up to Ken's arrival at the Escobita house with Gaelyn and Carol at about 1:40 P.M.

"What was your level of apprehension as you approached the house?" Nolan asked.

"It changed a great deal when I saw Kristine's car in the driveway," Ken said, "and then I went to full alert when I found—when I saw that the front door was part way open."

At that point, the trial was recessed for the evening.

The next day, when Nolan resumed his questioning, he asked Ken to describe the circumstances of his arrest on May 19, 2000.

"I was driving with John and Boots and Reina to Justin's college graduation," Ken said. "We were on Interstate 280 going to the north, and I was stopped—stopped by a combination of Highway Patrol and [the] Palo Alto Police Department, six or seven police cars. The entire freeway was closed. The photographers had been alerted and were there to take my picture while I was being arrested. I was looking down the barrels of six guns. First time in my life I had ever looked down the wrong end of a gun. And I said to John—"

"Objection," Fletcher said. Again he didn't want Ken veering off into some sort of narrative that would only generate sympathy from the jury.

But Nolan had another purpose besides this. After thinking about Ken's testimony the previous day—and watching the reaction of the jurors—Nolan feared that Ken was coming across as an unlikeable combination of arrogance and condescension. It was Ken's pedantic manner, so habitual to his personality. Since Fletcher hadn't even asked Ken a question yet, this was dangerous. Nolan wanted the jury to get the idea that Ken's demeanor on the stand was the result of his year in jail.

Fletcher tried to head this off with yet another objection.

"It goes to the state of mind of the witness," said Nolan. "His demeanor, his bias, his motive . . ."

Elia wasn't going for it. He sustained Fletcher's objection. The reason for Ken's manner was irrelevant, he said.

Nolan kept trying. "Your Honor, it's to explain his behavior on the stand. This is his testimony regarding how he is appearing right now, what he's trying to communicate to the jury." But Elia said it would be improper; judging Ken's demeanor would be up to the jury themselves, based on what they saw and heard, not on what Ken might tell them about life in jail.

Nolan wasn't about to give up.

"Last night after you testified," he asked, "did you go back to the jail?"

"Yes."

"Did you have a chance to think about how it felt to testify?"

"I did."

"Can you tell the jury what it felt like?"

"Strangely enough, it feels better to be able to talk about this, to be able to tell what happened as opposed to sitting there the last—the last four weeks and being frustrated [at] not being able to express myself."

This still wasn't getting there; Ken seemed incapable of shedding the role of being the man who was always in control. Fletcher decided to let this pass, reasoning that Ken was doing himself more harm than good, and Nolan decided to go on to something else. He asked Ken to tell what happened, from the moment he, Gaelyn and Carol had arrived at the house.

Ken described entering the house, calling Kristine's name, then checking upstairs. He listed every room he went into.

"Went downstairs," he said. "Turned down the hall to look in the family room and as I—passed the basement door, the door was open, and I looked in and the light was on. I went onto the landing, looked down in the basement and there was Kristine at the bottom of the stairs, face-down with her head at the bottom of the stairs. And I—immediately went into emergency mode and wanted help."

Fletcher sat transfixed. Ken, he realized, was coming across as some sort of robot. "Emergency mode," indeed—almost as if there were some sort of button that had been pressed.

"Ran out to the front door to call to the Sadies [Gaelyn and Carol], they were already starting to get out of their [sic] car. And I yelled, 'Come help me.'

"And I went back down the hall, down the basement stairs and tried to get around Kristine to get down to the bottom. It's a narrow staircase, a steep staircase. She was sprawled out and I had to kind of climb around her to get . . . down.

"At some point I saw the black shoe that was on the staircase and I began to evaluate what we had, what was wrong with Kristine. Her . . . hair was bloody, her head was by the bell, and she didn't seem to be breathing. I put my fingers on her carotid artery and there was no pulse. And I thought if I had heard of cases, what should I do? I was in a what-shall-I-do? mode to try and help her. Breathing, heavy bleeding, no heartbeat, heart attack and poisoning, those are the five hurry cases. And what we had was—We had no breathing and we had no pulse. We had some bleeding, but I couldn't tell what was going on. It was evident it was time for CPR. And all this is happening very fast, much, much faster than I'm explaining it."

"What went through your mind at that point?"

Ken said he decided to move Kristine to get her into position for CPR. He pulled on one of Kristine's arms, but he couldn't move her, he said. He was worried that Kristine might have a broken neck, and that moving her might kill her.

"What are you thinking about right now?" Nolan asked.

"I'm thinking about the scene where I was—where I was breathing into Kristine's mouth in the middle—in the middle of blood. There was—her lips had no—they weren't—they weren't like her lips, they were just—just flesh, and it was covered with blood, and it was a horrible, horrible scene.

"But I knew what I had to do, so I tilted her head back and held her nose with the finger of my right hand and breathed breath into her. And I got breath into her. I had never done this on a real person. I had done it on practice dummies in a CPR course, and I had always wondered whether it would actually be successful. And it was surprisingly easy to get that first breath.

"But there was a horrible gurgle, as if there was fluid . . . in the airway in the throat. It was kind of a rattle-y, gurgly sound. And it was identical to the sound—I had heard it only once before in my life—and it was the sound that Kristine's father was making when he was in his last five minutes in the hospital. And I knew right then that she was probably gone."

When the firemen finally arrived, Ken said, one of them told him that he'd done a good job.

"What did you do next?"

"The next thing I did was to—was to—was to get out of there," Ken said. "My hands were covered with blood. And on my way out of the basement, I stopped at the foot of the basement stairs where there was a pile of rags, and grabbed a rag. As I got on the basement stairs, the light was better. I looked at my hands and it was evident that it wasn't a job for the rag. And at the same time, I noticed there were buttons on the rag, and I put the rag—tucked the rag under my arm and went on up the stairs and into the downstairs bathroom.

"And I looked in the mirror, and my face, my nose and my mouth were all covered with blood. I thought the weirdest thing. I thought, Gosh, I'm covered with blood and I'm not hurt.

"So I washed my hands and I washed my face. And I looked at the towel and I thought, I'm not going to wipe my hands on that towel and get it bloody.

"I started to go into the kitchen and I felt—I felt faint, a little dizzy and a little nauseous. So I pulled out a chair at the kitchen table and sat down, put my head down between my knees for just—just a little bit, maybe fifteen seconds, until I felt better, felt like I could proceed. And I went over to the counter and pulled a paper towel off and started to walk out of the kitchen.

"On my way out of the kitchen I noticed the telephone. I thought about telling the boys and then I said to myself, I don't know what to tell them yet. Or I'm— I'm not— I'm not ready to tell them. And then I thought, Well, I'd better go down and see what's going on in the basement. Then I thought, No, I'm not going to do that, I need to stay out of the way. And then I thought, I've got to check on the dogs.

"We all—I thought we all came in the house just lickety-split, and I don't even know if the car doors got closed. And as I was going out the front door to check on the dogs, I noticed that the tennis shoes were by the front door. I picked them up and carried them out, opened the driver's door of the car, and, sure enough, the dogs were there, and it was all right.

"And just then Reina jumped off the console onto the driver's seat and grabbed the paper towel and ran off with it. And I put the rag under the driver's seat and put the tennis shoes down on the floor of the car, patted Boots on the head and went back in the house.

"And I looked at my hands," Ken continued, "and my hands were—there wasn't any—well, the blood was mostly off my hands, but still you could still see it. So I went into the bathroom and washed again. This time I dried my hands on the towel."

Nolan now interrupted. Wasn't this the first time that the jury had heard this explanation for how the shoes, shirt and paper towel had gotten into the Suburban?

Ken said it was; that he hadn't told the police this during any of the interviews.

"Did you go through a process recently in an effort to help you remember?"

"Yes, I did," Ken said.

The stage was now set for the next-to-last act of the Fitzhugh drama: the story of how Ken had come to be hypnotized, and what he had then remembered.

In April of 2001, Ken said, he'd been hypnotized by a psychiatrist, Dr. David Spiegel. This had happened at the jail at the insistence of Nolan and Pack. He'd never met Dr. Spiegel before that day, Ken said. After a video-camera was turned on, he said, the hypnosis process began.

What was this like? Nolan asked.

"The process I remember going through," Ken said, "was looking at a screen, looking at a movie screen, and going through the fifth of May. It was—it was a lot like looking at a movie. Under hypnosis I was conscious. It wasn't like a dream where you don't know whether or not you're dreaming. I knew I was in jail, I knew I was in the interview room, and the doctor was there, and the video camera was there, but there was—I'll tell you what it was like. It's like being in a movie theater watching a movie, and all of a sudden becoming part of the movie. You know you're in the theater, but you're not aware of it. You're in the middle of the action and so absorbed in the action that you're not really thinking about what's going on around you, although you know you're in a movie theater."

"Your Honor," Fletcher broke in, "may we have a question, please?"

Nolan now took Ken through all the events of May 5— both those he had talked of at the time, and those he'd remembered later, under hypnosis. He described all of the events at the house, the police questions, the request to search the house and Suburban, and the return to the police station for the midnight interview. Ken said he thought the police still believed that Kristine had died in an accident at that point, and that they were going to return the house to him. It was after the second interview that Justin had said he didn't like the way the police were acting, that he thought Ken should get an attorney, he said.

Ken said he'd had previous experiences with medical emergencies, and knew that the most important thing to do was stay calm. That was probably why everyone remarked on his demeanor in the basement, he said. As for shouting about the shoes in the interview that afternoon, Ken said he now believed he was reacting to a feeling of guilt—guilt for "not pressing harder to have Kristine get rid of the shoes.

"I was angry with her," he said, "for not getting rid of them. It was a horrible thing to feel anger toward my wife who had just died, but I did. And it was an outpouring of emotion that hadn't been released yet that day. That's the only explanation, that's the only thing I can figure out."

Nolan asked about the brass ship's bell. Ken said a week or so before Kristine's death he'd brought it into the kitchen to wash it, because he wanted to take a picture of it; he said he intended to put it up for auction on eBay. He'd washed it on the kitchen floor, he said. He had intended to take the picture, but had run out of time, because Kristine was due to come home from school, and he knew she wouldn't approve of the old bell being on the clean floor. So he'd picked it up and taken it into the basement, leaving it on the lower landing. Then, when he thought that Kristine had hit her head on the bell while tripping on the stairs, he'd felt guilty about that, too, he said.

How did the shoes and the shirt get into the Suburban? Nolan asked.

After the hypnosis, Ken said, he remembered picking up the running shoes near the front door, where he'd left them, and putting them in the truck, along with the shirt. He'd had a complete blank on this when the police had first asked him, he said, and it had only been when Spiegel hypnotized him that he'd finally been able to remember what actually had happened.

"How do you feel now, about Kristine, after finding out that Justin is not your biological son?" Nolan asked.

"I think Kristine is still—is still the fine lady that I knew for many years," Ken said. "She—I think of her as being a wonderful—a wonderful wife and a devoted mother and a dedicated teacher. None of those things have changed, but I do think that perhaps, being a human being, she had human frailties and temptations that we all face."

Was this devastating, or what? Asked how he felt about his wife of thirty-three years, tragically murdered by some unknown intruder, Ken's response was barely human. It did not go unnoticed by the jury that Ken never said that he loved his wife; and this, if any time, had been the time to do just that.

FLETCHER began his cross-examination of Ken later the same morning. This would last the rest of the day and well into the next, as Fletcher tried to show that Ken had repeatedly been deceptive, on matters great and small.

Fletcher began by pressing Ken about his recollections under the hypnosis. Wasn't it true that he'd conveniently remembered about the shirt and the shoes only when he'd realized that he had to think of some plausible explanation for them? Ken said that wasn't it; he'd only remembered what happened after Spiegel had helped him recall. Hadn't someone suggested these new explanations to him before the "hypnosis"? No, Ken said.

"I tried to think of every possible explanation," Ken said. But he simply had been unable to recall the events until the hypnosis.

Well, what about the blood that had been found in the kitchen?

"I believe there are two possible explanations," Ken said. "When I came into the kitchen with wet hands and sat down, I think blood might have come off of my clothes, my shoes and my hands. I also think that all the people traipsing through the house afterward could have trailed blood into the kitchen."

Ken said it was also possible that some of the blood found in the kitchen was animal blood, from a roast or something. This, of course, was silly; no one had been carving Kristine in the kitchen, that was for sure; after all it was her DNA in the kitchen, not some longhorn steer's.

Fletcher turned to the Fitzhughs' grand piano, which had been in the living room. The family had it tuned regularly, wasn't that true? Yes, said Ken. And hadn't Ken cancelled the regular appointment for the tuning that had been scheduled for May 5? Ken said that was so, but only because he wanted to be there when the tuner came. But hadn't Ken allowed the tuner in the house in the past when no one was there? Ken admitted that was true. Hadn't Ken later told the tuner that if he'd come on the fifth as originally scheduled, he [the tuner] might be dead, too?

Yes, Ken said.

Fletcher asked Ken why he'd put the running shoes under the seat on May 5.

"Because I was getting ready for the rest of the day," Ken said. "I had not yet figured out that the day that had been planned was over. I was still thinking that the gaming equipment for the party had not been picked up. I was still in a mode of going ahead and continuing with the rest of the day, which would mean having the shoes in the car, as they were supposed to be." The shoes were supposed to be in the Suburban, Ken said, in case he'd had to take Reina out to relieve herself.

Fletcher now brought up the time Ken had said he'd spent at the Family Golf Center. Ken said he thought he'd spent a half-hour to forty-five minutes walking over the ground.

So he'd spent an hour at the site? What took so long? Fletcher asked.

Ken insisted that he'd really spent no more than a half-hour there, that he'd actually left Palo Alto at 11:30 A.M., arrived at the driving range at 12:15 or so, then left to return to Palo Alto at 12:45 P.M., arriving at the Mason/Piraino house at 1:30 on the dot. Fletcher asked why he hadn't simply called Carol Gossett at the facility to see if anything at the property had changed over the previous year, and Ken said he needed to see the property for himself if he hoped to get the consulting work.

"Why do you think you suppressed the memory of the shoes and how you placed them in the car?" Fletcher asked.

"I think I felt guilt for not doing a couple of things that I was supposed to do for Reina," Ken said. "I was supposed to have the car seat in the car, and the dog was supposed to be in it. And I had not done that. I had agreed with Kristine that I would do that. Also, I was to be preparing Reina to go out if she needed to, and I had not done that, either."

"So you associated the shoes with guilt?"

"Yes."

Fletcher asked Ken why the dry-cleaning in the basement had plastic hangers, when, if it had come from the dry cleaners, it would have had metal hangers. To Fletcher, that showed that the dry-cleaning had already been in the house for some time when the murder took place, because all of the Fitzhugh family clothing in the basement had been hung on plastic hangers. It was, in Fletcher's view, an indication that the dry-cleaning had not been carried by Kristine, but that it had been added to the scene by the murderer.

Ken said he didn't know what kind of hangers the family used. In fact, he said, he didn't even know for sure whose clothes were in the dry-cleaning that were found under Kristine in the basement.

Why didn't he use the telephone in the basement when he'd first discovered Kristine? Why did he run out to get Gaelyn and Carol?

"What you did," said Fletcher, "is turn your back on your wife and walk out the front door?"

"Correct," Ken said.

Ken said he was trying to get help, because that was what he'd been trained to do.

Fletcher now turned to another area that held promise for the prosecution, at least as it affected motive: the Fitzhugh family finances. All along, Nolan had suspected that this would be where the motive would be asserted, so he was prepared for this: he had not asked a single question of Ken about his financial situation, in order to preclude questions from Fletcher about it.

But Fletcher now wanted to explore this area. He told Elia it was relevant to Ken's credibility as a witness—whether he could be shown to be a liar. "Mr. Fitzhugh told the detectives everything was comfortable and his business was fine," Fletcher said. "I would like to go into his credibility relative to those statements."

Elia said that much, at least, was allowable.

"You told the [police] officers that you were financially comfortable?"

"Yes."

"You had no problems?"

"Yes."

"Didn't anticipate any problems in the future?"

"Correct."

"Mr. Fitzhugh, isn't it a fact that your income—".

Nolan objected. Fletcher had the May 9, 2001, loan application in his hands, and was obviously going to ask Ken about it.

It was inappropriate, Nolan said; it wasn't relevant to the issue.

Elia asked for Fletcher's reasons for asking about the application.

"I will go briefly into the defendant's financial circumstances to show, in fact, they were in deep financial stress," Fletcher said. This related to Ken's credibility, he insisted.

"Credibility?" Nolan scoffed. "His credibility is not at issue at what his financial situation is. Otherwise, we're going to get into all his assets and expenditures . . . and frankly, Judge, I think we need an offer of proof, where it is going. If he can prove that, he should do it outside the presence of the jury."

Nolan was talking louder as he went on.

"Counsel, I am not deaf," Elia said. "I can hear."

Nolan apologized for getting excited.

Elia decided to discuss the whole matter when the jury took its forthcoming break; there was no point in tainting them any more than they already had been tainted, if the questioning wasn't going to be allowed.

Fletcher turned to the green polo shirt.

"Mr. Fitzhugh, this is your shirt, right?"

"It used to be my shirt."

"Well, it was your shirt on May fifth?"

"No."

"Whose shirt was it?"

"It was no one's shirt on May fifth."

"Well, where was it?"

"It was at the foot of the basement stairs."

"Had you sold the shirt?"

"No."

"Had you given the shirt away?"

"No."

"You owned this shirt on May fifth?"

"It wasn't a shirt."

"You owned this article of clothing on May fifth?"

"No."

"Tell me who owned it."

"I owned it, but it wasn't a shirt. It was a rag at that point."

This was an inane exchange, but from Fletcher's point of view it illustrated Ken's personality to a tee. Here he was, fencing over the shirt, trying to score points off Fletcher by caviling about his definitions.

Fletcher moved on. Did Ken remember how he'd gone up the stairs, hands raised "like a surgeon waiting to be gloved"?

"I don't recall that."

"You don't know where your hands were, but you remember what was under your elbow?"

He did, Ken said—"the rag [the shirt]."

Fletcher turned to the ship's bell.

"You're telling us that you lugged this bell from [the patio] into your kitchen, and that's where you decided to wash it off?"

"Correct."

"If you wanted to take this bell down into the basement, why didn't you take it down through the cellar door?"

"Because I wanted to photograph it first."

Fletcher asked why Ken hadn't washed the bell off in the patio area and then photographed it there. Ken said that wasn't the best place for the picture. Fletcher was trying to establish that Ken had put the bell at the base of the stairs before the attack on Kristine so that it would be there later, to give credence to the idea that the whole thing was an accident. This, of course, was evidence in favor of premeditation.

• • •

When the jury went out for their afternoon break, Elia returned to the issue of the Fitzhugh finances. Nolan said the whole line of inquiry was improper. Whatever Ken's financial condition was in May of 2000, the fact remained he had an ample asset in the form of the Escobita house to meet any contingency. Ken and Kristine, he said, habitually used the house as a source of cash, for the sake of liquidity.

"I expected they would bring it in as a motive, but they didn't," Nolan said. "Now at the last moment, to come in and raise the issue of whether or not he was properly using his assets, because he didn't have certain investments that he had before—or that they spent more money than the cash flow from their occupations—I am concerned about it, because I don't know where he [Fletcher] is going with this."

Fletcher said exactly where he wanted to go with it.

"The defendant has stated through his testimony . . . that his financial situation was good, and they were comfortable . . . Your Honor, the financial situation here was anything but good. In fact, they were living grossly beyond their income, and as I can demonstrate . . . come May of 2000, something was radically going to have to change about their circumstances."

Besides demonstrating whether Ken was a liar, Fletcher said, it also showed that Ken was under severe stress at the time of the murder, stress that had led to the death of Kristine.

If Fletcher wanted to raise these issues, Nolan said, he should have done it in his own case. It wasn't fair to grill Ken now on this, based on his statements to the police.

If the D.A.'s office had put this evidence on, said Nolan, the defense could have refuted it with their own testimony—testimony that showed both of the Fitzhughs had talked about selling the Escobita house and buying something new, somewhere else; that there had been any number of husband–wife discussions about the future, in which murder would have been seen as the least likely sort of financial planning. Nolan suggested that Fletcher's attempt to delve into Ken's financial affairs was half-baked, because he simply didn't have the information necessary to understand the whole picture.

Elia said he would not permit Fletcher to go into Ken's

financial condition in any great detail; but when Fletcher asked if he could still use it to impeach Ken on his own credibility, Elia said that would be appropriate. The crack thus left in the doorway would be exploited by Fletcher.

When the jury returned, Fletcher asked if Ken had in fact signed a loan application that claimed an income of $16,500 a month.

Nolan objected, and Elia summoned the lawyers to the bench for an off-the-record conference.

When this broke up, Fletcher temporarily abandoned the income line of inquiry. He turned to Ken's cellular telephone calls.

"Well, Mr. Fitzhugh, did you call home?"

"Yes."

"And did the phone ring?"

"I am not sure."

"Well, didn't you let it ring to find out whether somebody answered the phone?"

"Probably."

"You don't remember?"

"I do not remember exactly what happened with that call."

Now Fletcher returned to the hypnosis.

"Mr. Fitzhugh, in this hypnosis, you're never asked to go back and try to recall any of the events that occurred at the time when Kristine Fitzhugh was murdered, were you?"

"Correct."

Fletcher swerved back to the shirt and shoes once more. Ken now remembered putting the shirt under the seat, wasn't that right?

Ken said that was right.

"Okay. And the reason you put it under the seat was . . . ?"

"So that the next time I found it, I would not throw it in the rag pile."

"You put it under the seat, so the next time you find it, you won't put it under the rag pile?" Fletcher's tone was incredulous.

"Correct." The shirt's buttons made it ineligible to be used as a rag, Ken said.

"Mr. Fitzhugh, you put the shirt, wrapped up with Kristine's blood on it, under the seat, because you didn't want it out in the open, right?"

"No."

Why didn't he just throw it away? Fletcher asked.

"It had blood on it," Ken said.

"It had blood on it, right? That's one of the reasons you wanted to throw it away?"

"No," Ken said. "I didn't want to throw it away."

"You wanted to save the shirt?"

"Yes."

"Because it had buttons on it and it made such a good rag?"

"No."

"You were going to—you didn't even own this shirt, in your opinion, yet you wanted to save it, now?"

"I owned the shirt. It was a rag and I wanted to save it."

"You wanted to save it before the police found it?"

"No."

With this last exchange, the end of the day had been reached, so Elia excused the jury. When it was gone, the lawyers and the judge returned to the subject of the Fitzhugh finances.

Fletcher argued that he should be allowed to go into this matter, because Ken's own records had shown that while he was claiming an income of $16,500 a month, the family's income for the whole *year* until May 5 was only $11,000—almost all of it earned by Kristine alone. And the Fitzhugh tax returns for the preceding year, Fletcher said, indicated that the family had spent over $320,000 on an income of just over $28,000.

"The circumstances surrounding the death," Fletcher said, "and the circumstances that would indicate his mental state, and the victim's mental state, are critical to this case, and this, Your Honor, you know for all times, Shakespeare, everybody, money and sex, those are the things that draw people to critical junctures in their lives, where they do things that they would not otherwise do. And, Your Honor—"

"And excessive arguments by counsel," Elia gently chided.

"That's true," Fletcher admitted, somewhat abashed.

But only temporarily.

THE most striking thing about Ken's testimony under Fletcher's cross-examination—apart from his penchant for arguing with his interlocutor—was the sheer apparent rigidity of Ken's life: there were rules. Rules, rules, rules. The day had to be planned. He had to have the right shoes to take the dog out to relieve herself. The little dog had to have its own car seat. The buttoned shirt didn't belong in the rag pile. The bell shouldn't have been in the house. He had to be on time. Ken's entire life was governed by myriad little rules, and it seemed clear that he expected others to follow the same rules as well.

When the trial resumed in the morning, Elia, Fletcher and Nolan returned to the issue of Ken's money. The justice asked Fletcher what he intended to prove by using the loan application Ken had filled out on May 9, four days after Kristine's death.

Fletcher said Ken had signed the application under penalty of perjury, and had stated that his income was $16,500 a month. But it wasn't true, said Fletcher, and he could prove it. He had the Fitzhugh tax return for 1999, which showed a total family income of $30,655.

The D.A.'s office, said Fletcher, could prove that over the past few years, the Fitzhughs had depleted their investment accounts by nearly $400,000. Moreover, said Fletcher, the evidence was that on April 26, just nine days before the murder, Ken had asked for a credit check on himself—without naming Kristine as a co-borrower.

"I think this shows his premeditation regarding the murder of Kristine Fitzhugh," Fletcher said.

Nolan said the income figure was legitimate, not evidence of perjury.

"This is income that he takes from his assets," Nolan said. "Where does he get that money from? He gets it from himself, money that's already been taxed, so you don't have to put it on your income tax. And there's no misrepresentation at all about that money."

"Where's it coming from?" Elia asked.

"It's coming from savings," Nolan said. "It's coming from savings and trusts that have been set up, and other things like that."

Elia said that if Ken could demonstrate that he had enough in savings or investments to generate a $16,000-a-month income claim, he wouldn't allow Fletcher to go into the matter any further.

"No, we don't have that," Nolan admitted.

"Well, what do we have, then?" Elia asked.

"Where has he been getting his money?"

"That's what I'm asking you."

"He's been getting it from his assets," Nolan said.

"I'm not speaking Japanese to you," Elia said, "I'm saying this in plain English. If he can show that he has a trust income and savings income, whatever income, that is making up at least $16,000 or close to it, there's no problem. That's all I'm saying."

Nolan said that Ken intended to use the money he wanted to borrow to pay the $17,000 in monthly expenses, and implied that he did this frequently: borrowed against the Escobita house to smooth his cash flow. That was what the loan application reflected, that Ken intended to use the equity in the Escobita house to pay his bills.

"Maybe I'm coming from a different planet," Elia said, "but if I have $17,000 in expenses—I know this is Palo Alto, but if I have $17,000 in expenses and I have an income tax form that shows I make $2,000 a month, that's very complicated finances, to manipulate the whole process."

He still hadn't heard where Ken had the income to substantiate the $16,500-a-month claim, Elia said. He said Fletcher would therefore be permitted to ask Ken about the loan application as a matter of his credibility as a witness.

When Ken resumed the witness stand, Fletcher soon bore in on him about the money. Ken admitted that he'd told the bank he had a monthly income of $16,500, while at the same time he had told the IRS that his total family income for 1999 was $30,000.

"But we have a different definition of income," he told Fletcher. What he meant was, he said in answer to a question from Elia, that he had a sufficient equity in the Escobita house to repay the loan that he was seeking. In effect, Ken was using the Escobita house as a sort of private employer/bank.

But this appeared to be Ken's only remaining asset; when Fletcher produced documents that showed that Ken's investments had dwindled from just over $400,000 in 1998 to less than $20,000 by the time that Kristine had been murdered, Ken had to admit that this was true. He had, Ken finally admitted, consumed the principal on nearly all the investments.

In other words, the Fitzhugh aunts' money—itself inherited from D. E. Thompson, Marston Harding, Harvey Miller and Dr. Lane—had all been spent by the time Kristine was murdered.

CLOSING arguments began on the following Monday.

"It's been quite a journey, hasn't it?" Fletcher asked, as he opened.

"Sometimes people and places are deceptive. What is on the outside and what is on the inside are not necessarily the same. A beautiful home seems so perfect on the outside, and probably most of the time on the inside. But on the inside, on May fifth, lay the body of Kristine Fitzhugh, dripping with the blood from having been battered about her head and strangled. She looks in death nothing like she looked in life.

"The blood, the blood of Kristine Fitzhugh, leads us to her killer. The blood of Kristine Fitzhugh is on the defendant's shoes, the defendant's shoes in the defendant's car, the defendant's shoes in the defendant's car stuffed under the seat . . .

"Some people think motive is an element of murder. It's not. Imagine [what] a silly world we would live in if it was. We would somehow have to know what was going on in a person's mind before you could hold them accountable. We see people driving down the freeway, we know they're driving down the freeway, we see them, but we don't know where or why they're going."

There was no dispute that Kristine had been murdered, Fletcher said. The evidence showed that; and not only that, the evidence showed that the person who had killed Kristine had then moved her body to a place where people would think the death had been caused by an accidental fall.

"I cannot tell you which blow actually killed her. I cannot tell you exactly what weapon he used to cause the damage. None of those are required. In fact, you don't even have to have a body, but in fact, we do know that Kristine Fitzhugh was struck seven times on the head, and she was strangled. That was the cause of her death.

"This was staged to look like an accident, and part of the staging was the shoe. Staging is, by definition, purposefully altering the crime scene prior to police arrival that is intended to direct investigation away from the suspect.

"Who would do such a thing? It was done by a person who has a close relationship to the victim . . . for they are the one to direct the attention to be misdirected.

"Crime scenes that are staged are often flawed because the perpetrator doesn't have an opportunity or full knowledge to stage the scene properly. They're under stress, often criminally inexperienced, and don't know what a crime scene should look like. They make mistakes because they're in a hurry under stress. And it's hard to make things natural when in fact they are not."

Fletcher called the jury's attention to the way Kristine had been found: head first down the flight of stairs, with her legs behind her, dry-cleaning and school papers strewn beneath her. The entire scene was unnatural, Fletcher said, and showed that the murderous assault had to have happened someplace else.

"Is that the way somebody with an assault would end up, with the paperwork and dry-cleaning as neatly laid out? Yeah, it's laid out because it's staged. If this had happened anywhere on the stairs, these papers and dry-cleaning . . . would have been scattered about. That's common sense. That doesn't require an expert. That's common sense. As Bob Dylan says, you don't have to be a weatherman to know which way the wind blows. That is staging.

"Staging takes time. The people who stage have to be in control of the residence, because they're not going to stage a crime [scene] if they think they're going to get caught. We know that the perpetrator spent time in this house because not only did they have time to stage, but they had time to clean up.

"When you stage a crime, the idea is to misdirect. If you're the one who calls the police, the police are going to say, Well, you're the one there, you found it, [so] you need somebody else to come to be your witness, to be your prop, an unwitting prop. And that's exactly what happened in this case."

The sheer violence of the attack on Kristine showed that the crime was intensely personal, not the act of some wandering burglar, Fletcher said. The abundant evidence of the clean-up following the killing should by itself prove there was no burglar.

"If there was a clean-up, what does that tell you?" Fletcher asked. "That tells you something about the perpetrator. Their connection to the home, their control of the home, and their willingness to go through a clean-up for the purpose of misdirection. A burglar doesn't do that . . . a burglar is all about identification: get the heck out of here *right now!* Doesn't matter if it looks like an accident. Doesn't matter *what* it looks like. I'm out of here, not sticking around a house I don't have a connection with . . . it just doesn't happen. That's not what's going on in this case. What's going on in this case is the person who committed this crime is directly connected to the home, directly connected to the victim, and needs to make efforts to make it look like something it isn't."

Ken's demeanor at the time of the discovery of his wife's body was peculiar, to say the least, Fletcher told the jury, beginning even with his clothes on the day of the murder.

"The defendant is wearing white socks. Now, everybody's got their own quirks, but this was so unusual that everybody who saw him that day thought it was unusual. Angelina, Carol, Gaelyn, they all went, *That's weird.* Well, what do you wear white socks with? Tennis shoes. Why would you take tennis shoes off? They've got blood on them. He's in a hurry. These socks, you might not think much of them, but put them together with everything else, it all fits together.

"And of course there is no explanation for the shoes, the shirt or the towel. Eleven months, no explanation. Why no explanation? Because the only explanation is: I killed my wife. And that's not going to come out of this man's mouth, ever."

All of Ken's actions on the day of the killing, Fletcher repeated, were part of a script, a "macabre play" designed to throw suspicion away from himself, a concocted production in which he had assigned himself a starring role as a "victim."

What was Ken doing when Gaelyn and Carol hurried into the house after he had summoned them? He was standing at the top of the basement stairs doing nothing.

"Hasn't done anything," Fletcher observed. "This is somebody who knows she's dead. Let's face it: he knows she's dead. Why wait all that time?" If he hadn't already known Kristine was dead, he should have been down at the bottom of the stairs, trying to give Kristine assistance.

"This does not make sense. This is not shock. Remember him? He went into 'emergency mode.' He rattles off, on direct examination, all these semi-heroic events he's been involved in and kept his head all these times, but lo and behold, this time he can't figure out what to do.

"Your instinct, my God, the love of somebody, [you] pull her off the stairs, render aid. No—*I know she's dead, I'm going to play this out.* That's what's happening.

"I recognize," Fletcher went on, "that people all have a different reaction in given situations, but the fire people thought he was a doctor, right? Pointing to shoes and drycleaning, setting the stage, while, you know, 'trying to save his wife.' Gaelyn's down there. What's he doing? Pointing to shoes, pointing to dry-cleaning."

Fletcher shook his head. Ken's behavior gave away his lies—just as his statements about his financial condition were shown to be lies, as when he'd claimed $16,500 in monthly income when the real amount was less than $11,000 for the whole year, up to the time of Kristine's murder.

Fletcher played a portion of the first interview tape, when Ken had told the police that he had no financial troubles.

"Look," Fletcher said when the excerpt was over, "when caught, he starts spinning, and he got caught and he revealed himself for not being a credible person when confronted with things that make him look bad."

Ken lied, Fletcher said, again and again—about the timing of the events, about his whereabouts between 11:30 and 1:30, about the telephone calls he claimed to have made, about going to the Family Golf Center driving range, about everything important when it came to finding out who murdered his wife.

"It didn't happen that way, folks," Fletcher said. "That's

just not what happened. It's a lie. And trying to keep up with cell sites and all this going on, and the pressure of killing your wife, is hard."

Fletcher reviewed all of Ken's statements to the police, one by one: the telephone calls that he said he'd made, but for which there were no records; the movements of the brass bell, which seemed so nonsensical; his varying statements about his own shoes; the nonexistent cut on Kristine's hand; his claims about the rear gate, contradicted by Carol Piraino and others.

Then there were the omissions: glaringly, Ken's insistence that all was well between Kristine and himself, financially and emotionally, when there was evidence that, in fact, the Fitzhughs were in serious financial straits, having spent most of their liquid assets, and that a possible separation was in the offing, with Kristine possibly headed to Placerville, in Ken's own alleged words, none of which Ken had told the police. The contradictions between Ken's story and the facts, Fletcher said, showed that he was not to be believed.

FLETCHER'S argument had by now taken almost ninety minutes, and he was in danger of exceeding the two-hour limit he'd already agreed to abide by. As the jurors took their morning break, Justice Elia asked Fletcher how much longer he intended to go on. Fletcher said he thought he'd need another hour. Nolan complained that Fletcher was exceeding the agreed limits.

"Your Honor," Fletcher said, "we should do this right. If it takes—" But Elia cut him off.

"We always do everything right," Elia said. "I'm just saying that the summation shouldn't be all day."

Fletcher said he'd go as fast as he could, but there was a lot of evidence to get through. Nolan said he thought both sides should be held to the agreement. Elia said he would advise the jury if one side or the other was causing unnecessary delay, which was sort of like telling a group of hostages— the jurors—who they should blame if they weren't released on time.

Fletcher said he was doing his best. Elia said he'd give Fletcher another half-hour to wrap things up, "and then we'll see." Elia said if Fletcher exceeded the limit, he'd give equal time to Nolan.

When the jury came back in, Fletcher attempted to get started again by stepping back for a bigger picture, and trying once again to address the fuzziness of the motive for Kristine's murder. It appeared that he decided to move ahead to the end of his argument, even if it meant dropping some of the supportive points he had wanted to make.

"We never know why people do things, why they love someone or like who they like, and all the mysteries of life,"

Fletcher said. "That's probably what keeps it so interesting: we cannot predict what's going on [in] two people's minds. When you think about a little kid asking why, why, why . . . you don't have an answer, and we do not *know* why people do things. We think we know, we hope we know, and we search for that, because we want confidence. We want the world to make sense. We want tragedies not to be senseless. We do like letting the reality of the human condition get in the way of the truth—which is, he murdered Kristine Fitzhugh and we may never know why.

"There's evidence in this case of tension, of inner personal conflicts, but we may never know why, and it doesn't matter. Did he kill her? That's what matters. Did he murder her? That's what matters.

"Now, you heard from Robert Brown, and you know that when Kristine was murdered, a diamond ring that he had given her was embedded into her hand. We know that Robert Brown spent a great deal of time with Kristine, even taking trips when Kristine was pregnant with Justin, and lying on the sofa with the new-born child. This was a close relationship which seemed to belie so much of what we know of Kristine Fitzhugh, and what we know about Robert Brown. There is something that attracted those two people together and there was a bond. We may never understand that. That doesn't change the reality that there was."

There was no doubt that Justin was the biological son of Robert Kenneth Brown, Fletcher said. Just as there was no doubt that Brown himself believed that, as did others—including, Fletcher said, even people who also believed that Bob Brown was not otherwise a trustworthy person. The fact that Justin was Robert Brown's natural son was common knowledge in the circle of friends shared by Kristine and Robert Brown, Fletcher said, and so was the affair.

"Now, did the defendant know that?" Fletcher asked. "Well, it's interesting, he considered it, but he 'discounted' it. It's interesting. Everybody else knew it, [among] these close friends, but not the defendant—he claims. Did he know it, did he not know it? *I* don't know. If he didn't know it, and [it was] such a long-term affair, what does that say—okay?—

about his connection [with Kristine], and what was going on?"

Fletcher admitted that Brown was not a particularly good witness, in part because his version of his relationship with Kristine seemed to have several incarnations of truth. Brown's claim that Kristine had called him in January of 2000, to tell him that she intended to tell Justin that Bob was his natural father, wasn't part of his original story to the police, Fletcher agreed. But the jury had a reason to believe that this was true, and that was the testimony of Brown's aunt, Janet Moore.

"You might doubt Robert Brown," Fletcher said, "but nobody is going to doubt Janet Moore, that sweet little woman. She didn't stick up for Robert Brown." Janet Moore had absolutely no reason to lie about what her nephew had told her before the murder, that Kristine had told Bob she intended to tell Justin who his biological father really was.

The idea that Kristine intended to tell Justin the whole truth about his parentage fit with all of the known events, Fletcher suggested. "You know it fits, [and not] just because of Robert Brown. It fits because of wills [Brown's 1996 will naming Justin as his son had been put into evidence], it fits because of brains, fits because of Susan Cielo, fits because of DNA testing, it fits because of a relationship that extended [for] years. And there's Justin with Robert Brown's parents," Fletcher added, gesturing at the family snapshot that Janet Moore had provided. "Take a look at that picture.

"Now," Fletcher continued, "is that a good reason to kill Kristine Fitzhugh? Absolutely not. There *was* no good reason. But we know the defendant likes things his way, and he wasn't going to get it that way.

"Now, I can't tell you that . . . Kenneth Fitzhugh ran out and did this for any one particular reason. This is something, after meeting somebody [who was] sixteen, and spending the next thirty-five years [together]. There's a lot of water that goes under the bridge. And what it was, whether it was a buildup of three decades, or something fairly recent, we will never know. And the only way we will know is if he tells us, and we believe him, and that is not going to happen.

"And we are not going to let, when the evidence is compelling and proves the case, let the fact that somebody secrets their intentions from us, stop us from doing what is right, legal, lawful and appropriate, and that is find him guilty of murder."

Fletcher's decision to wind up quickly seemed to have caught Nolan short. He now had to address all the issues raised in the trial, and do so in a way that would at least cause the jurors to pause before rendering a verdict, if not come to the conclusion that there was reasonable doubt about Ken's guilt. This required a "big picture" approach, but that wasn't what Nolan now offered.

He spent the first fifteen minutes talking about the minutiae of the case—the fingerprint cards, the timing in the hallway, whether Ken had gone out to the Suburban, unnoticed, what Nolan's own job was—as if this last was pertinent to the decision the jury was being asked to make.

Nolan may have sensed that he was disappointing; he tried to step back to the beginning.

"Now," he continued, "what this case, in my opinion, deals with, and what I am confident [of], and what's been keeping me going all this time, is the fact that this case is an incredible example of the power of suggestion, power of accusation, the power of government, power of arrest, the power of criminal charges, the power of incarceration. And what I mean by that is, the defendant is in custody pending these charges, the power of publicity, and the power of calling somebody a murderer."

Nolan now told the jury that the whole case against Ken had been the result of a rush to judgment by the police and the prosecutors. It was up to the jury to determine the credibility of the witnesses, he said, and the defense had tried to show that not everything the state's witnesses had said could be relied upon as immutable fact.

"But the irony is that, from day one, we've been talking about shoes," Nolan said. "And we've been talking from day one, it's been shoes, bloody shoes, day one, bloody shoes, these shoes. I don't think you can say beyond a reasonable doubt that these shoes were worn by the perpetrator at the time the crime was perpetrated, based on the nature of the blood . . .

"So from day one, it's been the shoes, and day five when they found the shirt, it's been the shirt.

" 'Gee, Mr. Fitzhugh, explain, explain, explain, explain.' A horrible crime, a crime scene that's been contaminated, people going all over the place. Yet *he* is the one, he's the one who's been made to explain, explain, explain."

It was true, Nolan said, that motive wasn't a necessary element of the crime of murder. But, he said, "The lack of motive may tend to establish that the person is innocent."

The state had never proved beyond a reasonable doubt that Kristine had ever truly intended to tell Justin who his father was; and it certainly hadn't proven that Ken ever knew that, or even that he'd ever known that *he* wasn't Justin's father. The very fact that this had all come out only showed that once the government decided to charge someone with a crime, "they will investigate and investigate. And in this particular instance, they found a secret, a very, very deep secret . . . within the Fitzhugh family."

Nolan kept returning to the confusion that surrounded the initial minutes at the Escobita house, and the fact that it seemed at least possible that Ken had gone out to the Suburban with the shirt and shoes. But this didn't really address the major part of the evidence—the blood in the kitchen that seemed to show that the crime had taken place there, which in turn led inexorably to the conclusion that the killer had to be Ken and no other.

Nolan said he had his own theory about that. He said he believed that Kristine had been sitting at the kitchen table, when she'd gotten up to go down in the basement.

"She goes downstairs, she goes downstairs in those shoes, she is confronted downstairs, she is frightened, she turns around and runs, starts to run up the stairs. She is grabbed around the neck, she is pulled down. Now she hits her head on the bell, hard enough to crack her skull . . . She is now downstairs. And what is going on? Assuming it's a 'he,' you have clothing down there, you have somebody who's severely injured. You probably have a burglar, who is probably a three-striker [California has a law that three felony convictions automatically mean life in prison], who probably says: 'Oh my God, I came in here, there was nobody at the house, nobody was at the front door at 12:08, no cars in front, I can get in through this basement and see if I can work my way upstairs, see if I can find anything, and get out by the basement stairs.'

"Does she hear something downstairs? I don't think she would go downstairs if she heard something. She walks down the stairs between 12:08 and 12:35.

"This person now says: Holy, I get caught, prison for life, twenty-five to life, and she's severely injured." At that point, Nolan said, it was the burglar who staged the scene to make it look like an accident—because, said Nolan, the burglar wanted to buy himself some time, and did.

"Could I possibly be right? You know what? One of the worst things we have in society is the idea that somehow, you need to solve a problem. [That] somehow you need to find a solution to this. And you know what? You don't. All you have to do is say, 'We cannot say, based upon this case and this evidence, that we are convinced beyond a reasonable doubt that this man, in the middle of a Friday, on May fifth, 2000, went in and brutally killed his wife. We simply can't say it. It's a mystery."

The whole case had been skewed from the start by the state's unswerving devotion to their theory, Nolan said.

"This is a case in which the prosecution is constantly asking you to look through a keyhole, and they're putting what they want you to see right behind the keyhole. 'Take a look at that. Now take a look at this, now let's take a look at that . . .' It's your job to make sure that you're not hoodwinked by that kind of behavior. You've got to look at the whole picture . . .

"Look at the assault in this case. It's brutal. The idea that Mr. Fitzhugh committed the crime makes absolutely no sense. It's not supported by the evidence. It's a theory which they have spent considerable time [on] because, quite frankly, there is tremendous value in having people feel safe in this community.

"And that is not your job," Nolan continued. "It is not

your job. But it may very well be the job of law enforcement, and it may very well be the job of prosecution. What's the difference in property value? If the husband kills the wife, that's one thing. If the house could go for two-and-a-half million dollars, and an intruder kills somebody in their home, in a neighborhood, it creates problems. It creates problems for safety and environment and the community and everything else."

This was what Nolan's scattered, disorganized final argument had come down to: the police had blamed Ken Fitzhugh for the murder of his wife because they wanted to maintain the real estate values of a community many of them couldn't even afford to live in.

THE jury began its deliberations the following day, Tuesday, July 31, 2001. They began with what the jury foreperson later described as "just a total brain dump"—people began saying whatever came into their heads about what they had heard for the better part of a month. As the ideas came out, it soon became apparent that they fell into different categories, such as witness credibility and blood evidence, and the like. The jurors put up poster-sized sheets of paper for each topic, then listed their perceptions and recollections of the testimony under each.

By the end of the first day, it was apparent that no one believed that Kristine had died in an accident; nor did anyone buy the intruder theory. That left only Ken as the guilty party. But guilty of what? Manslaughter did not seem to be an option, since the severity of the attack seemed to show that someone definitely wanted Kristine dead. That left only murder. They each wrote this verdict on a piece of paper, and gave it to the foreperson.

"I want you to go around the table and say it," said the foreperson, Audrey Kenn of Sunnyvale. Kenn thought it was a lot easier to write something like that down than actually say the word out loud. "It's harder to say it than write it," she told the *Daily News* later. "Murder. Murder. Murder. That's where everything inside you has to agree, for it to come out. It's a sickening feeling. I wanted someone to come out of nowhere, to say, 'He's innocent. You have to let him go.' "

That wasn't going to happen. Most of the jurors had already concluded that Ken was a liar; the song-and-dance about the bloody shoes had not played well, and neither had his own testimony, so pedantic and, some thought, supercilious. But the experience of actually saying the verdict aloud was wrenching. "We went around the table, and each person said, 'Murder,' " another juror recalled. "It was so emotional. I had tears rolling down my face. When I said it, my stomach literally flipped."

But what sort of murder?

After another arduous effort, the jurors realized that they did not believe that Ken had actually premeditated the crime: it was simply too *ad hoc.* "We spent two hours going through our notes, wracking our brains, trying to find premeditation," said one juror, but in the end, it just didn't stand up. Ken was clever, everybody agreed to that. If he'd really planned it, it would have been much better organized.

"There was no doubt in any of our minds that he murdered her," she said. "With seven blows to the head, he intended to kill her. The savagery he used was so vicious, we felt he wanted to kill her."

That didn't mean that they didn't think that Ken hadn't tried to be smart after the killing, however, and in an altogether diabolical manner. Most believed that Ken had intended for Angelina Whitesell to discover Kristine's body, since Angelina was due to arrive at the Escobita house while Ken would have been busy taking Gaelyn and Carol Piraino to the gaming equipment place in the Suburban. This after-the-murder plan of Ken's was thrown awry, some said, by the telephone call from Phyllis Smith, which made him realize that he had to be seen to be doing something about Kristine's supposed disappearance, and the fact that Angelina was delayed in her trip from Concord to Palo Alto. Had Angelina found the body, some said, Ken's alibi would have looked much stronger.

Worse, some said, was Ken's decision to use Gaelyn and Carol as his witnesses. "I think he used his friends, the Sadies," juror Jenny Hope said. "What he did to them was unforgivable. He should go to jail just for that."

Some felt sorry for Brown, even though they didn't believe that Kristine had really made the much-debated January telephone call. They thought Brown was only trying to do something for Kristine; it was apparent to most that Brown cared deeply for Kristine in a way that Ken had not. And they didn't believe for a minute that Ken hadn't known that Justin wasn't really his son. In that regard, Ken's early "Freudian slip" about "her oldest son" seemed to be quite telling.

The whole experience had changed them, some of the jurors said.

"I don't think any one of us will ever be the same as the person who was selected," said Kenn. "Not better, just not the same. I look at little white-haired men differently. We all look at our neighbors differently. It looks like everyone is leading normal lives on the outside. Is this the truth or is it a façade?"

Truth or façade: in the end, that was the entire life decision that Ken and Kristine Fitzhugh had had to make, going all the way back to their earliest years together. In the end, both had opted for the façade. In one case, it was a fatal decision, and in the other, it was, in the end, a motive for murder.

DEL MAR, CALIFORNIA

In Del Mar, California, the ocean still beats against the red sandstone cliffs, just as it did more than eighty years ago, when the likes of D. E. Thompson and Marston Harding first arrived in the playground of the rich. The train still passes by along the edge of the cliff; the old hotel is still there, now shrunken and seeming much older than when it was the queen of the Pacific. The little cottage where Ken grew up is still there, although the garage on Pacific Highway, where his father Kenny worked for so many years servicing the automobiles of the wealthy, is long gone. D. E. Thompson's "new cottage" is still there, and so is Marston Harding's Castle.

The tale of Ken's troubles has made it down the coast, to the town where he grew up, and almost no one can believe that little, mild-mannered Ken Jr. could ever have committed such a violent crime; he just didn't seem to have it in him, everyone agrees.

And on the top of the hill, where The Castle still gleams in the sun, an old friend has returned: the Spanish chest, filled with all the silver, has come back. In the aftermath of his arrest, Ken has sold it to the man who now owns The Castle, and is engaged in restoring the fabulous dwelling that dreams, and façades, were made of.

ACKNOWLEDGMENTS

The author wishes to thank the following for their kind and patient assistance during the preparation of this book: Palo Alto Police Sergeant Mike Denson, who provided such a valuable inside look at his thought processes as he investigated the murder of Kristine Fitzhugh; Deputy District Attorney Michael Fletcher, who gave a significant amount of time in helping to get the convoluted events into some sort of coherent order; Don Terwilliger, of the Del Mar Historical Society, who provided irreplaceable background on the development of Del Mar, and its associated lore; the staffs of the California First District Court of Appeal, the Santa Clara Superior Court, and the San Diego County Superior Court, who provided invaluable assistance in tracking down the voluminous transcripts and documents that the Fitzhugh case spawned; David Price of the *Palo Alto Daily News*, who kindly permitted the author to use the excerpts of articles published in the newspaper; and finally, Kenneth Carroll Fitzhugh, Jr., himself, who provided the author with a valuable interview, even as he still maintained his innocence of a crime that had altered the lives of his family forever.